Alphonso Alva Hopkins

Wealth and Waste

The principles of political economy in their application to the present problems of

labor, law, and the liquor traffic

Alphonso Alva Hopkins

Wealth and Waste
The principles of political economy in their application to the present problems of labor, law, and the liquor traffic

ISBN/EAN: 9783337087029

Printed in Europe, USA, Canada, Australia, Japan

Cover: Foto ©Suzi / pixelio.de

More available books at **www.hansebooks.com**

WEALTH AND WASTE

THE PRINCIPLES OF

POLITICAL ECONOMY

IN THEIR APPLICATION TO THE

PRESENT PROBLEMS OF LABOR, LAW, AND THE LIQUOR TRAFFIC

BY

ALPHONSO A. HOPKINS, Ph.D.

Professor of Political Economy in the American
Temperature University

Of all wastes, the greatest waste that you can commit is the waste of labor. . . .

The first necessity of social life is the clearness of national conscience in enforcing the law that he should keep who has justly earned.—JOHN RUSKIN

[*Printed in the United States.*]

New York
FUNK & WAGNALLS COMPANY
LONDON AND TORONTO
1895

COPYRIGHT, 1895, BY
FUNK AND WAGNALLS COMPANY.

Registered at Stationer's Hall, London, England.

CONTENTS.

CHAPTER   PAGE
INTRODUCTORY, ... x

I.—POLITICAL ECONOMY DEFINED AND APPLIED, . . . 1
Dictionary Definitions — As Defined by Economists—Whether Abstract or Applied—Source and Object—Natural and Divine Law—Final Definition Analyzed—Derivation and Reference—Ethics and Economy—Economy and Prohibition—Economy and the State—Alcoholics and the State—Our Limitations—Divisions of the Subject.

II.—WANT AND PRODUCTION, ... 9
Natural and Unnatural Want—Want and Natural Law—Power of False Wants—Want and Labor—A Cause of Hard Times—Prime Natural Wants—Development of Natural Wants—Varied Forms of Production— Effects of Civilization—Increased Wants of Civilization—Want and Work—Labor Classified—Labor and Wealth—Labor and the Liquor Traffic.

III.—CHARACTER OF LABOR AND PRODUCTION, . . . 18
Labor's Purpose and Product—Unreproductive Quality—The Perfume-Bottle—The Brandy-Bottle—Immediate and Ultimate Production—The True Productive Quality—Unproductive and Reproductive Labor — Consuming Classes—Non-Productive Classes—Unproductive Classes Contrasted — Self-Supporting Non-Productive Labor—The Player and the Composer—Manual Labor and Mind Labor.

IV.—LABOR AND THE LABORER, ... 27
Definition of Labor—Labor and Sales—Painter and Portrait—Labor Further Defined—Player and Instrument—

| CHAPTER | PAGE |

Productive Labor—Inspirations to Labor—Creation of Utilities—Utilities and Wealth—Requisites of Production—Environment of Labor—Sobriety and Intelligence—Fundamental Economic Qualities—The Laborer's Character and Conditions—The Laborer's Foe.

V.—THE CREATION OF WEALTH, ... 38

Definitions of Wealth — Personal Wealth — Material Wealth—Natural Agents—Required for a Coat—The Poet to the Artisans—Natural Wealth—Wealth in the Mine—Partnership of Labor and Capital—Machinery and Production—The Machine and the Man—Intelligence and Wealth.

VI.—NATIONAL AND INDIVIDUAL WEALTH, ... 46

Individual Wealth—National Wealth—How it Comes—Millionaire and Mortgage—Division by the Astors—How Industry is Affected—The Relation of Industries—Natural Industries — An Unnatural Industry—Its Unhappy Effects—Four Years of Famine—An Industrial Parasite—A Threefold Law—Mutualities in Commerce—A Fungus upon Industry.

VII.—THE DISTRIBUTION OF WEALTH, ... 54

Problem of Distribution—The Distributing Agent—Labor and Capital—How Capital Comes—Law of Capital and Labor—The Mercury of Manufacture—Standard of Comfort—Employment of Capital—Proceeds to Labor—Labor's Pay from Liquor—Labor's Loss from Liquor—The Foe of Labor and Economy—Better Distribution Through Capital—Larger Demand for Labor—Greater Home Comforts.

VIII.—WAGE-EARNERS AND WASTERS, ... 62

Wages and Waste—Cost of the Family—The Massachusetts Margin—Where the Margin Goes—The Drinker's Yearly Average—Two Workingmen's Wages—Cost of Beer and Tobacco—The Gross Amount—Industry and Economy—Capital and Wages.

CHAPTER	PAGE
IX.—CHARACTER AND EFFECTS OF CONSUMPTION,	71

Consumption Imperative—Reproductive Consumption—Unproductive Consumption—The Reproductive Line—Where the Line Breaks—Song of the Beer-Barrel—No Nutriment in Beer—A Pint of Ale Analyzed—Results of Beer-Drinking—Effects on Human Life—Commerce a Mutual Benefit—Attitude of Economy.

X.—REPRODUCTIVE CONSUMPTION AND WEALTH,	81

Consumption and Capital—Congress on Economy—Wages and the Wage-Earner—An English Artisan's Demands—Labor Sober or Sodden—Wages and Wants—National Consumption—Capital and Wages—Liquor and its Laborers—Other Servants of Capital—Consumption of Raw Materials—Additional Laborers Possible.

XI.—WASTE OF LABOR AND PRODUCT,	90

Waste in Production—Fixed Capital and Waste—Fixed Charges and Profits—Sobriety and Production—Capital's Productive Power—Saloons and Capital—Capital's Decreasing Margins—Capital and Skill—Waste of Production—Waste of Products—Waste by Burning—Waste by Drinking—Waste of Labor—Waste of Wages—Production's Total Waste.

XII.—WASTE OF TIME AND LIFE,	98

Wider Field of Waste—Waste of Productive Time—Time of Producing Laborers—Time of Drunkards and Paupers—Time of the Defectives—Time of Liquor Laborers—Productive Life Wasted—Standard of Productive Life—Years of Life Discounted—Annual Aggregate of Loss—Through Premature Deaths—Cost of a Boy—Lost Capital in Manhood—Cash Value of a Man—Losing Human Investments.

XIII.—WASTE IN CARE AND SUPPORT,	106

Still a Wider Field—Care of Paupers—Cost of Almshouses—Cost of Incapables and Asylums—Cost of Criminals—Courts and Constabulary—Consumers of Wealth—The

| CHAPTER | PAGE |

Cause of Crime—Official Testimony—Municipal Statistics —Percentage from the Saloons — Net Charge to the Liquor Traffic—Recapitulation of Loss.

XIV.—RELATION OF AUTHORITY AND THE INDIVIDUAL, . . 115

A Selfish Relation—The Motive of Production—The Sovereign Element—Authority the State—Life and Revenue —Political Economy's Ideal—General-Betterment Law— Mill on the Roman Empire—Decadence under Turkish Rule—The Citizen Unit of Government—Human Solidarity—Advantages and Price of Citizenship—Man in the Mass—The Other Man—Moral Rights and Legal Limitations.

XV.—SOVEREIGN RELATION OF AUTHORITY, ... 124

Governmental Mastership—Society and Trade—Legitimate Liberty—Government and the Individual—Mill and the Liquor Traffic—Need of the State—The State the Sovereign—The State's Attitude—Genesis of License— Power of Restraint—Prohibition in History—Scotch Women Brewers—Early Features of Regulation—Regulation for Revenue—Early High License—The Logic of License—The Function of Government.

XVI.—THE NATURE OF LICENSE, ... 133

The Sovereign Relation Essential—Submission by the Liquor Traffic—Authority to Restrain—Source of Authority—License Defined—The Grant of Authority—We the People—Permission and Restraint—Prohibition Anterior to License—No Right in the Citizen—No Legislative Right—The Court on the Traffic—Judiciary on Prohibition—The Prohibition Principle—Prohibition versus License — License Unconstitutional — Groundwork of Government—Constitutional Declarations—Aim and Object of Government—License Properly Entitled.

XVII.—DUTY OF AUTHORITY, ... 143

The Interests Involved—Financial—The Income Side— Support for the State—Taxation Defined—Return for the

| CHAPTER | PAGE |

Tribute—Mill on Taxation—Immoral Sources of Taxation—The Regulation Claim—License Considered as a Tax—The Revenue Magnified—Who Pays the Tax—The Liquor Traffic Differentiated—License versus Tax—Taxing or Licensing Crime—The Ultimate Logic—Revenue from the Traffic—Direct and Indirect Taxation—Tax-Paying Liquor-Dealers—Annual Receipts from the Traffic.

XVIII.—AUTHORITY'S DUTY FURTHER CONSIDERED, . . 153

Authority and Regulation—The Claims for High License—From the Revenue Side—Regulative Claims Considered—High License in Iowa—High License in Missouri—The Volume of Drink—Effects Under High License—Facts in Comparison—Assessed Valuation of Property—Further Facts Compared—High License in Illinois—High License in Other States—Character of the Traffic—Comparison of Arrests—Authority and High License—Recovering the Bonus—Philosophy, Human Nature, and Fact—Breeding Contempt for Law—A Wisconsin Illustration.

XIX.—HARMONY OF MORAL AND POLITICAL FORCES, . . 164

Moral Interests Involved—Society and its Forces—Organized Moral Forces—The Home—The School—The Church—Supreme Function of Citizenship—Organized Political Forces—Test of a Law or Policy—The Saloon and Moral Forces—Contrasted Homes—Drink in Home and Neighborhood—What the Drinker Buys—Drink and Childhood—Saloon and School—Compulsory Temperance Education—The Saloon and the Church—Church Testimonies—A Cloud of Witnesses.

XX.—LOCAL OPTION ANALYZED, ... 175

An Old Economic Law—Early Local Suppression—Landlord Suppression—Logic of Local Option—Wrong in the Sale—A Moral Standard for the State—The Unit of Sovereignty—Right of Majorities—Centers of Immoral Sentiment—What Local Option Does—Effects of Local Option—Men and Methods Contrasted—The New Squat-

CHAPTER	PAGE

ter Sovereignty—Lincoln and Douglas—Supply and Demand—Hothouse Liquor Sentiment—Song of the Decanter.

XXI.—Demoralization by the Saloon, ... 136

Political Interests Involved — Existing Governmental Conditions—Effects of the License System—Demoralization of Conscience—Productive Citizenship—Harmonization of Forces—Inside the Saloon—Outside the Saloon—The Man Outside—In Michigan—In Texas—A Senator on the Saloon—Tennessee Convicts' Petition—Demoralization of the Press—General Palmer's Testimony—Another Witness—Demoralization of Manhood—*The Tribune* Testifies—Regulation versus Perpetuation—A Logical Indictment.

XXII.—Disloyalty of the Liquor Traffic, . . . 196

A Loyal Duty—Loyalty Defined—Defiance of Law—Proof of Disloyalty—As to the Sunday Law—Rebellion Against Law—Drink and Strikes—Former Effects of Strikes—The New Unionism—Inspiration of Strikes—Cooperation and Strikes—Beer at Buffalo—Wages and Drink at Homestead—Tramps on Communism—Anarchism and Beer—Saloons and Anarchists—The Cost of Strikes—Political Power in our Cities—Lawlessness—Phillips on City Rule—Danger to the Republic—City Reform Club's Testimony.

XXIII.—Need and Effects of Prohibition, . . . 207

Moral and Political Forces—City Control of the State—Uniformity of Law—Some Governing Principle—Morals and Law—Law a Moral Agent—Law and Popular Morality—Educational Power of Law—The Law Our Schoolmaster—Prohibition's Effects Limited—The Variable Policy—Permanent Policy Essential—Permanent Prohibition of Slavery—Constitutional Prohibition—Its Effects in Kansas—Iowa's Testimony—Prohibition in England—Town-Building on the Basis of Prohibition.

CHAPTER	PAGE
XXIV.—POLITICAL WAYS AND MEANS, ... 217	

Moral Reforms and Political Forces—How Reform is Made a Fact—Relation of Politics—Politics and Moral Questions—Political Party Defined—Basis and Purpose of a Party—What are Political Issues—Kinds of Issues—Principle and Its Application—How Issues are Presented—The Issue of Polygamy—National Policy Needed—The Issue of Prohibition—Policy and Platform—Supreme Issue and Compromise—The Tariff and Compromise—Blaine on the Tariff—Principle and Expediency—Progress of the World—Applied Political Economy.

XXV.—CITIZENSHIP AND ITS DUTIES, ... 227

The Sole Harmonizing Agent—The One Place to Harmonize—Focal Point of Political Power—The Ballot's Character—Ballots of Conscience—Garfield on the Suffrage—Defrauding the Suffrage—Saloon Sources of Fraud—Market-Place of Suffrage—The Poor Voter on Election Day—Whittier Revised—Loyalty of the Ballot—Party and the Ballot—Equatorial Party Lines—Contributions to the Commonwealth—Tribute to God and Government.

Civilization is the economy of Power.—*Baron Liebig*.

All Anarchy is the forerunner of Poverty, and all Prosperity begins in Obedience.—*John Ruskin*.

INTRODUCTORY.

AFTER many years of business and platform activities, during which I studied with special care those questions treated of in the following pages, I consented to serve the American Temperance University in the Chair of Political Economy and National Prohibition. I so consented, because of my profound belief that no more important branch of study is open to American youth; because I hold that Political Economy is related to Prohibition in the closest and most vital degree, and that the vital relation of both to government, and the perpetuity of government, should be carefully studied and thoroughly understood by those who go out from the higher schools of learning to take place and wield power in the work and progress of the world.

This book is the result of my direct preparation for the educational task which I thus attempted. My aim has been to present the subject-matter of it in such form as might both adapt it to popular perusal and make it of service, if desired, as a text-book for school use. The typographical style and sub-topical arrangement have been adopted with a twofold intention of directing the general reader's thought to, and fastening it upon, special definitions, propositions, and terms, and of similarly assisting both student and teacher, in and outside of the class-room, to their mutual profit and advantage.

It is the purpose of this book to carry on to their logical

application the accepted utterances of standard economists, rather than to formulate any new theories of economy or of civics. Its treatment of politics, where touched upon, is intended to be philosophical and patriotic, instead of partizan.

The Temperance Reform is more than a matter of sentiment, or a question of partizanship; it is rooted in some of the deepest and most abiding principles of natural, physical, moral, political, and economic law. With a sincere wish clearly and fairly to demonstrate what these principles are, how they relate to the individual, and how government may and must be affected by them, I now invite your thoughtful consideration, with me, of the comprehensive and intensely practical subject before us.

WEALTH AND WASTE.

CHAPTER I.

POLITICAL ECONOMY DEFINED AND APPLIED.

SEARCHING for definitions, let us turn first to the dictionary, and in Webster's we shall find:

DICTIONARY DEFINITIONS. "*Political Economy*—that branch of philosophy which discusses the sources and methods of material wealth and prosperity in a nation."

This definition, aiming at breadth and brevity, lacks explicitness. If sufficiently inclusive, it is too general.

The new Standard Dictionary thus defines the term:

"*Political Economy*—the branch of civics that treats of the nature of wealth and the laws of its production and distribution, including all the causes of prosperity and the reverse. It discusses labor, wages, population, capital, money, rent, value, trade, and the relation of government to industry and economic conditions."

This definition, while broader and stronger than the other, is also more specific.

Dr. John M. Gregory, in his work on "Political Economy," gives one of the best and broadest definitions offered by economists, in these words:

"Political Economy is the science of the industries. Its aim is to investigate and explain the nature, relations, and laws of these three constant factors and elements of the industries—human wants, work, and wealth."

Professor Arthur Latham Perry, of Williams College, one of our most authoritative political economists, with more brevity and less breadth has declared:

"It is **the science of exchanges**"; and has gone on to assert that "Political Economy has to do with men as buyers and sellers only"; still further declaring, on another page, that—

"Political Economy has to do with processes simply as these are related to sales."

AS DEFINED BY ECONOMISTS. Grant that Perry's limitations are proper, and we might as well accept in its narrowness a definition which once fell under my notice in a newspaper:

"Political Economy, the science of selfish interest."

Dr. Hargreaves has given us a better rendering than Professor Perry, in his "Wasted Resources":

"Political Economy, as a science, may be said to embrace the proper administration of the revenue of a nation, the management and regulation of its resources, labor, productions, and property, and the means by which the labor and the property of its citizens are protected and directed, as well as the best means of securing the success of each individual's industry and enterprise, and general national prosperity."

As a definer, I like Hargreaves better than Perry; he is broader, and more patriotic. You should fix his definition in your memory; we may have occasion to refer to or amplify certain parts of it farther on.

A multitude of definitions have been given by writers on philosophy and science; and it becomes rather difficult WHETHER ABSTRACT OR APPLIED. to select the most accurate and satisfactory, or to settle in one's own mind, after long pondering them all, what are the precise limits of the science which they define, or whether indeed it be a science.

Conceding it to be essentially an abstract science, as John Stuart Mill declares it, the question arises: "How shall it be applied?" or, "How widely may we apply it?"

If it has only become a science by becoming "a science of observation," as M. J. B. Say asserts, by what rules of observation are we to approach and master it?

If it has to do principally with laws laid down by the legislator, and not of nature, as De Laveleye affirms, is it not quite the opposite of abstract, and has it not the most concrete political application?

"Political Economy," says Droz, "is a science whose object is to make comfort as general as possible."

Being such, I am sure it must be founded on certain natural laws which condition comfort and make *that* possible.

The law of the legislator is for society—the State. As I see it, **Political Economy has its tap-root in the foundation of society, in the unit of the State—in the individual life;** and that rests, first and finally, on natural law.

<small>SOURCE AND OBJECT.</small>

Bossuet, speaking of politics, says "its true end is to make life easy and nations happy"; and De Laveleye supplements the remark by adding that "such is also the aim of Political Economy." But there surely are natural laws and divine laws upon which national happiness and well-being rest, and politics, political economy, can only secure the high end sought by bringing the law of the legislator into harmony therewith.

It has been well declared from the pulpit by Rev. Dr. C. H. Parkhurst (New York, Nov. 4, 1894), that the (Ten) "Commandments make out the biggest half of any system of political economy that has vigor enough to hold its own and win its way."

The law of the legislator must rest on certain divine and natural laws of human relation.

NATURAL AND DIVINE LAW. With this thought in mind, and as reflecting it in fair measure, I present one more definition, and one which, though very simple, has in it comprehensive breadth, and outreach, and force—one which, together with that of Dr. Hargreaves, before quoted, would form sufficient basis for a whole system of politico-economic laws. This final definition says that Political Economy is "the science which determines what laws men ought to adopt in order that they may, with the least possible exertion, procure the greatest abundance of things useful for the satisfaction of their wants; may distribute them justly, and consume them rationally."

FINAL DEFINITION ANALYZED. Note carefully in this definition what things are implied, viz:

(*a*) **A science,** that determines, fixes, something of great moment in the relations of men.

(*b*) **Laws,** determined by this science, adopted by men, in harmony with laws natural and divine, to secure certain important ends.

(*c*) **Labor,** a recognized necessity, to be minimized by results of Law, whereby "the least possible exertion" will yield the largest possible returns.

(*d*) **Want,** and the satisfaction of want with "*things useful,*" as the inspiration of work.

(*e*) **Distribution,** of abundance—in other words, the equitable allotment of wealth.

(*f*) **Consumption,** use, of whatever is distributed, earned, obtained, produced, in a rational and beneficent way.

Within the range of these things, implied by this definition, our study of Political Economy may fairly lie. Indeed the original derivation of the term anticipates and justifies this definition. It was first used by that old **DERIVATION** philosopher, Aristotle, and came of three **AND REFERENCE.** Greek words: *Oikos*, house; *nomos*, law; and *polis*, city or State.

It has direct reference, therefore, to individual property, in its natural and lawful relation to society and the State; to the methods and conditions under which property must be acquired, and maintained, and used; to the wise use and administration of property, in its relation to the general good.

And as all property is the product of individual life, conditioned by society and the State, I repeat that **Political Economy has the closest possible relation to individual life and natural law.**

Moreover, if it be a fact, as De Laveleye affirms, that "in ethics you find the true root of economic laws," and that "the end of ethics, the good, and the end of Political Economy, the useful, are inseparable," then the relation **ETHICS AND** of Political Economy to individual life is **ECONOMY.** plainly as intimate as is the relation of either to the State. For as De Laveleye well says:

"Ethics enjoins moderation in our needs, energy and conscientiousness in our work, fidelity to our engagements, thrift and prudence in the use of our income, and regard for justice in our relations with one another.

"There is not one of these laws," he continues, "that is not an essential rule in economy. Energy in labor insures abundant production; respect for justice, a fair distribution; respect for engagements, abundant credit; the spirit of thrift leads to the creation of capital, and the moderation of desires to a good use of time and property."

By such legitimate and logical steps we come to our study of Political Economy, from a distinctively and radically temperance standpoint; we deliberately link together, for closely related inquiry, two topics which have been studied in common far too little, and in our higher halls of learning scarcely at all—**Political Economy, and National Prohibition of the Liquor Traffic.**

ECONOMY AND PROHIBITION.

What the one is, we have seen in this introductory outline, as you may gaze upon a distant mountain chain, catching far glimpses of its important peaks; why the other should be, we may see, by and by, more clearly than is possible until Political Economy has been further revealed to us. Not much need be said about Prohibition, in this outline, definitive lesson, which barely brings us to the threshold of our subject, or the foothills of our mountain-chain.

It has been a source of growing wonder to me, for several years, that economists give little or no heed, in all their text-books and elaborate treatises, to the drinking habits of the people, as relating to production and consumption, and to the laws which concern the Drink Traffic. Scan the literature of Political Economy with watchful care, and rarely will you find an allusion to the drink habit as an important factor in the problems of natural and political law. Yet if, as the greatest French writer on economic science has said, " Political Economy and law underlie one another," it follows, beyond question, that **whenenever any element or influence enters life and the State to paralyze energy, to decrease production, to render distribution unfair, to impair** credit, **to pervert desire, to banish the** spirit of thrift, **and to destroy capital, Political Economy should find some law to eliminate that element or influence,** and to protect life and the State from its baleful effects.

ECONOMY AND THE STATE.

No one, it seems to me, will deny this proposition, unless he have more interest in or regard for such paralyzing, damaging, destroying element, or agency, than he has concern for the State, regard for humanity, and respect for himself.

We hold alcoholics, the liquor traffic, to be precisely such an element or influence as indicated,—paralyzing, damaging, destroying; and we claim that Political Economy, to insure the well-being of man and the prosperity of the commonwealth, must urge its abolition by and through and because of some underlying law. We hold National Prohibition to be that law,—the only law that logically meets the case,—the only law that is closely in correlation with the natural laws of human life and social relation,—the only law, concerning the liquor traffic, that can stand the tests of applied Political Economy.

Alcoholics and the State.

Boil down all the definitions that have been quoted, or that can be found, and admit, assert, that Political Economy is the Science of Selfishness, and still that science will demand the total Prohibition of the liquor traffic. Rid that science of every moral consideration, strip it of all sentiment, and make it as cold as a proposition in calculus, and still it will ban the liquor traffic from any status of deserved recognition by law. **Under the law, that traffic must be banished, or Political Economy is not a science, but a sham**: its principles are false and their pretended application a fraud.

We shall not be able, in our study, to take up the details of this science as minutely as these are presented in some of the college text-books. We may largely skip the consideration of values, and money, and credit, and tariff, and taxation, as these are generally discussed by the economists. We must con-

Our Limitations.

sider much that these men have largely missed, or mistakenly omitted. We must apply, in a deeper and wider way, some of the principles they have restricted: we may search for some which they have never found or have seldom confessed.

Let us go slowly, patiently, seeking step by step to see our way clear, finding illustrations that may throw light upon it, and so analyzing our subject, if possible, as to render it both easy and interesting.

DIVISIONS OF THE SUBJECT. It separates naturally into four distinct and important groups or grand divisions:

1. **Production and Wealth.**
2. **Consumption and Waste.**
3. **The relations to these, and to the Liquor Traffic, of Authority and Human Life.**
4. **The Duty of Authority toward the Liquor Traffic, in view of these relations and the momentous interests they involve.**

Minor subdivisions will as naturally shape themselves, and need not arbitrarily be made.

Production, the first part of the first grand division, separates readily into—

(*a*) Want.
(*b*) Work.

Wealth, the second part, as readily is resolved into—

(*c*) Creation.
(*d*) Distribution.

In the order of such analysis, and with such further analyses as may offer, we will proceed with our second chapter.

It will treat particularly of **Want.**

CHAPTER II.

WANT AND PRODUCTION.

"THE science of economy," says one writer, "is based on the notion of want."

Production is based on and inspired by the want itself.

Want is of two kinds; it is either

(*a*) **Natural** or normal, real and actual; or

(*b*) **Unnatural** and abnormal, false or fictitious.

As production is essential to wealth, and as human life and effort are essential to production, Political Economy demands that these shall be given the best possible advantage, and that, to yield a margin above Want's necessity, for the accumulation of wealth, want shall be normal and natural.

<small>NATURAL AND UNNATURAL WANT.</small>

The gratification of a natural want, in a natural way, ministers to life, and insures advantageous production.

The development of unnatural wants may impair life, disturb natural functions, and put production always at a disadvantage.

<small>WANT AND NATURAL LAW.</small> The gratification of a natural want must come easily within the scope of natural law.

Any want which, when gratified, renders the person less fit and able to work for the satisfaction of other wants must be unnatural and false.

The desire, the craving, for food indicates a natural want. Gratify, satisfy, that want, and strength is given wherewith to earn more food, and to satisfy other wants. To gratify that natural want of food, then, lies clearly within the scope of natural law.

Real wants are the voice of nature, making her requirements known. False wants are the demand of habit or the clamor of abnormal appetite.

The want of a man for his breakfast is a real want, and the provision of breakfast meets one requirement of natural law. The want of a man for his morning dram before breakfast is a false and fictitious want, the satisfaction of which violates natural law.

The hunger for bread is a natural hunger, and to satisfy it meets a natural law. The hunger for opium is unnatural, and to satisfy it must be dangerous, may be fatal.

Any want may be set down as unnatural when the desire which it compels will not find full satisfaction short of peril to life or health.

Every want is false that discounts health or imperils life to insure its gratification.

Yet false wants have the most real power over men. I have known a man to go hungry for bread, and starve his family, that he might buy opium. I have known another man to shut himself in his room of a Saturday night and drink two quarts of raw whisky between that time and Monday morning, taking no food whatever meanwhile.

POWER OF FALSE WANTS.

Of what benefit to production could such men be, with such wants gratified in such manner, through the indulgence of such habits? How could their wealth, or the wealth of those about them, be increased by them in any degree?

Between real want, the natural demand, and production, the necessary supply, stands Labor, an imperative necessity; and every false want, which detrimentally affects labor, in its quality or its quantity, decreases production and checks the accumulation of real wealth.

WANT AND LABOR.

Every want which, gratified, renders labor more or less impossible, more or less paralyzes production, and annuls a universal law. For labor is a prime natural condition—the necessity for it rests, primarily, upon all.

"Whoso will not work, neither shall he eat," said St. Paul; and in that saying is a law no man can repeal.

"If one of my subjects does not labor," said once an emperor of China, "there is some one in my country who suffers from hunger and cold."

Hunger and cold come every year when hard times come. What brings the hard times? Lack of labor; the inability of men to produce; the multiplication of wants, natural or unnatural, without a corresponding increase of supply, or the continuance of wants when the supply is for some reason greatly decreased.

Gratify and multiply those wants among men which discount production by discounting their power to produce, <small>A CAUSE OF HARD TIMES.</small> and the natural wants will go unsatisfied, hard times will follow. Fifty thousand men out of employment in Chicago means a curtailment of production, the logical and inevitable result of which is hunger and cold. And the natural, real wants of these 50,000 men will only be aggravated and increased by the 10,000 saloons of Chicago, which exist to create and stimulate unnatural wants and unfit men for production.

"Our children cry for bread!" was a conspicuous motto on one of the banners borne one day through the streets of Chicago by a procession of laboring men, another of whose mottoes was:

"Bread or blood!

Yet on the same day the same men paid for beer over $1,400! Enough to buy 28,000 loaves of bread: sufficient to feed 30,000 children one day at least.

"If one of my subjects does not labor," said that old

heathen Chinee, "there is some one in my country who suffers from hunger and cold!" and there wasn't a saloon then in his entire dominion! What would he say were he living and ruling in this country to-day?

The great, prime, natural wants are for **food, clothing, and shelter.** These can be magnified, exaggerated, developed, if you please, until in a sense they become unnatural, or at least abnormal; yet even then they need not necessarily, and will not inevitably, work harm or interfere with production. They may and they do stimulate production. They may and they do lead to the accumulation of wealth. They become in common esteem the indexes of wealth.

<small>PRIME NATURAL WANTS.</small>

The natural hunger of man may be satisfied with the coarsest food; but with the development of appetite, and the refinement of taste, the finest may become almost a necessity. The peasant may thrive on his oatmeal porridge, and may covet nothing better, while the merchant prince may crowd his table with delicacies unstinted: and one might say that the educated, magnified wants of the rich man are but abnormal developments of the poor man's needs; but is not production stimulated by the multiplication, the development, of want in this way?

Suppose that all the people were peasants, and satisfied with porridge? How the labor of the agriculturist would be lessened! How the number of tradesmen would be reduced! How "the butcher, the baker, the candlestick-maker" would find their occupations limited! How hard it would be to obtain supporting employment for the growing millions of men!

<small>DEVELOPMENT OF NATURAL WANTS.</small>

The coarsest and cheapest clothing may furnish protection and even comfort for the body; and the peasant, the poor man, may be satisfied with it, may find his natural want amply met by it. He may insist that the desire of the rich man, and the rich man's family, for fine raiment, like their desire for fine food, is exaggerated and unnatural; but what a wide range of productive labor is kept in operation thereby! From the sheep-ranch and the silk-worm's cocoon, to the tailor-shop and the *modiste*, that labor can be seen, actively engaged, as the direct result of the development into discriminative taste of a natural want or necessity.

The peasant, the poor man, may find comfort in his cabin, and his natural want or necessity may be met by **VARIED FORMS OF PRODUCTION.** the shelter it affords. He may not envy the rich man his palace; he may even condemn it as a sign of extravagance, or complain of it as a proof that wealth is distributed unequally; but how varied are the forms of productive labor which the palace represents, as compared with the hut of the Hottentot, or the "dugout" of the pioneer,—how manifold the kinds of work that have entered into it,—what a record it is, in wood, and brick, and stone, of the architect's thought, the artisan's handicraft, the workingman's wages —the genuine productiveness of labor—from cellar to chimney-cap!

From the forest to the carpenter's bench and the furniture factory; from the bed of clay to the mortar-bed and the bricklayer's trowel; from the quarry to the stone-cutter's yard and the final, finished wall—that record is written, and some proof of it you can find, if you search for it, in many a humbler home made more comfortable on account of the labor which went into the beauty of that palace and its cost.

Civilization multiplies wants. Wealth inspires **EFFECTS OF CIVILIZATION.** wants. But so long as the wants multiplied and inspired do not impair, discount or paralyze the work or the capacity for work necessary to meet these wants, they may be counted a blessing and not a curse.

Franklin's quaint philosophy was not final. He phrased it in verse more prosaic than poetical, on one page of "Poor Richard's Almanac," in 1746, as follows:

> "Man's rich with little, were his Judgment true,
> Nature is frugal, and her Wants are few;
> Those few Wants answer'd, bring sincere Delights,
> But Fools create themselves new Appetites.
> Fancy and pride seek Things at vast Expense,
> Which relish not to Reason nor to Sense.
> Like Cats in Airpumps, to subsist we strive
> On Joys too thin to keep the Soul alive."

As populations multiply, the means of support must increase. As labor-saving implements are invented, newly inspired wants become welcome. In other words, labor in some form must keep even pace with the needs of labor to maintain general thrift.

There is no danger that legitimate want will pauperize the world. Of such want comes wealth. But it must come according to natural laws. It must come of want that breeds work. All other want is against nature, a human violation of the divine plan.

Wants cannot be too numerous, if they be healthy and inspire healthy work.

"Man wants but little here below," sang the poet, generations gone by; and some philosophers have insisted that what the poet sang philosophy should teach. No political economist believes this who properly studies the possibilities of man and has faith in the world's progress. A Hottentot poet might sing it now, but the poets of civilization have come to see more widely and wisely.

INCREASED WANTS OF CIVILIZATION.

In the Cave Age, the Stone Age, every man's wants

were few and easily supplied. But then men were few, and of small account. With our teeming millions to-day, the whole situation is different. The fundamentals of Political Economy were as much a fact in the Cave Age of man as they are now, but the science had then little need of application. There were buyers and sellers then, perhaps, in their crude way, and exchanges of a sort were no doubt recognized; and this being so, Professor Perry's "science of exchanges" might well enough then have been in a kind of preexistent state, and his present definitions may have a certain *ex post facto* foundation.

We have come to the Age of Wants, and of wants that are necessities—civilized wants, that call for civilized work, and the skill, the genius, the capacity, of civilization.

It is **the Age of Work**, as well as of want; the age, let us confess it, when thousands want work who cannot obtain it, and are in bitter want because of this; when other thousands do not want work because unnatural wants have unfitted them for work, and through their idleness have made heavier and more burdensome the burdens of willing and capable workers.

<small>WANT AND WORK.</small>

That old Chinese was right. If one man does not labor, some other man must suffer from hunger and cold. Was it because of this that he, or another in place of him, 3,000 years ago, by royal mandate, uprooted every vineyard in all China and punished the sale of intoxicating liquor with beheading, by royal decree? Had he come to see, so many centuries before the existence of a saloon, that the fruit of the vine was the enemy of labor and interfered with production's natural law?

Under that natural law each must produce for each. Rousseau, the famous Frenchman, declared that human "laws should be so framed that labor should be always necessary and never useless."

Genuinely reproductive labor—which in China is made a religious duty, if not indeed an act of devotion—is everywhere a virtue; and, as De Laveleye puts it, "there is not a virtue which does not lead to true wealth, nor a vice which is not an obstacle to well-being."

Nearly all writers on economy classify labor merely as productive and unproductive. A better classification, it seems to me, would include also the word just used, and its opposite, and would make Labor—

<small>LABOR CLASSIFIED.</small>

Productive,
Unproductive,
Reproductive, and
Unreproductive.

All labor must be counted worthless that is unproductive, or that does not care for or protect the processes or fruits of production. But that which equally tells against national thrift is labor not *re*productive.

In other words, if the product of labor be not capable of transformation, through further labor or actual use, into some other product essentially valuable and necessary, the labor employed on it was not conducive to true wealth. Says Amasa Walker, in his "Science of Wealth":

<small>LABOR AND WEALTH.</small>

"If labor expends itself on objects that do not stimulate to further efforts, or serve as instruments to further production, but rather debauch the energies and corrupt the faculties, it is evident that reproduction will be lessened and debased, and the whole course of labor will be downward."

To nothing else can this language and the profound truth of it apply so forcibly as to the liquor traffic.

There is labor in this traffic, and an immense product flows from it; but what of its reproductive capacity? It **LABOR AND THE** has none. The greater the product the **LIQUOR TRAFFIC.** more it does "debauch the energies and corrupt the faculties," the more "reproduction is lessened and debased," and the less likely are men to make labor profitable and accumulate wealth.

Multiply this product as many fold as you will, and you do not correspondingly multiply wealth; for, as De Laveleye says, "things whose destruction improves the condition of mankind cannot be true wealth."

"Commodities consumed by false wants," he further asserts, "are false wealth. They are rightly called wealth, for they are bought and sold for large sums. But they are false wealth, for they are of no real good or use. Often they are worse than useless—they are injurious; worse than this, they are fatal."

A false want calls for alcoholic beverage; labor that is not legitimately reproductive supplies it; it is consumed; the consumer's energies are debauched, his faculties are corrupted; through him the course of labor sinks downward; and for him, for his fellow men, and for society, the production of which he shared was not in any sense a means of wealth, but a minister of curses.

CHAPTER III.

CHARACTER OF LABOR AND PRODUCTION.

LABOR which produces what meets a real want must be accepted as **Productive Labor**. Labor which does not thus produce we must class as Unproductive, or Un*re*productive.

Much labor is expended for the purpose of meeting wants that are developed, abnormal, but even this labor may be productive.

LABOR'S PURPOSE AND PRODUCT.

Into the perfume that you bought the other day at the drug-store went a considerable labor and a certain percentage of alcohol. The alcohol was a product of previous labor before it came under the perfumer's art. As perfume, it is now another product and the fruit of productive labor; but what is there about it *re*productive? Nothing. From time to time you sprinkle the perfume on your handkerchief, and presently it has vanished. There was in it no power for, no quality of, reproduction. Its purpose served in one form, it cannot serve a further purpose in the same or another form. If its production meant any addition to wealth, so much wealth has been wasted or dissipated.

Yet into the alcohol; into the distillation of that perfume which the alcohol absorbed and in turn breathed out for you; into the stuff from which the alcohol was made; and into the growing of the roses or the violets that furnished the precious drops of odor you so freely and completely expended—into all these went labor, and from it came a product—and forever disappeared.

UNREPRODUCTIVE QUALITY.

You wanted the perfume. It was a real want, of the

developed, educated, refined sort. You did not want it to quench thirst. You would not have used it for that purpose. No false want of the appetite of that kind has been created in you. But it was not a natural want nevertheless. No harm came of gratifying that want however, to you, or any one else. Some labor found employment because of it. It was productive labor, of the unreproductive kind which brings no ill.

Remember that we are speaking now of the perfume contained within that dainty cut-glass bottle you admired **THE PERFUME** so much and that you still possess. What **BOTTLE.** about the bottle itself?

A product of labor, surely; of skilled labor. It was made in a factory which labor built; it grew from a pile of sand that labor transmuted. Out of the fiercest fires it came, fed by coal which miners dug by the grimmest work far underground. Its crystal pattern was cut by skilful hands upon a grindstone which other hands labored to procure and shape in quarries far away. Though the perfume has fled from it, there is the pretty bottle still, for any future use you may see fit. It could be again melted and remade into a sauce-dish, if the glassblower should please. There is long use and possible reproduction in that fruit of productive labor.

Suppose into that bottle, or another less elaborate, had gone an alcoholic product of another sort—say, brandy. **THE BRANDY** There would have been as much labor back **BOTTLE.** of it as back of the perfume, perhaps. Then suppose a young man had bought it, and had drank it to satisfy an abnormal thirst, to meet a false want. Suppose the drinking had made him crazy drunk, and while in that condition he had committed a crime. Back of his deed would have been that productive labor—unreproductive as to final good, but awfully productive of ill.

Thinking of labor in this way, and the products of it, we may properly fix in mind two terms that will be of service—

Immediate Production,
Ultimate Production.

Immediate production meets an immediate want. Its product is direct, visible. It comes of labor which directly produces something of immediate use.

<small>IMMEDIATE AND ULTIMATE PRODUCTION.</small>

Put two jackknives into the hands of two boys. One uses his by the hour in aimless whittling, that yields only shavings and litter—unproductive labor, you properly say; the other makes a neat package of toothpicks in the same time, or fashions bracket on which to place his books.

Set a man carrying brick all day back and forth across the street. It is labor; and if you pay him well enough for it there is a sense (later explained) in which he is not an unproductive laborer, yet his labor is unproductive. Set him at paving the street with the same brick, and his labor becomes productive; it has in it, as had the brickmaker's, ultimate, as well as immediate, production, and of a useful sort.

Productive labor built Bunker Hill Monument, and if reasonably well paid the laborers were not unproductive; but there was no ultimate production, beyond some possible patriotic sentiment. Productive labor built the great factory's tall chimney, and through that comes ultimate production in whatever form of product the factory may turn out.

Where the product of labor is not immediate, to meet an immediate and legitimate want, the true productive quality of labor must be determined by ultimate production and what comes of that.

The alcohol which formed substantially all your perfume, in that handsome cut-glass bottle, came of labor immediately productive; and the ultimate production, as a perfume, wrought no ill. From the same alcohol, under different treatment, could have been made the brandy I suggested, from which, as the ultimate, might have come murder.

THE TRUE PRODUCTIVE QUALITY.

Productive labor reared the large and fine laboratory of my friend, Alfred Wright, in Rochester, N. Y., whose perfumes have been so long and so widely known; productive labor reared the great Bartholomay Brewery in the same city, whose products are not less widely known. That is to say, labor in one case produced a laboratory, and in the other case a brewery—two buildings or sets of buildings for further productive purposes, in both of which further labor should be employed, the ultimate production of both to satisfy taste or appetite; the fruits of one to yield delight or pleasure only, the fruits of the other to harm all who partake of them, to breed want, inspire wickedness, and consume wealth.

It has been said that all labor is *un*productive which is not in its product *re*productive. In the ultimate that is true. There is a very vital sense in which, however, unproductive labor may be productive, and productive labor may be unproductive. To understand clearly what seems a paradox, you must think of labor in two lights—

UNPRODUCTIVE AND REPRODUCTIVE LABOR.

Labor as of the individual;
Labor in the aggregate.

You must also regard the fruits of labor in a twofold aspect—

As to the individual;
As to the community.

Labor as of the individual determines whether the individual man is **productive** or **non-productive**; whether he be **a producer** or **a consumer**. Labor in the aggregate must show whether a class, a community, or an entire people produce and care for more than they consume.

There are whole classes of men who rank as consumers only. They labor, but they do not produce. It depends on the fruit of their labor whether they be or be not of the unproductive class.

CONSUMING CLASSES.

Bear in mind two facts, viz., that, whether of the individual or in the aggregate, *to be productive—*

Labor must produce, or

Labor must care for production;

and that, whether labor produces or cares for production, to be productive—

The laborer must produce, or must earn, more than he consumes.

The man whose keeping costs society more than, through productive work or wages, he contributes to society, is a non-producer, whatever quality or character may pertain to the fruit of his work.

No labor is, in its ultimate, of productive value to society, the fruit of which begets a non-productive class, a class of consumers whom society must support.

The laborer upon the farm who receives less in wages as his share of the farm's production than he and his family cost the community for their keeping, is non-productive; he and they consume more than they contribute. The laborer in the brewery who receives less in wages than he and his family cost for their support is non-productive in a far greater degree, for the fruit of his work tends to build up a non-producing class.

NON-PRODUCTIVE CLASSES.

Two distinctively non-producing classes, in fact, are the direct result of productive or non-productive labor in the brewery, the distillery, and the saloon,—**the drinking class,** who through drink are rendered unable to earn or to produce as much as they consume; and **the constabulary class,** made necessary to care for and control these, who are non-producers entirely, and a burden to all the rest.

There are other non-producing classes—teachers, preachers, doctors, lawyers, actors, etc. All of these labor; none of them produce; all are consumers. Without the producers all of them would starve. Yet some of them care for production and are essential to it.

Teachers and preachers are a necessary aid to the mental and moral development of mankind. Such development is required for profitable production. Wealth cannot be extensively created without it. Says Mr. McDonell in his "Survey of Political Economy":

"Wherever there is a great store of wealth, there must be a people living under moral restraint."

Says De Laveleye:

"Order, security, liberty, justice, above all that organization of responsibility which assures to the industrious the fruits of their labors,— these are necessary conditions of the development of wealth."

To these the teachers, the preachers and the lawyers largely contribute. **Moral restraint among men** is

UNPRODUCTIVE CLASSES CONTRASTED.
 directly due to the inculcations of preachers and teachers; thrift is born of well-directed intelligence, and is dependent on order, security, liberty, justice. These non-producing classes appear necessary to moral progress; and some one has well said that—

"Moral progress always brings with it an increase of prosperity; but material progress, unless accompanied by an equivalent progress in morality, is always the forerunner of decline."

The progress of immorality, the existence of disorder, the feeling and fact of insecurity, create, or make imperative, the constabulary class of non-producers, the necessity for which makes more difficult the work of those other non-producing classes.

How much a given community shall produce, and how rapidly it shall accumulate wealth, must depend on **the ratio of producers to non-producers.** Its moral status will have much to do in determining that ratio.

Better for the moral status of a community, all will admit, that ten per cent. of the population be teachers and preachers than that ten per cent. be saloonkeepers and gamblers; and as much better for the material progress, also, as all experience and statistics prove.

SELF-SUPPORTING NON-PRODUCTIVE LABOR. All non-productive labor is not a burden to the productive classes, though none but productive labor can create wealth.

I heard Paderewski play the piano, not long since, before 3,000 people who had paid an average of a dollar apiece to hear him play. His hour of play, for me, was an hour of work for him, which represented years of severe, patient toil preceding. It was not productive labor, because nothing was produced save melody, harmony—as elusive and fleeting as the perfume you bought and which vanished. It was not productive labor, yet the laborer, the artist, is not unproductive or non-supporting; his fingers win him, from his fellows, more than he costs the community for support.

But suppose nobody would pay Paderewski to play for them. Suppose, in consequence, that he had to be maintained at a poorhouse as a charge on the public. He might play every day to his fellow paupers; he might work as hard at the piano, and as long, as he does now; and yet he would then be an unproductive laborer, belonging then, as now, to an unproductive class. He does not now create wealth, but he shares in the distribution of it, as a pauper could not. And he works as hard, as many hours of every day, as does the most untiring productive laborer whose labor produces wealth.

When he *plays* a piece of music, for the public's entertainment, his labor is unproductive; when he *composes* a <small>THE PLAYER AND</small> piece of music, for publication and sale, his <small>THE COMPOSER.</small> labor is productive. He thus exemplifies in his one person the two kinds of labor of which we have chiefly spoken.

As a player he is unproductive. As a composer he is productive—he creates wealth. He supplies a want of an educated, refined taste. He adds to the store of accumulated musical publications, for which there is a demand and for which men and women will pay. He makes work for other men, who become fellow producers with him— the paper-maker, the engraver, the printer, the publisher. As a composer he is more than the marvelous artist whom I heard play; just as the Mendelssohn, Mozart, Handel, and Bach, of whom we know to day, were more than the grand organists who played for the generations gone by, and who were known by those names.

The player and the composer, whether in two persons or in one person, represent both **Manual Labor** and **Mind Labor.** As a rule Mind Labor reaches beyond the immediate thing produced, and comprehends the later <small>MANUAL LABOR</small> mental or manual employment of others; the <small>AND MIND LABOR.</small> fruit of manual labor may be consumed in a day, or be but the idle surplus of years to follow, neither affording further occupation of labor nor furnishing the means of further production in any form.

The author dictates a book. The stenographer takes down the author's dictation in "shorthand," and transcribes it in a neat style into readable pages, on a typewriting machine. It was mind labor with the author; it was manual labor with the copyist. The latter's task ended when the copy was complete; but the author's production, the fruit of mind labor, will furnish employment for compositors, and paper-makers, and printing-presses, and binders, and booksellers, for weeks or months to come.

Edison in his workshop labors with hand and brain. Manual skill as an artisan is matched by patience as an inventor. He produces the telephone and the electric-light. Now a thousand men in a single shop are at work multiplying telephones and making incandescent apparatus; but the labor of each is manual, not mind, while Edison's labor, back of all theirs, made all theirs possible, and opened the door of a mammoth new industry, which to-day is building dynamos by the thousands, stretching electric-wires by the millions of miles, weaving street-cars like shuttles across all our cities, and supplying occupation for a whole army of laborers all over the world.

CHAPTER IV.

LABOR AND THE LABORER.

SOME of the references in our last chapter suggested some questions and comments which may well be considered before we pass on to the consideration of wealth.

What is Labor?

The different kinds of it have been stated; some of the relations of it have been referred to; the fruits of it have been emphasized; but no exact definition has been attempted. Should not one be given?

One answer might be that in defining and explaining the several kinds of Labor, we have sufficiently shown the meaning of the general term. Political Economists have, as a rule, acted on this assumption. You will scarce find a definition of labor, as an inclusive word, in all their pages. Mill, the most extensive writer on Political Economy since Adam Smith, who founded the science, does not give one; neither does Marshall, the most compact writer, in some respects, who has covered this field.

DEFINITION OF LABOR.

The only exact definitions of Labor by economists which I can now recall and care to quote are by Professor Perry, whose definitions do not always satisfy, and by Mr. W. H. Mallock. Distinguishing between "Labor" and "Ability," in his little book on "Labor and the Popular Welfare," Mr. Mallock makes all production the result of **human exertion,** and this he divides into the two terms thus given. In effect he declares that **Labor** is manual exertion, and that all other exertion is **Ability;** which thought he amplifies in this definition:

"Labor is a kind of exertion on the part of the individual which begins and ends with each separate task it is employed upon ; while ability is a kind of exertion on the part of the individual which is capable of affecting the labor of an indefinite number of individuals."

Speaking of Labor as "the second requisite of Production," Perry says:

"Labor is any human exertion that demands something for itself in exchange."

He puts this in italics, as if it were to stand, unmodified, the positive, final statement of what Labor is. As a negative statement, not italicized, he adds this:

"Every person puts forth more or less of muscular and mental effort without any expectation of a return for it. This is not labor. Nothing is labor that does not look to a sale."

Further on Professor Perry says:
"All labor is offered over against some desires of other men;" still further carrying out his market-and-sale theory.

But, in my opinion, a large per cent. of the wealth of the world has been created by Labor that in its production had no thought of sale.

Take the settlers of the West. Each man who went pioneering far out upon the prairies or the plains built himself a home. He did it with the toil of his own hands, and with no regard for the "desires of other men." It was to shelter his own family, and not "for sale." He turned the prairie sod, primarily, to secure food wherewith to feed his own; neighbors and a market were out of reach, and "sales" were out of question. By so much as the value of the home he built, and the land improvements he made, he added wealth to the nation. And who shall say he did not labor, though during those first pioneer years he scarcely sold a thing?

<small>LABOR AND SALES.</small>

Barring the dollar a day to which the Irishman referred, **Perry's idea of labor** would in some sense fit the Irishman's when he wrote to his friend in the old country:

"Pat," he said, "come to Ameriky! It's here I am gettin' a dollar a day for jist carryin' a boxful of brick to the top of a tall buildin', and the man up there does all the work!"

"Nothing is labor that does not look to a sale," says Perry; and if that be true, hodcarrying would not be work if the hodcarrier were not paid for it. But I surmise that Professor Perry would find it laborious if he were forced to engage in it, even without compensation.

A thousand cases could be cited of production coming from Labor that does not look to a sale. Take one:

PAINTER AND PORTRAIT.

An artist paints a picture of the wife of his friend. His friend wants it; has ordered it; will buy it and pay for it when finished. Perry would admit this to be labor on the part of the artist—it looks to a sale. But suppose the artist wants a picture of his own wife, to hang upon the walls of his own home. He paints it, even more painstakingly than he painted the portrait of the other woman. Shall we say he does not labor, now, because he would not sell this latest canvas,—because he did not paint it for sale?

If we had not already classified Labor as Productive and Unproductive, and if we were seeking a definition in the fewest possible words, we might say:

LABOR FURTHER DEFINED.

Labor is any effort to produce; or

Labor is an agent of production.

In the light of the classification stated, and of the best reasoning of all economists, we must accept the declaration of John Stuart Mill, that—

"Labor is indispensable to production, but has not always production for its effect. There is much labor, and of a high order of usefulness, of which production is not the object."

Suppose, then, we say:

Labor is any effort to produce, or to care for the fruits of Production, or to assist in making Production possible under the best possible auspices, or to secure for the Laborer wherewith from the effort of others to satisfy desire or want.

"Production," says Perry, "is always effort, but it is not every kind of effort that is Production." And then he speaks of his boy at the piano as making irksome effort to play, but "unproductive effort," because the boy does not intend to sell the skill he may acquire, while the boy's teacher makes "productive effort" in teaching him because of the compensation involved.

According to Perry, if Paderewski were to play an hour or more to a great audience without pay, his playing would not be labor; if he had practised all his long years before coming to America, for the purpose of giving free concerts, his practise would not have been labor; the quality of what a man does must depend on what he gets or expects to get for doing it.

"But," says one, "you declared Paderewski's labor PLAYER AND productive as a composer, and unproductive INSTRUMENT. as a player. Did he not produce by his playing the greatest sensations of delight? Was it not, then, productive?"

John Stuart Mill has answered this question. He says:

"All labor is, in the language of political economy, unproductive which ends in immediate enjoyment, without any increase of the accumulated stock or permanent means of enjoyment."

The sensations produced by the player's performance

upon the instrument ended with his performance. Without the instrument he could not have produced them. The piano was made to gratify a refined taste for music, not to meet a natural want or necessity; but the maker of the piano, in producing the instrument, produced real wealth; it can be bought and sold; it is a commercial commodity, an "increase of the accumulated stock or permanent means of enjoyment."

The sensations produced by the playing of Paderewski ended in immediate enjoyment; but when, as a composer, he produces a musical composition, he adds to the "permanent means of enjoyment," he supplies a merchantable commodity. The sensations of his audience, when he plays, could not be sold or bought; they are not wealth, according to any definition of what wealth is; and Mill has declared, and with him all economists agree, that—

PRODUCTIVE LABOR.

"**Productive labor is labor productive of wealth.**"

I think it possible for music to produce sensations that would help or hinder productive labor, yet this fact would but indirectly alter the player's unproductive status.

I have read of a musician who played hour after hour, day after day, a droning, die-away set of pieces, which were heard plainly in a large room adjoining, where a large number of tailors were plying their needles, before sewing-machines came generally into shop use. The boss of that shop saw that his workmen were keeping slow time to the slow tunes, and were accomplishing less than they should accomplish. He went to the musician and paid him to play all the liveliest airs he could, and the workmen kept pace with these, to their employer's great gain.

INSPIRATIONS TO LABOR.

A farmer in haying-time fed his men meagerly, buttermilk and whey being their chief diet at the start. Going out in the field he found them slowly singing—

> " Buttermilk and whey,
> Faint all day "—

and swinging their scythes in slow time to their own music. He changed his supplies for them, and going to the field again he found them briskly moving through the grass, each man's scythe swinging to the brisker measure—

> " Ham and eggs,
> Take care of your legs."

The **effect of stirring band music** upon an army of men during a toilsome march or just before entering battle has often been cited, and of its inspiring benefits in the way of courage and cheer there can be no doubt. Yet who would call the members of a band productive laborers? Even the army cheered on by them could be counted in the productive class but indirectly, and so far as directly engaged in the protection or defense of productive labor's results.

De Laveleye says that "labor is man's action on nature to the end to satisfy his wants."

Mill holds that "we should regard all labor as productive which is employed in creating permanent utilities."

Again he says: "Labor is not creative of objects, but of utilities." And borrowing from M. Say, he declares that CREATION "what we produce is always an utility." In OF UTILITIES. his opinion, and according to his limitation,

Utilities are of three kinds:

1. Those fixed and embodied in outward objects.
2. Those fixed and embodied in human beings.
3. Those not fixed or embodied in any object, but consisting of a mere service rendered.

The first kind, he holds, come of "labor employed in investing external material things with properties which render them serviceable to human beings."

The second kind come of labor "employed in conferring on human beings qualities which render them serviceable to themselves and others"; and in this class he includes all concerned in education of every sort, in caring for the sick "as far as instrumental in preserving life and physical or mental efficiency," and "governments, so far as they aim successfully at the improvement of the people."

The third kind come of labor expended "without leaving a permanent acquisition in the improved qualities of any person or thing"; and in this class of utilities he enumerates the service rendered by musical performers, actors, showmen, the army and navy, and all agents of government "in their ordinary functions, apart from any influence they may exert on the improvement of the national mind."

Utilities of this third class, Mill insists, "cannot be **UTILITIES** spoken of as wealth," concerning which he **AND WEALTH.** further declares:

"It is essential to the idea of wealth to be susceptible of accumulation."

Yet utilities of the second class—viz., those fixed and embodied in human beings: the skill, the intelligence, the energy, the character, of the producers of a country—may be and are properly "reckoned part of its wealth," in the opinion of Mr. Mill.

What are the essential requisites to production of wealth?

Natural Agents,
Labor, and
Capital.

The first and the last of these we will consider when we **REQUISITES** come to the second part of this first great **OF PRODUCTION.** division of our study—Wealth. Labor we have been and still are considering.

Now what are the requisites of productive labor? I answer *First, as to the laborer:*

(*a*) Adequate preparation and fitness for the labor to be done.

(*b*) Intelligence ample to insure this, with opportunity given.

(*c*) The spirit of industry joined with skill and character.

(*d*) Ambition to produce, for the satisfaction of want or the accumulation of wealth.

(*e*) Effort where the necessary natural agents are at convenient command.

Place the best laborer in the world upon a desert island and his labor will not be productive.

Put an idle, unambitious savage in a garden of the richest natural fertility, and he will be no more productive. **ENVIRONMENT** Place amid the best opportunities, and in **OF LABOR.** command of the finest natural forces, a man who is little more than an idiot, and he may be willing to work but almost unable to produce.

Select a man of fair intellect, but put him at effort for which there has been no preparation, and the productiveness of his labor will be discounted greatly.

Intelligence and sobriety must unite with ambition and opportunity to insure productive labor.
SOBRIETY AND All economists recognize this. Character is **INTELLIGENCE.** widely declared an economic quality.

Mill has more to say in regard to this than most of the economists. Listen to him:

"The moral qualities of the laborers are fully as important to the efficiency and worth of their labor as the intellectual. Independently of the effects of intemperance upon their bodily and mental faculties, and of flighty, unsteady habits upon the energy and continuity of their work, it is well worthy of meditation how much of the aggregate effect of their labor depends on their trustworthiness."

Going out still farther upon this line Mr. Mill says:

FUNDAMENTAL ECONOMIC QUALITIES. "The advantage to mankind of being able to trust one another penetrates into every crevice and cranny of human life: the economical is perhaps the smallest part of it, yet even this is incalculable. To consider only the most obvious part of the waste of wealth occasioned to society by human improbity, there is in all rich communities a predatory population, who live by pillaging or overreaching other people; their numbers cannot be authentically ascertained, but on the lowest estimate, in a country like England, it is very large. The support of these persons is a direct burden on the national industry. The police, and the whole apparatus of punishment and of criminal and partly of civil justice, are a second burden, rendered necessary by the first. The exorbitantly paid profession of lawyers, so far as their work is not created by defects in the law of their own contriving, are required and supported principally by the dishonesty of mankind. As the standard of integrity in a community rises higher all these expenses become less."

And thus we might quote from Mill a page or two more as to the **needs and benefits of character,** of trustworthiness, in productive labor and the production of wealth.

Professor Laughlin, of Harvard, says:

"The amount of wealth produced in a country will depend on the following causes: First, not merely on the number of the laborers, but on their physique, their intelligence and skill, *and their moral character.*"

Marshall, stating the function of Political Economy, says:

"Last, but *not least,* it traces the connection that there is between the character of the workman and the character of his work; as the work is, so is the worker; *as the worker is, so is the work.*"

With special reference to the laborer's personal habits Marshall declares:

THE LABORER'S CHARACTER AND CONDITIONS. "The prevalence of intemperate habits in a country diminishes both the number of days in the week and the number of years in his life during which the breadwinner is earning full wages. Temperance increases a man's power, and generally increases his will to save."

Second, as to the Laborer's Environment:

(*a*) A demand for the fruits of labor that shall induce it, for support of himself or others.

(*b*) Custom or law that shall insure to him the benefits of his labor in fair proportion.

(*c*) Security for himself and his own, while he labors, against unjust interference.

(*d*) Helps to his intellectual and moral progress, so that he may come to the best of his capacity.

(*e*) Safeguards from whatever would hinder such progress, would weaken his physical and mental powers, would rob him of his working-time or his well-earned wages, or would in any way unfit him for the best effort as a producing agent.

(*f*) A government guaranteeing him such law, and security, and helps, and safeguards, with that liberty to which he may be entitled as a citizen without imperiling these for any other, and thus insuring to him, by equally providing for all, the demand for his labor or the fruits of it, upon which he as a productive laborer must depend.

In view of these conditions, which are vital to the laborer and essential in his environment, **the liquor traffic is a direct foe to the productive laborer,** **THE LABORER'S FOE.** a constant enemy to his production of wealth; and the government which cares for him and his future, which must support him if he is unproductive and on which to so great an extent he must depend for productive opportunity, owes it to him, and to itself, to deny that traffic rights and recognition as a legitimate business, whether licensed or otherwise.

The positive prohibition of that traffic is demanded of government in behalf of labor and wealth. More of the reasons why, will be shown as we study the Creation and the Distribution of Wealth. Our next chapter will treat of its *Creation.*

CHAPTER V.

THE CREATION OF WEALTH.

WHAT is Wealth?
We might answer:
The gain of production over consumption.
The proof of productive labor.
The surplus after supplying Want's necessities.
The accumulation of means wherewith to supply Want.

But not one or all of these answers will cover all the meaning of wealth, as the word is used by economists **DEFINITIONS OF WEALTH.** uniformly. Each of them would be good in their sight as far as it goes, though I have never seen either given, in just the form I have used, by any economist; but neither goes far enough.

De Laveleye comes near to the last one when he says:

"**Wealth may be defined as everything which answers to men's rational wants**"; but even this falls rather short of meeting the broadest idea of wealth.

Perry prefers the two words, Value and Property, to what he calls "the old and poor word 'Wealth'"; but other economists do not abandon it.

Marshall subdivides it, or what it includes, into

Material Wealth, and
Personal Wealth;

and the former he speaks of as—

"The material sources of enjoyment which are capable of being appropriated, and therefore of being exchanged"; while speaking of the latter he says:

PERSONAL WEALTH
"'Personal' or *non-material* wealth consists of those human energies, faculties, and habits—*physical, mental and moral*—which directly contribute to making men industrially efficient, and which therefore increase their power of producing material wealth."

"In goods or wealth," says De Laveleye, giving elasticity to his own definition, "must be included **all that is good for the advancement of the individual and of the human race.**" And he goes on to add:

"From this idea of wealth it follows that besides *material* riches there is also *immaterial* riches, such as knowledge, manual skill, or the taste for work. The growth of riches is not an unmixed benefit, unless it be accompanied by the growth of justice and morality."

Grant that there are two kinds of wealth, in the language of Political Economy, it follows that the creation of one must depend upon the existence and preservation of the other.

MATERIAL WEALTH
Material wealth, while it may come from natural sources, *under natural law must come through labor alone*—through the productive effort of "those human energies, faculties, and habits—*physical, mental, and moral*"—which constitute personal or immaterial wealth, the result of temperance and sobriety, and form the basis of all profitable production.

We have already seen that there are three requisites to production—Natural Agents, Labor, and Capital.

Between the first and the last stands Labor, the intermediary, striving to make from one yet more of the other.

The four great natural agents are—

    Land, Water,

    Electricity, Climate.

As Professor Laughlin says: "No single article of wealth is produced for which something is not taken from nature, either in the form of materials or of forces."

The taking of it is labor; and the production of any single article which may meet any person's want or add to any person's wealth, may employ the labor of many persons and the natural agents in many parts of the world.

<small>NATURAL AGENTS.</small>

Newcomb, in his "Principles of Political Economy," illustrates this in this way with regard to a coat:

"In the first place, sheep had to be reared, pastured, and sheared, in order that the wool necessary for the coat should be obtained. The breeding of the sheep required a considerable expanse of land on some Western prairie or in the interior of Australia. It is obvious that without land there could be no grass, and therefore no wool. Now, land in its original state is a gift of nature, which men cannot make at all.

"In the further process of manufacture a factory had to be erected and machinery of brass and iron employed. A particular kind of earth was necessary to make the bricks out of which the factory was built, and the iron had to be extracted from iron ore. Both these materials had to be taken out of the earth, and their ownership is associated with that of land. If the machinery was run by water-power, a river was necessary; if by steam-power, coal had to be dug from the earth to make the fires which produce the steam."

<small>REQUIRED FOR A COAT.</small>

You will observe that this illustration covers two great natural agents—*Land and Water*—by direct reference. The other two are sufficiently implied; for proper *Climate* is essential to the raising of sheep—in the Arctic zone they would freeze to death in spite of their wool—and the great woolen factory would be lighted now with *Electricity*, of course.

A more poetical illustration, which covers even a wider range of work and natural supply, has been given us by Whittier, who sang thus on one occasion to the shoemakers:

<small>THE POET TO THE ARTISANS.</small>

> "For you, along the Spanish main
> A hundred keels are plowing;
> For you, the Indian on the plain
> His lasso-coil is throwing;

> For you, deep glens with hemlock dark
> The woodman's fire is lighting;
> For you upon the oak's gray bark
> The woodman's ax is smiting.
>
> "For you, from Carolina's pine
> The rosin-gum is stealing;
> For you the dark-eyed Florentine
> His silken skein is reeling;
> For you the dizzy goat-herd roams
> His rugged Alpine ledges;
> For you, round all her shepherd homes
> Bloom England's thorny hedges."

Ah, how many things, and persons, and countries, and climates, and conditions, and kinds of work, may enter into the making of a single pair of shoes! But only a poet or a political economist (who would ever have supposed these two so much allied?) could take such account of them. No doubt there may be poetry in the production of wealth, even though there be little or no wealth in the production of poetry.

Natural agents may in a sense be considered natural wealth, and are indispensable to the creation of

NATURAL WEALTH. wealth. Of the four mentioned, land and water are commonly reckoned as wealth, and are commercially conveyed or exchanged. It might be accurate enough to define land as private wealth and water as public wealth, but each definition would require a modifying clause in some cases.

Each of these two natural agents has close relation to the other. In a well-watered region the land will be worth more, whether as private or public wealth, than in a dry and barren region—worth more because it will produce more. A direct addition to the value of land is made and fixed, in Colorado and some other parts of the West, by water-rights, which great irrigating companies convey.

Apart from land—from which, however, the separation can be but nominal—the gold or the diamond in the mine **WEALTH IN THE MINE.** is as near to being natural wealth as anything which you can name. Close akin are silver, iron, and coal.

But of what actual value is the gold-mine unworked? To be sure, it can be sold. For it, if you own it and sell it, you may obtain a large sum of money. In this way it may add to *your* wealth, to your surplus or accumulation, wherewith to meet *your* increasing wants.

Yet it has not so far added one dollar to the world's wealth. No part of the money paid you, or value received in exchange by you, has come from the mine you sold. You merely transferred to another man your *opportunity for increasing the general surplus*. Until he fulfils the opportunity and becomes an actual producer, there is no productive value in that mine.

The gold-mine, the silver-mine, the iron-mine, the coal-mine, furnish a few of **Labor's opportunities for part- PARTNERSHIP nership with Capital** in the production of **OF LABOR** wealth. Outside that partnership no wealth **AND CAPITAL.** is produced. Inside of it production is limited by or dependent upon certain conditions of labor that grow out of certain conditions of want. Large capital, controlling unskilled labor, may in some cases fail to produce wealth. Skilled labor, rendered incompetent by, or heavily discounted on account of, bad habits, the result of false wants, may waste capital and wreck the creation of wealth.

It may be superficially assumed, in these days of multitudinous mechanical devices and the constant increase of machinery for production, that Labor's share in the partnership, Labor's part in the creation of wealth, is much less than formerly, and is likely to disappear.

It is true that machinery has in great measure supplemented, or been substituted for, the work of human hands. But take the most marked instance of which I have ever heard, where machinery, unaided, carries on the work of production to meet the wants of men.

I read of it a few years ago. It is or was found in a small factory, in a little English manufacturing town somewhat remote from productive centers, the name of which I do not recall. The machines in that factory make or made only one sort of thing—such cord as is used for window curtains, or was used in connection with them before spring appliances came into vogue, and is yet used for picture-hanging, etc.—a cord of peculiar weave. These machines are so complete in themselves that they require practically no attendance; and it was said that the whole factory could be set in operation Monday morning, and run day and night until the week's end without any supervision whatever, each machine caring for itself and mending its own breaks. The report which I saw of it said that regularly at night the doors of the factory were closed, but the work of the factory went on until morning unattended.

<small>MACHINERY AND PRODUCTION.</small>

A marvel of mechanics indeed! A triumph of the inventor's art! A far step, and the ultimate perhaps, toward thought by a machine—the embodiment of brain in brass and steel!

Yet back of the machine was man, the inventor of it; man, the maker of it. And back of it were other factories where the maker and the inventor labored, and other machines which colabored with them; and back of all, those natural agents from which all production must come, and the creation of all material wealth.

<small>THE MACHINE AND THE MAN.</small>

I have seen silk and carpet-weaving machines that came

as near to thinking as anything in metal could come; but back of each were human hands, a diversity of hand labor; back of each were laborers of many kinds, from the coal-miner, the iron-miner, to the most skilful machinist money could hire to cooperate with the inventor's brain.

Bear in mind, also, that much of the work done by machinery could not be done so well by hand labor, and is done to meet a want that handicraft, in the direct application of it, could not supply—a want in one sense widely created by the machinery devised wherewith to meet it.

Until the cheapness of window-cord was made possible by the machines to produce it, the want of window-cord was not universal or was not extensively recognized. Until carpet-machines rendered fine carpets cheap, the want of fine carpets was not commonly felt, and coarse rag carpets, or no carpets at all, fairly well sufficed.

The better the machine the better the man.

By which I mean that the higher the grade of mechanical devices, the higher the order of human wants; the more finely developed "those human energies and faculties," the more wisely regulated those "habits" upon which depend the supply of those wants and the creation of wealth. A Hottentot could not have constructed a sewing-machine; a Russian serf could not have invented a McCormick reaper and binder.

The greater the immaterial wealth of the people, the greater will be their aggregate of material wealth.

In other words, the more perfect the development of intelligence in a people, the more universal their skill, the more completely at command their physical and mental powers, the more industrious their habits, the more generally and successfully they will appropriate natural agents to meet their natural and

INTELLIGENCE AND WEALTH.

cultivated wants, the more widely they will accumulate surplus over the demands of all wants, the more prosperous and wealthy they will become.

Ignorance and indolence go hand-in-hand with poverty all over the world. Poverty is want but ill supplied. Wealth is everywhere recognized as more than the immediate supply of want.

CHAPTER VI.

NATIONAL AND INDIVIDUAL WEALTH.

WEALTH has been subdivided into material and immaterial, or personal; and we have made incidental reference to certain kinds of it as public and private. A further and final classification should be considered,—
**National Wealth, and
Individual Wealth.**
The latter term is quite distinct and different from the term *personal*, previously employed. The word *personal* was used as really synonymous with *immaterial*, to differentiate personal wealth from material wealth. But *individual* wealth may be either personal or material. In economic language, as generally accepted, it may consist of personal skill, intelligence, character, habits; or it may consist of houses, lands, bonds, or any evidence of ownership in any form of material wealth whatsoever.

<small>INDIVIDUAL WEALTH.</small>

Save in so far as natural agents constitute natural wealth, and as they have not been appropriated to individual use, **national wealth is the aggregate of individual accumulation**; and one might plausibly assume that Economy should consider the individual alone, letting the aggregate of individualities take logical care of itself.

<small>NATIONAL WEALTH.</small>

But Political Economy, though its tap-root be in the individual life, deals with man in the plural; and man in the plural must be regarded very differently from the single and isolated man. If there were but one man in every county, every state, and he were fenced off on all sides from his fellow-man, the functions of Political Economy would cease in large measure, to say the least. As it is, the science of economics must deal with men in the mass.

Individual wealth may come of both production and trade; National wealth can come of production alone.

The Nation—the aggregate of individuals—does not buy and sell. It may be said, also, that the Nation—the aggregate—does not produce. But what is produced in the Nation—what has been produced and still exists—is the national surplus, the national store of individual accumulation; while it may frequently change hands, by way of trade, and the man whose portion of it is large to-day may find it small to-morrow.

<small>HOW IT COMES.</small>

However much the conditions of international commerce may influence the growth of national wealth, such wealth results only from production, and not from trade. The multi-millionaire, however, may have come into possession of vast individual wealth without producing a dollar of it. It may not be the product of his mills, his factories, his lands; it was produced, and *it does exist, in the nation*, of which he is a unit; it forms **a part of the national wealth.** Production gave it to the nation; trade insured it to him.

Suppose the millionaire holds a mortgage upon the poor man's farm.

It represents a thousand dollars, if you please, that the rich man loaned the poor man wherewith to buy that land. It is that much, or little, of the rich man's individual or personal wealth. Now suppose, further, that in a fire which attacks the office of the rich man that mortgage is burned; and, as it has not

<small>MILLIONAIRE AND MORTGAGE.</small>

been recorded or witnessed, no proof is at his command of the loan he made. Unless the mortgagor be honest and admits the debt, the mortgagee must lose that particular thousand dollars of his wealth; but has anything been lost to the national aggregate? Certainly not. The land remains. It is worth no more, no less, as a natural agent, than before the mortgage burned. If its owner now consider himself worth one thousand dollars more than previously, this does not affect the aggregate of individual accumulations.

Burn the mortgages upon a thousand or ten thousand farms to-day; wipe out in this or any other way all evidences of indebtedness upon them and all claims against them, and the national wealth would not be depleted one penny. The distribution of it would be changed, that is all.

Compel the great Astor estate in New York to be subdivided, if you had the power; parcel out its many thousands of houses among its many thousands of tenants, and give each a good title to the place where he now resides—would you have altered the aggregate of national wealth? Certainly not. You would merely have transferred the possession of certain millions of property in the nation. One family might be made poor by the change; thousands of other families would be made well-to-do.

DIVISION BY THE ASTORS.

"National wealth," says Marshall, "includes the wealth of the individual members of the nation; but in estimating it, any debts due from one member of the nation to another may be omitted altogether. On the other hand," he goes on to remark, "**account must be taken of the internal and external political organization of the nation** in so far as this affects the freedom and security of its industry."

HOW INDUSTRY S AFFECTED.

"*Its industry,*" as here used by Marshall, means *all forms of industry*, or, as the more common terminology puts it, *industries of all kinds*. Division of labor into various lines has come about naturally, as insuring the most profitable production and the largest possible creation of wealth; and under such division great industries have grown up, each more or less distinct and separate from the other, though all closely related and more or less interdependent, while **the creation of national wealth is determined by the relation which every industry bears to all other industries.**

If there be any industry which detrimentally affects the security and well-being of any other industry, the national **THE RELATION** wealth suffers from it; and injury to national **OF INDUSTRIES.** wealth, in what it is or fairly should be, is a direct wrong to every individual who should share in that wealth.

We have heretofore stated (in Chapter III.) that how much a given community shall produce, and how rapidly it shall accumulate wealth, must depend on the ratio of producers to non-producers. We may now go a step farther on this line, and say that **how rapidly a nation shall accumulate wealth must depend on the mutual helpfulness of its industries.**

According to Perry, in one of his italicized summaries, " History affirms that all industries are equally natural; **NATURAL** and hence no one has the right to subsist **INDUSTRIES.** at the expense of the others."

If there be any industry, then, which does subsist at the expense of the others, it must be unnatural. Being unnatural, it directly antagonizes natural law. Being in antagonism to natural law, the law of the legislator should be against it, should forbid it, should prohibit it.

The liquor traffic sins against legitimate industry of

every sort. **Legitimate industries should and do favorably affect each other,** while the liquor traffic un-favorably affects them all. The more it flourishes, the more they must decline. It stands alone, the monumental robber of every other industry upon earth.

<small>AN UNNATURAL INDUSTRY.</small>

Its profits are taken from the merchant, and the manufacturers behind him; from the butcher, and the cattle-raisers behind *him;* from the farmer, the miller, the baker, the builder, the shoemaker, the printer, the teacher, and the preacher. Every honest producer suffers from the liquor product. The country suffers from it in its individual production, in the well-being of its producers, in the aggregate of its wealth, in its imports and exports. More than low tariff, or high tariff, or no tariff at all, it depreciates American industry, interferes with American commerce, and discounts the fruit of American labor. And yet the great leaders in our great political parties have not learned this fact, or are not statesmanlike enough to confess it.

The scholars, or some of them, are finding it out and asserting it. In a notable article which he published in *The Forum* for September, 1892, further referred to in this volume, Prof. J. J. McCook, of Hartford, Conn., thus testified:

<small>"Now, I am not a total abstainer, either theoretically or practically, and I have always voted in favor of license. It is needless to say that I do not belong to the Prohibition Party. But anybody who can see must know that, considered merely as a question of social economy, of dollars and cents, of tax-bills and public convenience generally, the drink question is the question of the day. The tariff wrangle is a mere baby to it. If intelligent, steady-going people could be induced to spend upon the drink question a fraction of the time and money they employ upon the other, we might hope for some real improvement in its treatment."</small>

In hard times the injustice done legitimate industries

by the presence of the liquor traffic is more marked even than when times are easy. The years of 1809-10 and 1813-14 saw great scarcity in Ireland. By wise forecast, and as wise authority, the distilleries were stopped, and note the result:

ITS UNHAPPY EFFECTS.

In the better years of 1811-12 and 1815-16—better but for distillation and unchecked drinking—the average consumption of spirits was 7½ millions of gallons; in those years of want, and the prohibition of distilleries, the consumption fell below 4¼ millions.

But, it may be said, the people had no money wherewith to buy, and of course other industries suffered in like proportion.

Not so. In those four years of famine, free from drink in fair degree because the distilleries were closed, the Irish people bought and paid for haberdashery, iron, hardware, and cotton goods, to the amount of £253,657, or about $1,268,285, *more* than in the four years of plenty named; of tea and sugar 773,911 pounds *more* were bought by them than in those good years. They used 1,356,070 *more* yards of drapery, and they slept under 33,401 *more* woolen blankets.

FOUR YEARS OF FAMINE.

So for the shopkeeper, the ironmonger, the cotton-maker, the merchant, and the woolen manufacturer, those years of want became years of prosperity, because an illegitimate industry was in part prohibited, and could not feed as a parasite on the legitimate industries. The distiller, no doubt, uttered loud complaint of hard times, and the barkeeper, it is probable, cursed Prohibition as loudly as does his lineal descendant in America to-day.

AN INDUSTRIAL PARASITE. Any parasite industry, magnifying the false wants of mankind and maintaining itself at the expense of other industries, is a foe to the creation of individual and national wealth. Whatever of so-called wealth such an industry may create is but false wealth—as false as the want it meets and magnifies—and can not really enrich the world.

Let us quote again De Laveleye's declaration, that—

"Things whose destruction improves the condition of mankind cannot be true wealth."

Dr. Oliver Wendell Holmes once declared—

"If all the drugs in the world were thrown into the sea, it would be vastly better for mankind, but might be bad for the fishes."

Paraphrasing the genial Autocrat's remark, we may as truly declare: "If all the liquor in the world were thrown into the sea, it would be vastly better for mankind, but very bad for the denizens of the great deep."

All being true which previously in our study has been asserted, there follows a law of Political Economy, logical and fundamental, which I have never found set forth by any economist, as I remember, but which in my opinion no man can set aside, viz:

<small>A THREE-FOLD ECONOMIC LAW.</small>

Every industry must produce its equitable share of the State's wealth, must receive its equitable share of the distribution thereof, and must bear its equitable share of the State's burdens.

Only as this law is observed can the creation of individual wealth go forward in a natural fashion to equitable results. Legitimate industries hold commerce with each other, just as the workers in each industry maintain trade relations with their fellow men.

As between individuals, so between classes and industries—each party to an exchange of products should receive an honest *quid pro quo*.

What Perry says in an entirely different connection applies here:

"Commerce is an exchange of goods for the mutual BENEFIT of the respective Owners."

The emphasis is Perry's own, and upon that word *benefit* all recognized principles of Political Economy would lay especial stress. All the products of labor should be for the immediate or ultimate *benefit or well-being* of all persons into whose possession they may come or whose wants they may supply. By the exchange of these products no man should be made poorer in person or in purse.
_{MUTUALITIES IN COMMERCE.}

The creation of wealth should be for the common weal. The very term "commonwealth," applied so often to an organized State or body politic, is proof of this fact. The creation of wealth should not be for a class, either of consumers or producers. Any class of consumers not actually required in reproductive effort, or in caring for the fruits of production, or in the diffusion of intelligence and morals, is a fungus upon industry, a hindrance to industrial progress, a curse to organized society.
_{A FUNGUS UPON INDUSTRY.}

The existence of such a class violates the fundamental law of Political Economy to which we have just referred. Such a class comes directly of the Liquor Traffic; which is, indeed, the progenitor of more than one such class. That traffic does not, never did, never can, produce its equitable share of the world's wealth. While that traffic remains, an equitable division of the world's wealth is impossible. Until that traffic is terminated, or exterminated, the burdens of the State cannot be equitably borne.

As to the latter statements, we will present further consideration and illustration later on, taking up as next in order the *Distribution of Wealth*.

CHAPTER VII.

THE DISTRIBUTION OF WEALTH.

WHILE the proper Distribution of Wealth is a requirement of Political Economy, it is also a great social and financial problem, growing more difficult every day. While such distribution is more general now in America than in any other civilized country, it is not here an equitable fact—it never can be until conditions are changed.

<small>PROBLEM OF DISTRIBUTION.</small>

Monster individual fortunes are piling up among our people in a way which excites the alarm of economists and patriots; the great needy class grows larger and needier. And where is the remedy? Statesmen will seek it, by and by, in the halls of legislation. They must find it, first, in the principles of Political Economy—in the natural laws underlying this Science of Economics.

<small>THE DISTRIBUTING AGENT.</small>

What must be the natural **Distributing Agent of Wealth?**

Wages.

What is it that *commands* wages?

Labor.

What is it that *pays* wages?

Capital.

What is Capital?

The third requisite of Production, as we have seen; but this fact is not a definition.

Perry defines it as "any valuable thing reserved for future use in Production."

Marshall says: "Capital is that part of wealth which is devoted to obtaining further wealth."
From what does Capital come? *From Labor.*

LABOR AND CAPITAL. While it is true, as Mr. Mill says, that "Industry is limited by Capital," it is equally true that **Industry creates Capital.** Idleness must feed upon it. The more idleness, the less capital.

The more idleness, the more unevenly will that wealth be distributed which remains.

"Capital," says Mill, "is the result of saving."

Saving what? The *earnings received from Capital* for services rendered, or *the direct products of Labor.*

"The growth of Capital," says Marshall, "depends upon the *power* and the *will* to save."

HOW CAPITAL COMES. The *power* depends upon the *ability to earn*, the *opportunity for earning;* the *will* depends upon the *habits of the laborer*, upon *his self-control*, and upon *his surroundings.*

Many a man has the power to save, is given the opportunity, feels the desire, but is mastered by his environment, and acquires no capital when otherwise he could and would. For thousands on thousands of such men, wages do not fulfil their natural function as the distributing agent of wealth.

Grant that the laborer has both ability to earn and will to save, and that his environments do not interfere with his will and wish, how shall he be sure of his opportunity?

Through the **Law of Demand and Supply,** which Perry says "is the most comprehensive and beautiful law in Political Economy."

It is the law under which Capital operates; the law upon which Labor depends. It is the law which establishes honest partnership between Labor and Capital, according to the terms of which must follow all distribution of profits.

Whatever to-day checks Demand, will to-morrow affect Supply. It may be insisted, as Mr. Mill does insist, that LAW OF CAPITAL "what supports and employs productive AND LABOR. labor is the capital expended in setting it to work, and not the demand of purchasers for the produce of the labor when completed."

But Capital will not long set Labor at work, or keep it at work, when demand for its production has ceased. In spite of Mr. Mill's theorem, Capital will not long demand Labor, when Capital's patrons do not demand the fruits of Labor. Stop the wearing of silks, and the silk-mills will soon cease the manufacture of silkstuffs. Stop the building of railway cars, and the plush-mills will soon stop the making of car-plush. Stop all demand for cotton goods, and the cotton-mills will soon close, the cotton-fields will become cornfields.

Demand is the sensitive business atmosphere, according to which rises and falls the mercury THE MERCURY of **manufacture and trade**—of supply, as OF MANUFACTURE. Capital affords it.

Demand, as to the standard articles of production, must depend upon what Marshall calls the **Standard of Comfort,** what is by other economists called the **Standard of Living,** and that will chiefly depend upon the distribution of wealth—upon the wages which Labor is allowed.

Skilled labor will always receive more than unskilled. The higher the grade of intelligence the more reliable the habits and character, the greater the skill.

An expert stonemason will command three times the per diem pay of a hodcarrier. But if the stonemason, STANDARD getting three dollars a day, is drunk four OF COMFORT. days in the week, and the hodcarrier, receiving but one dollar a day, soberly works the whole six working days, the skilled laborer is no better off than the unskilled. In such case the standard of comfort in the home of the mason and of his attendant will be the same.

A million such homes would make only one third the demand for home comforts that should result from the labor of a million sober men with skill to earn as wages three dollars a day each.

Since, under natural law, all men should labor, **that capital is best employed, and best serves the creation and the distribution of wealth, in whose reproduction the largest possible amount of labor is engaged,** and in the returns for which labor has the largest share. This fact alone would militate against employment of capital in the manufacture of spirituous and malt liquors, even were there no ill effects to follow their use. An English authority, Frederick Powell, says:

EMPLOYMENT OF CAPITAL.

"It has been computed that in the manufacture of a pound's worth of intoxicating liquor, sixpence only falls to the share of the laborer, while the amount paid for labor in the manufacture of articles of utility reaches on the average to about 8s. 6d. to the pound."

This statement is explained by another, which tells how one gallon of gin (a favorite English drink) containing over 50 per cent. alcohol, after being reduced by the seller to 37 per cent., is retailed to the drinker so as to yield 22s., of which latter sum government claims 10s. for revenue; the manufacturer pockets 2s. 6d. for raw material, expenses and profits; the retailer keeps 9s. for *his* profit, and the laborer gets that single paltry sixpence remaining!

PROCEEDS TO LABOR.

In America the laborer's proportion of proceeds is greater, but in striking contrast to the proportion he derives in other industries.

Dr. Hargreaves has shown (in "Wasted Resources,"

page 86) that, in 1870, the 2,110 laborers then engaged in manufacturing liquor in Pennsylvania were paid $993,354 **LABOR'S PAY FROM LIQUOR.** in wages, while their product was valued in first hands at $11,692,528—giving labor about one twelfth of the manufacturer's income.

By another table (W. R., p. 101) he shows that cotton and woolen and shoe products, valued at $295,039,452, employed 323,206 persons (though such products are largely made by machinery), and paid $78,249,052 in wages, or about one third the valuation.

By still another table (W. R., p. 109), Dr. Hargreaves demonstrates that of every $100 which we pay for boots and shoes $22.85 goes for labor; for furniture, house fixtures etc., $22.76; for hardware, $20.99; for cotton goods, $15.94; while of $100 spent for liquors, labor receives but $1.94.

Accepting one sixth of a product's valuation as **the average share of labor** in all reproductive industries— **LABOR'S LOSS FROM LIQUOR.** and this is not a high figure—and estimating that the annual drink bill of this nation is but $700,000,000 (which is concededly a low estimate— too low by at least $300,000,000), to render the manufacture of liquor as directly profitable to labor as other lines of production, to insure the average equitable distribution of returns from such manufacture, it should pay to workingmen annually $116,666,666.66, whereas they receive on the basis of that drink bill less than $14,000,000—a clear, direct loss to labor in the distribution of wealth of over $100,000,000 every year.

Admitting these estimates to be true, and saying no word about the loss to laborers involved in drinking the product whose production loses them so much—conceding, just now, that they could drink it all without any damage to their earning capacity or without discounting their power and will to save—it must be admitted, in turn, that **liquor production antagonizes the best interests of labor, is ever at war with the welfare of workingmen, and is hostile to the true teachings of Political Economy.**

Put only $700,000,000 of the amount yearly paid to the Liquor Traffic into genuinely productive industries, and the $100,000,000 additional that it would annually pay Labor would support 200,000 laborers' families, or a round million of men, women, and children. Save the whole $700,000,000 only out of the round billion which our people annually pay for alcoholics, and it would fairly support 1,400,000 families, or quite 7,000,000 souls.

<small>THE FOE OF LABOR AND ECONOMY.</small>

And this only as the direct effect of supplying that amount of money to that number of people every year. Suppose that one year the $700,000,000 be invested as capital for productive and reproductive purposes, to remain thus invested, while subsequent years devote a like sum annually to the purchase of what such capital produces, how many millions more would be supported by the wages paid? How many more families would find a higher standard of comfort because of this happier distribution of wealth?

Who will figure this out?

Dr. Hargreaves, in his "Worse than Wasted" (p. 66), has made estimate of a fair division among other industries of $800,000,000 annually expended for liquor, on the basis of the census of 1880, and he apportions $471,000,000 of this for food and food preparations, giving to—

<small>BETTER DISTRIBUTION THROUGH CAPITAL.</small>

Flour and grist mills........................$252,592,856
Bread and bakery........................... 32,912,448
Slaughtering and packing meat............... 151,781,206

Cheese and butter..............................$12,871,255
Coffee and spices.............................. 11,462,447
Food preparations (so called).................. 1,246,612
Canned fruits, vegetables, etc................. 8,799,788

What an army of men and women the production of these things would require and maintain!

To them he adds:

Boots and shoes...............................$84,025,177
Carpets.. 15,896,401
Cotton goods................................... 96,045,055
Mixed textiles................................. 33,110,851
Woolen goods................................... 80,303,360
Worsted goods.................................. 16,774,971

—making a total of less than $800,000,000, while the liquor bill last year reached about $1,100,000,000.

The mind can not grasp what all these figures mean, in their wonderful outreach through the distribution of wealth, **PROBLEM OF DISTRIBUTION.** by the payment of wages for work, and the purchase of what work brings into being. No man can imagine the benefits resulting from the expenditure of such a vast amount in this better and wiser way.

Take an item or two, and see what analysis reveals. Select the item of **Boots and Shoes.** You cannot realize what those figures represent—$84,025,177.

At lowest prices over the retail counter, they would call for nearly or quite 10,000,000 pairs of boots, and 30,000,- **LARGER DEMAND** 000 pairs of shoes—enough to keep 5,000,- **FOR LABOR.** 000 of men and boys and 15,000,000 women and girls comfortably shod every year—enough to keep half the shoe factories in America running about all the time, and most of the tanneries.

Take the **woolen goods** item, of over $80,000,000. Inspect that. What does it show?

Over 1,000,000 pairs of blankets; over half a million

woolen coverlets; 48,000,000 yards of cloth, for men's clothing mostly; 12,000,000 yards of various dress goods, and more than a half-million shawls.

Add to these the round billion of yards of **cotton goods** covered by that $96,000,000 item for such, and can you conceive what this expenditure would mean for the woolen mills and cotton factories, for the sheep-growers of the North, and the cotton-planters of the South?

Some important items were not included by Dr. Hargreaves in either list, noticeably **Coal and Furniture.** A full hundred millions might fairly be appropriated for these in equal division, leaving still another hundred millions out of the billion-dollar drink bill.

Fifty millions worth of furniture, stoves included, would call for immense supplies of lumber and iron, and an equal figure for coal would mean marvels of comfort in the homes of drinking men and of miners, where comfort now is little known.

<small>GREATER HOME COMFORTS.</small>

There are 150,000 saloons in this country, with an average of at least 40 patrons for each.

This would give 6,000,000 of drinkers, representing at least 5,000,000 of homes. In every one of these homes the standard of comfort is detrimentally affected by the habit of drink, because the earning capacity is discounted, or the earnings are misappropriated, or both.

There can be little serious question that the larger demand, in these five millions of homes, for the necessities and comforts that fair work and fair wages would supply and the power and will to save would insure, would match the greater production, give to Labor its own, guarantee to Capital its proper returns, and so establish the common weal in every commonwealth; for labor would be in demand, the wages of labor would be certain, the distribution of wealth would everywhere be more equitable.

CHAPTER VIII.

WAGE-EARNERS AND WASTERS.

INTO the great problem of the proper Distribution of Wealth enter, as finally determining factors, **Consumption and Waste.**

While Wages form the distributing agent, they do not alone solve the problem of distribution. If to-day I give or pay you one hundred dollars, and you to-morrow throw it in the flames or otherwise destroy it, the proper distribution of wealth, as between you and me, has not been consummated. I am poorer than I was, if I gave you the money without adequate return; you are no richer.

<small>WAGES AND WASTE.</small>

It is not what a man can earn, but *what he can save*, that determines his individual wealth. If he earn little, but deny himself much that he may save a little, he will in time acquire more or less of wealth; and yet for him there may not have been a fair distribution because of the unthrift all round him, and the unfairness resulting from unwise production, and from unequal partnership between capital and labor.

As to national wealth, everything depends upon the ratio of consumption to production. **All Consumption is not Waste,** but a vast proportion of it is. Much productive labor is wasteful, as to national wealth; it produces less than it consumes.

Statistics have shown in Massachusetts, where these matters have been more carefully studied than perhaps in any other State, that the average annual cost of maintaining one laborer's family is $488.96. If this one laborer earn more money than this every year, he is productive in the sense and to the extent of increasing national wealth. If he and his consume more than they earn, they count as non-producers, or among the wasters of wealth.

<small>COST OF THE FAMILY.</small>

The farmer's products may and will reproduce muscle, bone, tissue, and the varied means of life; but if he and his annually eat up and wear out more value than he brings forth, they are non-producers, and do not increase wealth.

The artisan may produce articles of lasting beauty or utility; but if, through idleness or insufficient skill, he does not or cannot earn self-support, and therefore lives partly on credit or charity, he is unproductive.

Neither of these men adds to the world's wealth; both subtract from it. Without either, in a material sense, the world would be better off.

Massachusetts has told us what the average laborer's family costs the State, and also what are the average yearly earnings of such family. If the cost, as cited, be larger than in some other portions of the country, so are the earnings, for in Massachusetts more members of the family are wage-earners than in many other States—the number of cotton factories and other mills employing young hands assures this.

Yet even in Massachusetts the average yearly earnings of a laborer's family are but $534.99—only $46.03 *more* than the cost of that family's support. So that the question of **whether the average laborer shall remain a producer and add to the State's wealth, or a consumer and a waster of it, turns on a dangerously narrow margin.**

<small>THE MASSACHUSETTS MARGIN.</small>

Whatever in any degree diverts him from labor or detracts from his skill, whatever discounts confidence in his trustworthiness and makes uncertain his employment, whatever impairs his strength and renders doubtful his health, may wipe out the small surplus of $46.03 that places him in the producing class, among the creators of wealth, and may put him over in the non-producing class, among the wasters, where he does not belong.

It has been demonstrated beyond all question that the Liquor Traffic does this.

Father Mathew, the great Irish temperance reformer, visited England, after a wonderful work in his own country, and in the great manufacturing town of Waterford he induced 60,000 persons to sign the pledge. Just previous, the corporation of Waterford had made examination of the **homes of the poor** and working classes, and had estimated the value of all their household and other property at £100,000.

<small>WHERE THE MARGIN GOES.</small>

Two years later the same authorities made a similar examination among the same people, and a like estimate showed them the possessors of household and other property to the amount of £200,000.

The power and the will to save had come with abstinence from drink; and though no doubt thousands, in those two years, had gone back to their cups, the difference, in favor of those who had not, reached a clear half-million of dollars in that short time.

The margin in Massachusetts of the earnings of an average laboring man and his family over the yearly cost of their support was shown to be but $46.03.

Dr. Dorchester, in his comprehensive book, "The Liquor Problem," has estimated that the **annual cost for liquor** to the average laboring man who drinks is $49.34—a figure just a little in excess, you see, of the margin given. But to get even this low average of annual cost, Dr. Dorchester not only places the

<small>THE DRINKER'S YEARLY AVERAGE.</small>

total yearly cost of liquor drank in this country at but $700,000,000—he estimates the number of drinkers at 15,000,000—two and a half times my conservative estimate, allowing forty drinkers to a saloon.

The more drinkers, the less the cost to each. While the total number of drinkers estimated by Dr. Dorchester, I have no doubt, is too high, the average cost as he computes it is surely too low. I have no doubt that 50 per cent. should be added, at the least.

Even if we leave the average annual cost of drink at the figure which Dr. Dorchester gives for each individual laboring man, when we consider that man and his earnings alone, leaving out the earnings of his family, there appears a decided balance against him. In Massachusetts the average earnings per individual, without regard to age or sex, during the year 1893, in a total of seventy-five industries affording employment, were but $434.17— less by $54.79 than the average annual cost of a laboring man's family to the State. Clearly, then, the average laboring man, as the head of the home, does not entirely support it, but must be assisted by other members of the family; and while he requires of them (and they are generally his young children, who should be in school) the average annual contribution of $54.79 toward their maintenance and his, he *taxes their earnings* in addition for all the cost of the liquor which he annually drinks. As the head of the home, there should be no deficit between what he individually earns and what the home collectively costs.

My friend, Mr. P. A. Burdick, one of the most efficient workers in the temperance reform which this country has developed, and whose death while in his prime was a great loss to humanity, used to tell a little incident that well illustrated the **loss to one laboring man** through bad habits and the gain to another through habits of saving and thrift.

Both men earned fair wages. They were skilled workmen, employed in a wagon-shop. Burdick was introduced to one of them by another workman who had signed the pledge.

"Tell me how it is," said this man to Burdick, "that Mr. D. has paid for a home worth $1,200, has sent his three children to school for four years, and has a $1,000 bond laid by for a rainy day. We have worked here together in this shop for fifteen years, and I have been paid the most wages. He has received only $2 a day, and I $2.50. I can't understand how he has a home and $1,000 at interest, and I have neither."

TWO WORKINGMEN'S WAGES.

"Don't you save anything of your wages?" asked Burdick.

"No. Sometimes at the year's end I am $35 ahead, and sometimes that much in debt."

"Have you any children?"

"No."

"Do you drink?"

"Not much; only beer, and I buy that by the quart, so I get it cheaper than by the glass."

"How much do you use a day?"

"You see that pail? Well, I get that full twice each day, and it costs me twenty-five cents a pail. It don't amount to much."

"Do you get your pail filled on Sunday?"

"Yes, just the same as on week-days."

"Now if you will multiply 365, the number of days in a year," said Mr. Burdick, "by fifty cents, you will see that it does amount to something. It amounts to $182.50."

Burdick figured it out on a piece of pine board.

"Well," said the man, "that is so. I never reckoned it up before."

"Do you use tobacco?" further inquired my friend.

"Yes, smoke and chew both. Get my box filled every morning, which costs five cents, and smoke three five-cent cigars a day. I wonder how much that amounts to?"

Burdick put the figures before him—365 multiplied by 20, the amount spent each day, amounts to $73 a year.

COST OF BEER AND TOBACCO.

"Then both beer and tobacco cost me $255 a year, do they?" asked the man, mentally summing up these items.

"They do. Is there any other habit you indulge?"

"I don't know whether you'd call it a habit," and the man hesitated, "but I never work on Saturday. I take that as a holiday."

"How do you celebrate your holiday?"

"Well," he answered, shamefacedly, "I might just as well make a clean breast of the whole matter. I generally sit in the bar-rooms, and now and then play a game of pedro for the beer, to amuse the boys."

"How much do you think amusing the boys costs you every Saturday?"

"Oh, half a dollar, I guess, would cover it."

"Don't you know it costs you three dollars every Saturday instead of fifty cents?"

"No, I can't see it so."

"Let me show you," said Burdick, and he figured away on the pine board. "If you should work every Saturday, you would earn $2.50; if you don't, you are short $2.50 and the fifty cents you spend, which comes out of Friday's wages. Don't you see?"

"And now," the temperance lecturer went on to say, "let us sum up the whole business:

For beer one year	$182.50
For tobacco one year	73.00
For lost time one year	130.00
For amusing the boys	26.00
Total	$411.50

"If you had saved this sum every year and put it in a savings bank at 6 per cent. interest, how much would you have now, do you suppose?"

"I have no idea," answered the man; "but I can see now how Mr. D. has laid up money, for he neither drinks, uses tobacco, nor plays cards, and he works all the week. Figure it out, Burdick, in full: I want to know just how big a fool I have been."

THE GROSS AMOUNT.

And soon the pine board showed the total, "$9,676.07"—an astonishing sum, surely.

"Bring out your pledge," said the man, as he stood looking over my friend's shoulder and saw the result, "and put it all in—liquor, tobacco, and cards! I'll quit the whole or none. Almost $10,000 I have squandered, and never dreamed I was the only one to blame."

He took the pledge, and took the pine board—and kept both. The board he framed, and hung it up over his work-bench, in daily reminder of what he had done.

Now these two laboring men fairly exemplified Production and Wealth, Consumption and Waste.

Both were skilled workmen, but the wages of neither were large. The one having the larger pay was no better off now than fifteen years before: in all that time he had barely kept even with the world. The one getting the smaller wages had become a capitalist—he had money at interest. The better man, as to work and wages, was worse off as to personal wealth—skill, and character, and habits—because of his indulgences. He was fifteen years nearer the point inevitably before him when his earning capacity would in part or altogether cease.

Industry is the father of capital, but Economy is its mother. Industry creates it; Economy nourishes it.

INDUSTRY AND ECONOMY. Capital can be preserved and can profitably reproduce itself only through the constant care of Economy.

Both to the employer and the employed, to the capitalist and the laborer seeking to create capital, Political Economy comes with a lesson growing more eloquent every year, and illustrations becoming every year more abundant. True Capital is not the millions in bonds, reposing in the safe of the railroad king, which turn no mill-wheels and feed no looms; it is the surplus of a production which can and does continue reproducing itself, at the hands of labor fairly sharing in such surplus, and fairly entitled thus to share by reason of intelligence, sobriety, steady application, and honest interest.

What I have said before, let me repeat: That capital is best employed, and best serves the State, in whose production the largest possible amount of labor is engaged, and in the returns for which labor has the largest share. So employed, Capital fulfils the highest requirement, Labor serves the supreme law, and Wages perform the divine mission of Political Economy by insuring a proper distribution of Wealth. For there can be no other system of distribution so just and so complete as this. Wages must form the final basis of equalization; but **wages will not equalize wealth when hand in hand with wages goes waste.**

CAPITAL AND WAGES.

That all men shall earn wages is the primal law. That the wages of some shall become capital, and in turn pay wages to others, is a law secondary and essential. That wages form a legitimate share in all legitimate industries, nobody doubts; and that the prosperity of the State depends upon the most perfect distribution of wealth, through the wisest employment of capital, the most equitable apportionment of Labor's proceeds and the most provident use of Wages, is too plain a fact for further need of elucidation.

CHAPTER IX.

CHARACTER AND EFFECTS OF CONSUMPTION.

WANT, and Production to satisfy it, imply **Consumption**. Were there no consumption, there would be no want. Were there no want, there could be no wealth. As De Laveleye says:

CONSUMPTION IMPERATIVE.

"All production is in obedience to the demand of Consumption."

But, as has been said, all Consumption is not Waste.

Consumption is of different kinds. It may be broadly classified as—

1. **Unproductive;** and
2. **Reproductive.**

Or we might say—

1. **Consumption for enjoyment;** and
2. **Industrial Consumption.**

All that Labor secures through Production is wealth; and Xenophon's aphorism is as true now as when he uttered it: "No wealth is useful save to him who can put it to a good use."

Putting it to **use means its consumption,** since to use wealth is necessarily to consume it. Consumption may be swift or slow; but slowly or swiftly, consumption consumes. Whether the consumer shall lose his wealth or retain it depends upon whether his consumption is unproductive or reproductive. One or the other it cannot escape being. Says the great French economist: "Consumption is bound to be reproductive, under penalty of destitution or death."

REPRODUCTIVE CONSUMPTION.

"When everything goes into the mouth," also says De Laveleye, "the result is destitution."

Which means that unproductive consumption pauperizes the individual, burdens the State, and impairs national wealth. Let us see what reproductive and unproductive consumption are.

I own a cotton factory. I invest capital in the raw cotton, and my factory consumes it. But that factory turns out a product, in cloth, more valuable than the crude stuff carried into it. It was reproductive consumption.

Or I am a boot and shoe manufacturer, and my capital purchases a large quantity of leather. As leather it is cut up and consumed, but there comes a more valuable product in boots and shoes. It was *re*productive consumption.

Or I am a baker, and buy many barrels of flour. It is consumed as flour, and from my ovens as flour it can never reappear. But the product is thousands of loaves of bread—Reproductive Consumption.

Or I am a farmer, and in my fall seeding I consume scores of bushels of grain. But my labor and nature's bounty return me hundreds of bushels instead—again, Reproductive Consumption.

All consumption is *re*productive which appropriates substance in one form to bring forth equally or more valuable substance in another form, or to insure a still larger supply of substance in the original form.

All consumption is *un*productive which appropriates substance in one form and reproduces it in a form less

UNPRODUCTIVE CONSUMPTION. valuable, or in a form which, if nominally of more value, *has in itself no powers or qualities of reproduction.*

And all consumption which thus reproduces a less valuable form of wealth, or reproduces a more valuable form without the powers or qualities of further reproduction, is ultimately and absolutely **waste.**

It must be remembered that our English verb *to consume* takes from its Latin derivative, *consumere*, a double meaning—*to use, to employ*, and *to waste, to destroy.*

The question naturally comes up, How far do reproductive uses extend, or what constitutes actual destruction?

As a baker, my flour is reproductively employed in making bread. You buy my bread and eat it. Have you destroyed it?

The cotton which I bought for my cotton-mill passed through reproductive processes, and the cloth which came of it you bought and consumed. Is it destroyed? You bought the boots and shoes that were reproduced in my boot and shoe factory from the leather consumed there: you have worn them out and cast them aside. Was the leather wastefully destroyed in such consumption and use?

Your thoughtful answer to these questions is in the negative.

My flour, you say, is reproduced in the tissues of your body; and the body itself is a reproductive agent. But,
THE REPRODUCTIVE LINE. that it may employ itself reproductively, it must be clothed, and the cloth used to cover it was not destructively consumed, since of such use came the means to buy other clothing; and the boots or shoes worn out were not wasted, since they made possible more service and the purchase of more shoes.

And you thus establish **a reproductive line** from the farmer's wheat in his bin to his growing crop, from his harvest-field to the baker's, and from the baker's to your own reproductive labor in the shop or in the field. Consumption has kept even parallel with the whole line, but it has been reproductive or industrial consumption. *There has been no waste.*

Now, I ask you to go with me, a farmer, while I sow my grain. Yonder ripples the wheat-field, and from it runs just such a reproductive line as mentioned. But barley is a sure crop, and always commands a good price, and this spring my usual area of barley shall be sown.

I consume ten bushels of seed—my capital—that I may by and by reap 300 bushels of product. Thus far it is reproductive consumption, surely. I sell my product, and get my pay, and for me the reproductive processes go on.

But my barley reaches the brewer, with a halt at the maltster's between. It is malt when it finds the brewer's vats—another product, commercially more valuable; and soon it flows out in still another form, valued commercially yet higher, perhaps, and doctored with vile drugs to give it "body," and "bead," and "age," and that nameless Oliver-Twistish quality calling for *more*.

[WHERE THE LINE BREAKS.]

But here **the reproductive line suddenly breaks.** This latest product has in it no powers or qualities of reproduction. Productively, it is the ultimate. Used, employed, it is so much substance wasted and destroyed, in swift, absolute, unproductive consumption at the last.

If I drink it myself, it gives me no renewal of strength for my productive labor; if my neighbor drink it, it is no more helpful to him. If you drink it, you cannot say of it what you said of the flour, of the cotton, of the boots and shoes. It restores no wasted tissue; it brings no means to buy other clothing; its use was absolutely and finally a waste—and worse than waste.

[AT THE BEER BARREL.] Thinking once of the barley-field and the results of it, these verses came to me, as if they were sung by

A BARREL OF BEER.

I'm a barrel of beer! I'm a barrel of beer!
Growing prouder and mightier year by year!
My beginnings were back in the barley-field,
By the sun and the rain from the soil revealed ;
I was innocent then as a babe unborn,
While I rippled and waved in the breeze of morn ;
Now I'm altered, and old, but a ruler here,—
      I'm a barrel of beer!

I'm a barrel of beer, just a barrel of beer,
But of me and my power some men have fear!
From the grain-field fair, by the breezes kissed,
I was borne to the vats where the serpents hissed—
Through the doors of a malthouse wide I went,
Where I gave up my soul in a sad lament ;
Now I'm altered, and old, and my end is near
      As a barrel of beer.

I'm a barrel of beer, I'm a barrel of beer!
I am coveted, now, for my gay good cheer!
I am scepter and throne for the thirst of men ;
I am mightier, now, than the sword or pen,
For I bow men's brains, and I bend their will,
And I would not scruple to starve or kill,—
I compel my bidding, through love or fear
      Of a barrel of beer!

I'm a barrel of beer, but a barrel of beer!
You may fancy it strange, and may call it queer,
That a royal man should before me bow,
And should do my bidding, as men do now.
Some are sitting to-day in the Chair of State,
And you praise them much, and you call them great,
But they bend to me as I laugh and leer,—
      Me—a barrel of beer!

I'm a barrel of beer, but a barrel of beer,
Yet the law of the State, and the speech of seer,
And the words of God, are as weak things, all,
To the Christian cowards who fawn and fall

At my strong behest, when their aid I claim
And require it swift in their party's name,
While I sit in my place of power, and jeer,—
    I, a barrel of beer!

I'm a barrel of beer, but a barrel of beer!
When the day shall come that I disappear,
When out through the faucet I glide and flow,
With the devils all dancing to see me go,
And into the stomachs of men I glide
Bearing curses and imps on my foaming tide,
Will the end of the reign and the power be near
    Of a barrel of beer?

I'm barrel of beer, but a barrel of beer!
And there are some men with a hope sincere
And a purpose plain to dethrone me yet ;
There are mourning mothers who can't forget
How their sons went down to the depths of sin,
Where the mocking tortures of hell begin,
And greater with God may be one woman's tear
    Than a barrel of beer.

I'm a barrel of beer, I'm a barrel of beer!
My beginnings were back in the sunshine clear,—
In the soft, brown beauty of waving grain,
And the rippling streamlet that sought the main,
And I would I were innocent now as then
To the vision of God and the taste of men,
For then I could never be lingering here
    As a barrel of beer.

Liebig, the great German chemist, is on record as testifying that in two gallons of the best Bavarian beer there **NO NUTRIMENT IN BEER.** is not so much nutriment as could be taken up on the point of a knife-blade; and that the man who should drink two gallons of such beer (the most nutritious known) *every day for an entire year* would obtain no more nutriment than is contained in a five-pound loaf of bread, or in three pounds of meat.

Figuring forty gallons to the barrel of beer, the drinker would get out of every barrel about the same nutritive constituents as he would derive from four ounces of bread, or between two and three ounces of meat.

Some years ago the Rev. Dr. Dunn, of Boston, in a pamphlet on "The Evils of Beer Legislation," thus declared:

"Much has been said of waste and extravagance, but we know of no instance or example that will bear any parallel with the prodigality that is practised in converting barley into malt, and malt into beer."

After asking what there is to support and strengthen a man in a pint of ale or beer, Dr. Dunn answered in these words:

"Its contents are fourteen ounces of water, part of an ounce of the extract of barley, and nearly an ounce of alcohol. The water and alcohol immediately go into the veins, and while the alcohol *poisons*, the water, if not needed, unnecessarily *dilutes* the blood, overcharges the vessels, and loads the kidneys and bladder, while there remains less than an ounce of indigestible extract of malt, which has been 'grown,' scalded, boiled, embittered, fermented, and drenched with water and alcohol, till it seems unfit for the brute, far less the human stomach. Yet this is all that is left in the stomach to be digested. No wonder that all beer-drinkers feel a constant pain and sinking in their stomach, and that they are always craving for more drink!"

A PINT OF ALE ANALYZED.

If mere unproductive consumption were all, or the worst, that is chargeable against the manufacture of beer, while Political Economy would condemn it, from the purely material side, the severest condemnation might be spared. But the evils and waste that result from beer-**drinking** exceed many fold any loss in the **manufacture**. Proof by the volume could be brought forward in evidence.

In 1830 the Parliament of Great Britain passed a Beer Act, now famous, or infamous, in the history of liquor legislation. It was to do great things for the working-classes of England; and it did, but not in the way ex-**RESULTS OF BEER-DRINKING.** pected. Only two weeks after its passage Sidney Smith wrote of it: "The new Beer Bill has begun its operations. *Everybody is drunk.*"

Not long afterward the London *Globe* printed this editorial testimony:

"The injury done by the Beer Act to the **peace and order** of the rural neighborhoods, not to mention **domestic happiness, industry, and economy,** has been proved by witnesses from every class of society to have exceeded the evils of any single act of internal administration passed within the memory of man."

One American instance, as illustrating in this country this reference to peace and domestic happiness in rural neighborhoods abroad, will be pardonably sufficient.

Almost under the shadow of a great brewery, in a rural neighborhood of western New York, adjoining a pretty village, lived not many years ago a German laborer and his wife, in a neat cottage, well kept. When perfectly sober he was a kind husband and a good citizen. He never drank anything stronger than beer, as was finally proved, but always after taking that he was bad-tempered, surly, unkind.

On a summer Sunday morning the entire community was appalled by the discovery made at this man's home. Upon one end of the pretty piazza, in front, lay the murdered wife; at the other end lay the dead husband. He had killed her, and then killed himself; and the cause of it all, as was amply shown by the coroner's inquest, was the small empty beer-keg found close by his side—or the contents of that keg before he emptied it.

A thousand cases of like nature could be cited to show that the waste of grain and of effort in producing beer is not nearly so bad as the **waste of human life** that fol-

lows consumption of it. As to the utter uselessness of beer for sustenance; as to its damaging effect upon tem-
EFFECTS ON HUMAN LIFE. per, and character, and the physical system; as to its baleful influence upon domestic peace, and social order, and morality—chemistry, and human experience, and common observation, testify as with one voice and in perfect accord. And what, then,. should Political Economy declare?

"Nothing," Professor Perry would answer, in the logical line of his narrow definition: "Political Economy has to do with nothing on earth but sales."

And so, as I sold my barley for a good price, and the brewer bought his malt at a price he could afford to pay, and somebody bought his beer, to the brewer's and the barkeeper's profit, according to Perry, Political Economy has no more interest in the matter.

But remember what Perry afterward said, with all the emphasis of italics and small capitals, that "*Commerce is*
COMMERCE A MUTUAL BENEFIT. *an exchange of goods for the mutual* BENEFIT *of the respective owners.*"

And recall that statement of De Laveleye when he said: "In '*goods*' must be included all that is *good* for the advancement of the individual and of the human race."

Now, if Political Economy be but the Science of Sales, and if sale be but an exchange of *goods* for mutual *benefit*, how, then, would Professor Perry treat the sale of that which is not *good*, or which does not inure to *mutual benefit?* How shall we have a Science of Sales that relates only to sales of a certain kind?

How shall we divorce Political Economy, as a mere
ATTITUDE OF ECONOMY. Science of Sales, from the sales that do not confer mutual benefit, unless by the laws of Political Economy and of the legislator we declare that *such sales shall not be?*

"It goes almost without saying," says Perry in another place, "that **persons** are more important in Political Economy than **things;** that the buyer is of more consequence **economically as well as morally** than that which he buys, and the seller than that which he sells."

Surely a Science of Sales must consider those objects most important economically. Surely *our* Science of Economics must insist that Production and the sale of things produced shall not lead to sure waste of persons and of things, the absolute destruction of individual and of national wealth.

CHAPTER X.

REPRODUCTIVE CONSUMPTION AND WEALTH.

As Wages are, and must be, the distributing agent of Wealth; as Wages must be paid to Labor, the second re-
CONSUMPTION quisite of Production, which begets Wealth;
AND CAPITAL. and as Labor creates Capital, by which Wages must be paid and more wealth created; **Political Economy requires that in the use of Capital, in the employment of Labor, for the payment of Wages, there shall be the largest possible amount of Reproductive Consumption.**

Through such consumption alone can a fair standard of Wages be sustained, the employment of Labor be general, and Wealth's distribution be fair.

Over this question of Wages, considered indirectly and directly, our statesmen have wasted an immense amount of time. A great tariff debate continued several months in both houses of the Fifty-third Congress, and the central topic was "Industrial interest, National prosperity." The core of the whole question was the conservation of Capital, or the guardianship of Labor, the protection of Wages. On the last day of that debate, in the lower house, when so-called Protectionists (Republicans) and so-called Free-Traders (Democrats) put forth their recognized ablest leaders to speak for them and to rally their voting ranks (February 1, 1894), the Hon. Thomas B.
CONGRESS Reed stood as Protection's final champion
ON ECONOMY. among the Representatives, and made a speech that was printed in full by his party press the next day. In that speech, evidently prepared with care, and

intended to be the master effort of that debate, Mr. Reed sneered at Political Economy and economists, as now and then a politician does, but gave half-conscious recognition, nevertheless, to politico-economic laws.

In the course of that speech Mr. Reed said:

"I confess to you that this question of wages is to me the vital question. To insure our growth in civilization and wealth, we must not only have wages as they are now, but constantly and steadily increasing. This desire of mine for constantly increasing wages does not have its origin in love for the individual, but in love for the whole nation."

A few minutes before this confession Mr. Reed had thus declared:

"The increase of wages which the service-seller ought to have, and the only useful increase he can ever get, will be by the operation of natural laws, working upon the opportunities which legislation may aid in furnishing. The increase will never come from the outside, will never be the gift of any employer. *It must come from the improvement in the man himself.*"

Partially explaining how, through such improvement in the man, increase of the man's wages may come, Mr. Reed went on to say:

"Man is not a mere muscular agent, to be fed with meat and give forth effort. Man is a social being. He must have whatever his neighbor has. He cannot grow unless he does. Every growth implies a larger consumption of consumable wealth,—I mean whatever is made by man and contributes to his enjoyment, whether it be a loaf of bread, a novel, or a concert. The more a man wants of consumable wealth the more his wages are likely to be. But by wants I do not mean any wild longings for what is beyond his reach, but such wants as are in sight, and to supply which he has such longings as will make him work."

WAGES AND THE WAGE-EARNER.

You see that in part, at least, the great speech of Mr. Reed sounds as if he had read our preceding pages. Let us follow him a little further:

"This question of wages is all-important as bearing upon the question of consumption. All production depends upon consumption. Who are the consumers?

"In the old days, when the products of manufactures were luxuries, the lord and his retainers, the lady and her maids, were the consumers, a class apart by themselves, but to-day the consumers are the producers. Long ago the laborer consumed only what would keep him alive. To-day he and his wife and their children are so immeasurably the most valuable customers that if the shop had to give up the wealthy or those whom it is the custom to call poor, there would not be a moment's hesitation or a moment's doubt."

Now, in this last utterance Mr. Reed fairly recognized two facts:

The enormous proportionate increase of "those whom it is the custom to call poor."

The higher standard of living among that class so greatly increased.

This elevation of the standard of living in the home of the average laboring man has "come from the improvement in the man himself." What it means in relation to the law of supply and demand has been referred to in former chapters. How widely this law is put to the test, in the home of this man, nobody realizes until some one calls to it our specific attention.

In a recent address at Birmingham, England, Sir Edwin Arnold, speaking of the average English artisan's domestic condition and comforts, swept the wide range of supply and demand, and hinted at the multiform varieties of labor involved, the extent of capital employed, and the like, in these words:

AN ENGLISH ARTISAN'S DEMANDS.

"Observe his dinner-board : Without being luxurious, the whole globe has played him serving-man to spread it. Russia gave the hemp, or India or South Carolina the cotton, for that cloth which his wife lays upon it. The Eastern Islands placed there those condiments and spices which were once the secret relishes of the wealthy. Australian downs sent him frozen mutton or canned beef ; the prairies of America, meal for his biscuit and pudding ; and if he will eat fruit, the orchards of Tasmania and the palm woods of the West Indies proffer delicious gifts; while the orange groves of Florida and of the Hesperides cheapen for his use those 'golden apples' which dragons used to guard.

"His coffee comes from where jeweled humming-birds hang in the bowers of Brazil, or purple butterflies flutter amid the Javan mangroves. Great clipper ships, racing by night and day under clouds of canvas, convey for him his tea from China or Assam, or from the green Singhalese hills. The sugar which sweetens it was crushed from canes that waved by the Nile or the Orinoco ; and the plating of the spoon with which he stirs it was dug for him from Mexican or Nevadan mines.

"The currants in his dumpling are a tribute from classic Greece, and his tinned salmon or kippered herring are a token from the seas and rivers of Canada or Norway. He may partake, if he will, of rice that ripened under the hot skies of Patna or Rangoon; of cocoa, that food of the gods plucked under the burning blue of the equator.

"For his rasher of bacon, the hog express runs daily, with 10,000 grunting victims, into Chicago; Dutch or Brittany hens have laid him his eggs, and Danish cows grazed the daisies of Elsinore to produce his cheese and butter."

In such poetic prose an English poet and a world-wide traveler has told us of the broad field which is drawn upon by an English artisan's demands.

But Sir Edwin does not say that these demands are **the result of sobriety;** of the steady labor of a sober man; **LABOR, SOBER OR SODDEN.** of the fair wages paid that man for skilled work; of productive consumption, by thousands of other men, for the behoof of this man and thousands of others besides. He need not say it; it is all implied.

Suppose, now, instead of the sober artisan at his dinner-board laden with the fruit and other products of so many lands and representing the toil of so many hands, you have the besodden laborer, with but his brown loaf and his mug of beer. And suppose you multiply this man by a million, what do the man and the multiplication mean?

"All production depends upon consumption," says Mr. Reed.

Curtail by 75 per cent. the normal consumption in one million of homes, and how must Production be affected?

If "the more a man wants of consumable wealth the more his wages are likely to be," as Mr. Reed affirms, is <small>WAGES AND WANTS.</small> there not the closest relation between his wages and his wants? And must it not, then, be true that the less he *wants* of consumable wealth the less will his wages be? *If the brown loaf and the mug of beer satisfy his wants, will they not measure his wages?*

Let one more quotation from Mr. Reed suffice:

"We are nominally 70,000,000 people. That is what we are in mere numbers. But as a market for manufactures and choice foods we are potentially 200,000,000, as compared with the next best nation on the globe. Nor is this difficult to prove.

"Whenever an Englishman earns one dollar, an American earns one dollar and sixty cents. I speak within bounds. Both can get the food that keeps the body and soul together, and the shelter which the body must have, for 60 cents. Take 60 cents from a dollar, and you have 40 cents left. Take that same 60 cents from the dollar and sixty and you have a dollar left, just two and a half times as much. That surplus can be spent in choice foods, in housefurnishings, in fine clothes, and all the comforts of life—in a word, in the products of our manufactures. That makes our population as consumers of products, as compared with the English population, 200,000,000. Their population is 37,000,000 as consumers of products which one century ago were pure luxuries, while our population is equivalent to 200,000,000."

Why are we equivalent, comparatively, to 200,000,000? Why are we, as consumers, potentially so strong?

Because of our standard of living; because of our demands, as consumers of consumable wealth.

<small>NATIONAL CONSUMPTION.</small> But are we potentially so strong as Mr. Reed's figures affirm? He considers all our 70,000,000 people as consumers in the larger proportion

which his comparison indicates. He takes no account of the half or wholly idle class, multiplying with dangerous rapidity, who consume but a small per cent. of what they should, yet who are consumers in the sense that they produce nothing, and are a growing waste of the public wealth.

Mr. Reed argued eloquently for **Consumption**; he gave no heed to **Waste.** Into the great economic problem, which he and his fellow Congressmen were trying to solve in that great debate, the great factor of Waste did not enter, to their recognition. Day after day, hour after hour, their oratory flowed forth, giving reasons for the widespread want, and the growth of our great needy class, and not a man of them saw or dared assert **the greatest reason of all.**

That reason lies in the violation of economic law. The largest possible amount of Reproductive Consumption has not been secured. The conditions that would secure it have not been provided for and insisted upon; they were not even mentioned, in that great debate, by the statesmen who took part in it. Was it because these conditions would seriously affect a great political power on which these statesmen depend?

Capital and Wages are essential to Reproductive Consumption. Without Capital, Wages cannot be paid. CAPITAL AND WAGES. Without Wages, Reproductive Consumption is impossible. With a constant and enormous increase of laborers, and a growing increase in the proportion of unskilled labor, the tendency of Wages is downward; there is **a growing momentum of waste.** Increase in the unskilled class means an increase in the saloon class. Increase of that class makes of less and less account the difference between an Englishman's wages and an American's. Whether the surplus of a man's earnings, over the bare support of the man, be sixty cents a day or a dollar and sixty cents, cuts little figure in his case, when all that surplus, whatever it is, goes into the till of a saloon.

Multiply the man by six millions, and say that he spends but the sixty cents of surplus on each working day of the year, and the saloon takes from him and his class, allowing that its doors are closed and that its patronage ceases every Sunday, **the enormous sum of over $1,126,000,000 that should be spent in the lines of Reproductive Consumption.**

Labor must earn Wages. Capital must pay Wages. Wages must distribute Wealth. **The more wage-earners, then, the better** will be the **distribution of Wealth.**

Apply this more than $1,126,000,000 which are annually spent for liquors in this country to the purchase of articles consumed in Reproductive Consumption, and how many more wage-earners would be supported by providing this new supply for this new demand?

According to a table in *The Voice* of January 25, 1894, the number of men employed for one year in the manu-

LIQUOR AND ITS LABORERS. facture of liquors consumed to the amount of $1,014,592,500 was 37,033.

This figure was reached by learning the total number employed in making malt liquors in 39 cities, and distilled liquors in 2 cities, counting the establishments, and finding the average employed by each, then multiplying this average by the total number of establishments.

This table further shows that in the manufacture of
OTHER SERVANTS malt liquors but $\frac{61}{100}$ of a man is employed
OF CAPITAL. for every $10,000 in retail value of the same, and but $\frac{12}{100}$ in the manufacture of distilled liquors, while for every $10,000 in retail value of useful articles produced

by seven other industries the average number of men employed is as follows:

    Bread and bakery products.......................... 3.36
    Boots and shoes................................... 5.03
    Cotton goods...................................... 6.89
    Silk goods.. 4.86
    Woolen goods...................................... 5.40
    Lumber and mill products.......................... 4.08
    Iron and steel products........................... 3.52

It is further shown by this table that in the manufacture of $10,000 retail value of liquor, the **raw material demanded** is, for malt liquors $1,213, and for distilled liquors $647, or an average of $930; making a total, at CONSUMPTION OF this average, of raw material consumed in RAW MATERIALS. producing the liquor drank for one year of but $94,357,103, while the average value of raw material demanded by the seven legitimate industries mentioned for the manufacture of goods to the retail value of $10,000 is $4,774; and at this rate, if these other and useful goods took the place of the liquors, the raw material demanded would aggregate $484,366,460—an *increase in the demand for such raw materials of over $390,000,000 every year.*

The average of men employed for the manufacture of useful goods to the retail value of $10,000, in the seven legitimate industries, is $4\frac{73}{100}$—nearly thirteen times greater than the average employed in the manufacture of liquor; and according to these figures, if the money spent for drink were spent instead for such goods, *their increased manufacture alone would call for 443,275 more men.*

For producing the **greater amount of raw material required** by this increase of such manufacture, it is conservatively estimated that our country would require still more men to the number of 650,016. So that, if the more than $1,126,000,000 wasted yearly by our people in the unproductive consumption of liquor were spent for useful articles of food, clothing, and shelter, it would require 443,275 more men in the factories to meet the demand for manufactured goods, and 650,016 more men outside the factories to produce the raw materials for their manufacture—*it would pay wages to and distribute wealth among a grand additional total of 1,093,291 men!*

<small>ADDITIONAL LABORERS POSSIBLE.</small>

And this, it must be borne in mind, is taking no account of the handling and transportation and sale of the goods additionally produced; of the increased number of railroad men, teamsters, boatmen, merchants, clerks, etc., who would be called for in putting these goods through the channels of trade into the consumers' hands.

When Ireland closed her distilleries, in the hard years we have told about, she demonstrated that such figures and statements are not the idle estimate of theorists and of dreamers, but are the actual, the logical, outcome of applied Political Economy.

CHAPTER XI.

WASTE OF LABOR AND PRODUCT.

In the further study of Consumption and Waste we may group our thought, figures, and facts around the following five subdivisions:

1. Waste *in* Production.
2. Waste *of* Production.
3. Waste of Productive Time.
4. Waste of Productive Life.
5. Waste in the Care and Support of Productive Life Wasted.

Waste in Production can come variously. The more you employ Capital in manufacture without profit, and with loss, the more waste will result.

Wealth, as employed in Production, is denominated **Fixed Capital** and **Circulating Capital;** and more and more, as mechanical devices multiply and manufacturing is concentrated into great establishments, the proportion of Fixed Capital increases. The greater such increase, the more care is required to prevent Waste.

FIXED CAPITAL AND WASTE.

Capital must earn profit on Capital, or Waste is certain. Large manufacturing concerns regularly "charge off" every year, from any profits they have made, a certain per cent. to cover wear of machinery and other depreciation. Unless their gains be in excess of this, there are no net profits. Without net profits there are pretty certain to be net losses. Net losses mean Waste.

A large amount of **Fixed Capital** invested in any business must mean a large amount of **Fixed Charges** in the conduct of that business. The larger these fixed charges, in proportion to output, the smaller the margin of profits. The smaller this margin, the more will Capital be affected by the character and habits of the wage-earners employed by Capital.

The fixed charges of that wagon-shop went on every Saturday when that laborer was idle of whom Mr. Burdick told—rent of the shop, interest on the money invested in its equipment, cost of fuel for heat or steam-power, pay of a superintendent, and insurance. And the profit of the shop was decreased by whatever net sum should result from the labor of one man fifty-two days in one year.

<small>FIXED CHARGES AND PROFITS.</small>

If there were only twelve men employed in that shop, and if each one of them lost one working-day each week, the time lost would equal 624 days in one year, or just about the full number of working-days for two men in twelve months. By so much, then, as the business of that shop should profit from two men's work in one year must it lose, at least, from the partial idleness of the whole twelve men. If to run the business and meet the fixed charges required all the profits or proceeds of the work of ten men, then the idleness of two men one day out of six meant the loss to the proprietor of his entire normal net returns.

In 1867, the Messrs. Ames, of North Easton, Mass., great manufacturers of shovels, etc., produced in the months of May and June, with 375 men employed, *8 per cent. more* than in the same months of the year after with 400 men working the same hours, under the same conditions as to the manufacture itself.

<small>SOBRIETY AND PRODUCTION.</small>

Why did this great factory of the Messrs. Ames thus

show such a percentage (about 14 per cent.) one year in favor of the smaller number of men that year employed?

The inside conditions were different only as affected by the conditions outside. In 1867 Massachusetts had a prohibitory law; the town of North Easton had no license and no saloons; the 375 men were all the time at their sober best. Saloons came, with repeal of Prohibition, the year after, and the 400 men were the victims of saloon influence.

"We attribute this large falling off entirely to the repeal of the prohibitory law," said the Messrs. Ames, "and the great increase in the use of intoxicating liquor among our men in consequence."

If they were paid for piecework, the loss to their employers was less than otherwise it would have been; but even then, it was easy to be computed. The fixed charges of that plant were constant. As much money was required for machinery, the interest upon it and the cost for superintendence were as great, the wear and tear upon the whole "plant" were as considerable, for the output 14 per cent. less than the year previous, in proportion to the number of men, as for the larger output possible. *In the larger output might have been the largest part of a year's possible profits.*

Economy nourishes Capital; and Capital can preserve itself, and profitably reproduce itself, only through the constant exercise of economy.

The employment of drinking men in large concerns where system largely prevails, and where machinery is largely operated, may and does impair the producing power of Capital by curtailing the capacity of large lots of machinery; and in these days, when machine products form so large a proportion of manufacture, and when great business "plants"

CAPITAL'S
PRODUCTIVE
POWER.

require so vast outlays of fixed capital in machinery, the necessity for sober heads and steady hands exists as it never before existed, and inability to secure these must mean loss to capital, waste of wealth, and comparative decrease of production as never before it could.

The larger the "plant" the greater will be the loss from intemperate workmen in it, not alone because of the greater number employed, but because the fixed capital, in machinery, etc., will, as a rule, exceed in proportion to laborers that of smaller "plants," where thorough system cannot so take the place of service; and because **the greater the ratio of Capital to service the more competent must Labor be to make Capital productive.**

These facts have been plainly recognized by manufacturers. Some years ago one large corporation in Pennsylvania, having its works located in a license town, actually contracted with the saloon-keepers to close their saloons for an entire year, and paid them a good bonus to do it, considering this wise business policy to prevent waste where 4,000 men were at work.

<small>SALOONS AND CAPITAL.</small>

The narrow margin in manufacture of almost every kind, which has come about because of such active home and foreign competition, has compelled the most rigorous care in conservation of raw materials, in spite of which the margin decreases and the profits for capital diminish year by year.

In every branch of industry it is the same. Time was when they separated the cotton-seed from the cotton all through the Cotton States, at great expense, and then threw the seed away as worthless. Now they save the seed and make oil of it, or soap from it, and pay the cost of taking out the seed by such saving; but cotton production is even now of so little profit that cotton is no longer king.

Once the butcher business in this country was conducted altogether by a multitude of men, each operating in a small way, without care for the saving of odds and ends, and with comparatively large profit for each; now a few men, conducting vast killing and packing establishments, furnish beef and pork for half the people on our continent, and their gains come from the careful saving of every part of every animal killed, from pig's feet to snout, from ox-hoof to horns.

<small>CAPITAL'S DECREASING MARGINS.</small>

Everywhere *Capital seems on a universal bent to save itself from waste*—except as waste comes from the human appetite for alcoholic liquor.

Division of Labor, as to which economists in general have much to say, is but one method for conserving Capital and saving time. The most effective employment of time, while men are actually engaged in Labor, has been and everywhere is now the problem of Capital; but more and more "piece-work" is made the law of manufacture, piece-wages become the law of distribution; and the constant, effective use of machinery, by the constant application of the most effective skill, is Capital's only safeguard. Skill comes by Division of Labor—the daily repetition of a day's task by men who make their work perfect through practise. But what is gained for Capital, in Production, through the greater skill that such Division of Labor insures, may be lost to Capital by the demoralization of skill through Drink.

<small>CAPITAL AND SKILL.</small>

Waste of Production may be **direct,** through the destructive use of raw materials, or **primary products;** or **indirect,** through the unproductive use or consumption of **secondary products.**

If the farmer in the far West, after raising his year's

crop of corn, having given to it his year's labor, heaps it in his field and then deliberately burns every bushel, it is **WASTE OF PRODUCTS.** wanton, deliberate Waste of all the work and all the primary product. If, when he has heaped it in his field, he fails to gather it into bins and it rots there, it is equal Waste. If, when he has gathered it into bins, there be no near market, and the railroads charge him for transportation more than the remote market will yield, and he can find for his corn no other use than as fuel, and so burns it up at last, it is finally Waste. Raw material, primary product, has gone to complete destruction in this way, and a season's work is also wasted.

But suppose his corn is raised, and binned, and presently sent away. In the distillery, as raw material, it finds use; from the distillery, as a secondary product, it comes forth again; and as such secondary product, called whisky, it is totally consumed. Is not the waste as complete? Is it not a greater waste, because of the additional work wasted? Is it not better to waste raw material only, if any waste there must be—even if we take no account of the effects of waste?

Some years ago, in Minneapolis, a great flouring-mill exploded, from spontaneous combustion, and thousands of **WASTE BY BURNING.** barrels of flour were destroyed. Was this not indeed a greater waste than would have come had the Dakota wheat-field caught fire a few weeks earlier and had the wheat from which this flour was made been burned then in that field?

In the twelve years from 1870 to 1882 there were drank in this country (not counting drugged and "expanded" liquors) the enormous amount of 5,086,263,323 gallons of alcoholic liquor. Deduct foreign and American wines and foreign distilled spirits (into which went no American grain), and we have an aggregate of 4,849,975,961 gallons manufactured from the raw material or primary product of American fields. Divide this by twelve, and it shows 404,164,663 gallons as the annual average of liquid consumption during those dozen years—a positive annual waste of secondary product to that amount.

The Brewers' Journal says that one bushel of grain will make three gallons of liquor. Dividing this annual WASTE average amount by three, we get 134,721,554 BY DRINKING. bushels of grain as the **annual average waste of primary** (farm) **product** resulting from the business of the brewer and the distiller. Multiplying this by twelve, we have the total waste of grain for twelve years, in the enormous aggregate of 1,616,658,648 bushels.

Vast as was this direct loss by waste of the raw material alone, this was not all, nor the worst. Into the raw WASTE OF material went the sum of labor to produce LABOR. it—so much additional waste. If we estimate the grain at one dollar a bushel, and reckon one man to every $600 of raw material, or every 600 bushels of grain, we shall find that into this waste of labor every year went the work of 224,536 men; and if you estimate the yearly wages at only $300 for each man, the aggregate for the twelve years will be $808,329,600. Had not the work of these men gone into this waste, it would have added that much more to the wealth of the world.

Add the waste of work to the waste of work's product, and you have a total waste of Production, during the period of twelve years, amounting to $2,424,988,248.

Nor is this all, nor the most. For the aggregate of WASTE grain above shown, in its liquid form, the OF WAGES. drinkers of America paid an annual average of $718,795,894, or in twelve years $8,625,550,728. (In this is included the grain consumed in 21,214,032 gallons of foreign distilled liquors, which cannot easily be separated.) Here the secondary products were wasted to this appalling amount, plus the labor to produce these from the raw materials before estimated. Allowing that it took but 30,000 hands annually to turn these raw materials into secondary products, and estimating that each hand could earn on an average but $300 a year, the total of wages thus additionally wasted will reach in the twelve years the considerable sum of $108,000,000.

So the waste of Production on account of the Liquor Traffic along these lines alone foots up:

Raw materials	$1,616,658,648
Wages for these	808,329,600
Secondary products (liquor)	8,625,550,728
Labor on these	108,000,000

Making a huge total for only one dozen years of $11,158,538,976

PRODUCTION'S TOTAL WASTE. As absolutely beyond realization as these figures are, they would be immensely increased should our twelve years' term begin with 1893 and end with the year of grace or of drinking disgrace 1894.

7

CHAPTER XII.

WASTE OF TIME AND LIFE.

Waste of Productive Time was alluded to in the last chapter but incidentally, and with reference only to
<small>WIDER FIELD OF WASTE.</small> time spent in producing what is wasted. This consideration barely crosses the borderline of this extensive field of Waste. A hint of what may be found, if we fully traverse this field, was given in that testimony by the Messrs. Ames. Four hundred men, according to their testimony, produced 8 per cent. less in one year than 375 men produced the year previous—a decrease in the average annual production per man of about 14 per cent. **Loss of capacity** must no doubt be credited with a part of this decrease; loss of time with the rest, and by far the most. If we count an even 10 per cent. for such loss of time, how stupendous must be the total of this waste!

Allow, if you please, that there are only six million of drinkers in this country, and that of these there are only
<small>TIME OF PRODUCING LABORERS.</small> one million of male **moderate drinkers** who class as producing laborers in lines of work likely to be affected, as in the Ames establishment. Ten per cent. of their time would equal the full time and pay of 100,000 men. Count their earnings at but $600 per man each year, and the time-waste in cash computation foots up $60,000,000 yearly.

At least 10 per cent. of the 6,000,000 drinkers are **habitual drunkards,** wasting practically their whole time because of drink. Assume that they waste but half of it, and that the time of each man should be worth $600, and the annual time-waste figures at $18,000,000.

For the year 1880, 67,000 **paupers** were reported to the Census Office as inhabiting the almshouses, and the number of **inmates of the prisons and reformatories** that year was returned at 70,000. Here, then, are 137,000 more men whose time is wasted; and on the same basis of time-value, the time-waste annually for these is $82,200,000.

<small>TIME OF DRUNKARDS AND PAUPERS.</small>

By the Census of 1880 the total **inmates of charitable institutions** in this country reached 400,000. Deducting 137,000 paupers and prisoners already accounted for, we have 263,000 insane, idiotic, or otherwise "defective" persons, whose time is a waste, and whose defectiveness and incompetency are due in more or less degree to the Drink Habit, in themselves or their progenitors. Credit but one half of their defectiveness to this cause, and the time-waste of this class on this account reaches the yearly sum of $78,900,000. Cut this in half, to allow for the idiotic and other incompetents who are not of and who never reach mature years, and the figure still stands at $39,450,000.

<small>TIME OF THE DEFECTIVES.</small>

But the largest item of Waste of Productive Time is yet to be shown. There are in round numbers not less than 500,000 **persons engaged in the manufacture, handling, and sale of intoxicating liquors** in this country. The careful estimate of these by Dr. Hargreaves in 1874 made the number 545,624 —it has not been reduced since then. Call it 500,000, still, for easy computation, and multiply it by $600, the time-value of each man, and the time-waste will sum up $300,000,000; for the business of these men is not finally reproductive: their labor adds nothing to the public wealth; they *must be counted as* **unproductive**, and their time as

<small>TIME OF LIQUOR LABORERS.</small>

wasted. They are consumers, supported by the producers, much of whose time and product they waste likewise.

But what shall we say when we come now to consider the **Waste of Productive Life?**

Human life, as the basis of all Production, and as the central, starting point of Political Economy, must figure in the estimate.

Born into the world a helpless non-producer, and grown to manhood a consumer chiefly, at the world's expense, *every man, as brought to his producing capacity, is but an investment of the world's wealth for possible returns.*

<small>PRODUCTIVE LIFE WASTED.</small>

Kill him off before his dividend-paying life naturally ends, and you must consider the investment more or less a loss. How great the loss depends upon how early you kill him. But the loss can be computed. There is a **standard of productive existence** among men, and there is a known failure of men to reach that standard by reason of Drink.

Scientific men and men of business have labored along different lines to determine what this standard is and should be, and have reached quite the same results. The men of business chiefly interested in this matter are insurance men, who have obtained, by the most careful compilation of statistics, a reliable set of facts. They show that the actual "*expectation of life*" on the part of a drinking man is less by some years than the "expectation of life" on the part of a total abstainer—in other words, that the drinker will die sooner, after a certain age, than the non-drinker. Based on this showing, some of the most carefully managed insurance companies in the world regularly charge a higher premium to the moderate drinker than to

<small>STANDARD OF PRODUCTIVE LIFE.</small>

the total abstainer, while the hard drinker is refused insurance altogether.

The British Medical Association, a purely scientific body, has made investigations that are very interesting and valuable. Upon the basis of these investigations, Mr. E. J. Wheeler, in his admirable book on Prohibition, says: "We may assert broadly that those who become intemperate after the age of twenty-five lose, on an average, ten years out of the thirty-five that they otherwise have to live, and that the free drinkers lose five years out of the thirty-five."

Marginal note: YEARS OF LIFE DISCOUNTED.

The thirty-five years after such given age constitute the normal **"expectation of life."** How much of life, thus normally expected, is cut off, wasted, in this country?

Comparing the per capita consumption of liquors in Great Britain and in the United States, and estimating from this comparison and from the number of such drinkers in Great Britain, Mr. Wheeler declares that out of a population in the United States, January 1, 1889, of 65,000,000, there were 2,480,000 hard drinkers, 120,000 of whom die every year. Multiply the latter figure by ten, the number of years by which each intemperate life is curtailed, as Mr. Wheeler concludes from the British Medical Association reports, and the result is 1,200,000 **years of productive life annually wasted because of drink.**

Dr. Hitchcock, long president of the Michigan State Board of Health, a few years since made some interesting figures which bear directly upon this point. According to *his* estimates, the annual loss of productive life in this country by reason of the *premature* deaths caused by alcohol reaches 1,127,-000 years; and accepting these figures, because they are smaller than those we take from Mr. Wheeler's estimates,

Marginal note: ANNUAL AGGREGATE OF LOSS.

and reckoning the productive power of an able-bodied person at only $500 instead of $600, as previously computed, we have here a loss or waste annually of $563,500,000.

Through premature deaths of the insane and the idiotic, made so by reason of alcohol, Dr. Hitchcock estimates a **THROUGH PREMATURE DEATHS.** total further loss in effective producing life annually of 418,167 years, which, on the same low basis of productive power, he puts at $209,083,500.

Let us pursue this line of thought a little further. We have said that every man, as brought to his producing capacity, is but an investment for possible returns. How much does the investment represent as an average, and when do the returns begin? We must needs answer these questions before we can determine whether the returns are sufficient to make the investment pay.

One estimate brings the average young man to the age of twenty-seven years before his care and keeping cease to be a cost to the community, and he, ceasing to be a consumer, becomes a producer. There are no statistics which absolutely prove this, to my knowledge; but approximate estimates can be made as to the **cost of a young man** before he may reasonably be expected to pay his own way. I asked a friend yesterday, who has very good judgment of things in general:

"What would you figure as the cost of a boy for the first five years of his life?"

COST OF A BOY. He considered a moment, and then said: "Fifty dollars a year."

"And what for the next ten years?" I asked further.

"About twice as much."

Then I remembered a subheading in "Economics of Prohibition," by Mr. J. C. Fernald, entitled "Cash Value of a Man," and referring to that I found the same estimate precisely—fifty dollars a year the first five years, one hundred a year for the next ten years; cost of the fifteen-year-old boy, $1,250. To this the book mentioned adds $200 a year for the next six years, bringing the total cost of a young man at twenty-one up to the considerable sum of $2,450.

Lop off the odd $450, as possibly the young man may earn that much before he is "of age," and leave his cost lost capital in manhood. at the round figure of $2,000. He will do exceeding well if he actually maintains himself during the next four years. Kill him before he is twenty-five, and what is the result? Positive, total loss of the cash investment which he represents. Kill him after he is twenty-five and before he is thirty-five, and he has at his average best returned but a portion of the money invested in him—he may have done little more than return the interest upon it. If, after he reaches his producing capacity, he never does more than barely maintain himself without further cost to the community, the total cash investment which he stands for is a total and absolute loss and waste.

Every young man, then, killed by the saloon before he is twenty-five, or so affected by saloon influences before that age as to be incapable afterward of producing or earning a surplus beyond his support, represents not only a waste of productive life, but **a direct loss and waste of cash capital in manhood.**

It may fairly be assumed, I think, that one half of those 120,000 hard drinkers who die annually have never returned to society, by their surplus production over their cost of keeping, one dollar of the cash capital invested in them. We may, then, estimate on the death of 60,000 men every year who were **a non-paying investment,** whose original cost is a dead and unredeemable loss. Multiply 60,000 by $2,000, and what is the cash aggregate? $120,000,000!

Do you think that in thus estimating **the cash value of a man,** Political Economy oversteps its boundaries and enters the field of curious speculation merely? Let me remind you that such value once and for generations had its full recognition in this country, and that the relations of Drink and the Liquor Traffic to such value, and the effect of both upon it, were clearly understood, and were plainly asserted in social and statute law.

In the days of slavery, an able-bodied slave found ready sale at from $1,500 to $2,000. For what did the owner CASH VALUE pay who bought him and who paid that OF A MAN. sum? **For what he had cost and for what he could produce.** The older he grew, after midmanhood, the less he would bring. To protect him in health and value, and to guard his habits of industry, to insure his productive power for the normal period of a human life, it was made a penal offense for another man to give or sell him intoxicating liquor.

For him, the slave, was Prohibition, upon the selfish basis of Political Economy, which recognized and protected his productive life.

Now, if it be fair to estimate as a total loss of the original investment in manhood those hard drinkers who die annually—and who doubts it?—must we not add to such loss all, or at least a part, of the idiotic and otherwise "defective" who die? We have reckoned in their loss of Productive Time: we cannot ignore the loss through them of what should have been Productive Cash Investment.

Take their total, already given, of 263,000, and still assume that only one half the number became "incapables" directly or indirectly through Drink—131,500. Then assume that only one half of this number—65,750—should be counted in this item at the full cash-investment figure before accepted ($2,000), and the total is $131,500,000 *cash investment loss* on their unfortunate and expensive account.

LOSING HUMAN INVESTMENTS.

Allowing that 10 per cent. of these "incapables" die every year, the annual distribution of this total loss would increase the annual aggregate of Waste by $13,150,000.

I know of no way in which we can compute the waste of Productive Life directly and remotely due to the Liquor Traffic, through murder, and crime, and sickness; through the poverty which Drink begets, and the mortality, among children especially, that comes of bad living conditions and insufficient food and brutal parentage.

Inside the jails, and penitentiaries, and poorhouses, and asylums, the representatives of cash loss in Manhood Investment and of Time and Cash Waste in Productive Life are appallingly numerous, and the aggregate of all their loss and waste is immense; but out sidethose institutions, where it is little considered and impossible of even approximate estimation, such loss and waste are enormous, and must be in general terms included, though otherwise it cannot be set down.

CHAPTER XIII.

WASTE IN CARE AND SUPPORT.

WE come now to consider:
Waste in the care and support of Productive Life Wasted.
This classification must be treated as having more elasticity than a strict limitation of its language would allow.

The phrase "care and support of Productive Life Wasted" is meant to cover a somewhat wider field of <small>STILL A WIDER FIELD.</small> Waste than the prisons, asylums, and almshouses afford. Inside this field, however, the waste and loss are very serious.

Let us **begin with the almshouses,** and accept 67,000, the number already stated, as the aggregate of paupers <small>CARE OF PAUPERS.</small> therein maintained. To figure the annual cost of maintaining each one at $100 would be a moderate estimate. The net cost to the State each year for each pauper cannot be less; and the amount spent upon each, economically considered, is a total waste, however it may be regarded from the humanitarian point of view. The figures representing this waste stand at $6,700,000 each year.

The cost of the almshouses themselves must be taken into account. *All this cost is dead capital.* Dead capital, <small>COST OF ALMSHOUSES.</small> forever remaining such, is dead waste. I cannot readily ascertain how many almshouses there are in this country. Many States possess one for each county; in some States there are but a few, of the larger sort, each costing, of course, a much larger sum. Reckon but twenty, on an average, to each State, and the average cost of each at but $20,000, and the total is $17,600,000. Exact figures would no doubt greatly increase these.

Consider next the 263,000 **other "incapables"—idiotic, insane,** etc.—whose care costs double, at least, **COST OF INCAPABLES AND ASYLUMS.** the care of paupers, and the estimate of whose care every year can not fall below $52,600,000. Put the building cost of asylums to accommodate these at only $500 for each person accommodated, and the total of unproductive or dead capital, representing so much actual waste, is $131,500,000.

But again we have held the largest item for the last, inside this narrow field. There are **the prisoners—**and **the prisons.**

Of the former, 70,000 prisoners, at an annual cost of $200 each for care and support, mean an annual waste of $14,000,000.

Of the latter, there are some fifty large penitentiaries, at least 2,200 jails, and an indefinite number of police prisons, the total cost of which has been set down, in a work by J. P. Altgeld, of Chicago, on "Our Penal Machinery and its Victims," at $400,000,000!

And it is with regard to these penal institutions, erected at such enormous outlay, and the prisoners maintained **COST OF CRIMINALS.** within them at such great annual expense, that our term "care and support of Productive Life wasted" must be given elasticity. In the "care and support" of prisoners, of criminals, must be included the care exercised by society, in self-defense, that makes prisoners of those who violate law, and that relegates them to the criminal class, to be punished and supported as such.

It is through this kind of "care," outside those institutions where the later "care and support" find exercise, that appalling waste is incurred. The authority last quoted ("Our Penal Machinery") estimates that there are 2,500,000 arrests in this country every year, and that the cost of police is on an average $24 to each arrest. Accept this estimate, and we must place over in the Waste Aggregate another annual item of $60,000,000, for there is **nothing productive in police effort;** a constabulary is made up of non-producers.

Walk along the streets of any town you please, and in the uniform of every policeman you meet is a consumer, who adds nothing to the wealth of the town, but steadily subtracts from it. Policemen are unproductive members of society.

You may say that they make other members of society secure in their avocations, that they guarantee safety to
<small>COURTS AND CONSTABULARY.</small> industrial pursuits, and are thus productive factors.

Suppose we grant this. We may still insist that to the extent which these men are made more necessary by causes which need not exist, and in the degree to which with such causes removed they could and would be spared, their unproductive service is a loss and a waste.

With them, upon the same plane of unproductive service, in close relation to them and largely existing because
<small>CONSUMERS OF WEALTH.</small> they exist, are the **courts of justice,** the officers of the law who do not perform police duty,—judges, and constables, and sheriffs, with all the paraphernalia of justice connected therewith—an army of men outside the jails, apart from the prisons, wearing no uniforms; unrecognized upon the street as consumers of the public wealth, but never producers of it; whose time is all wasted, so far as real production goes; in the "care and support" of whose productive life wasted the

waste of public wealth goes unremittingly on, and who, in just the proportion that they are necessitated by causes that should not exist, represent only **so much loss and waste on such unproductive and pauperizing account.**

What is this proportion, for which the Liquor Traffic must answer to Political Economy? In how great a degree is that traffic responsible for the prisons and the prisoners? for the cost of both? for the "care and support" required by crime and on account of crime inside and outside prison walls?

The answers given by different authorities differ, and yet within the limits of their variation there is surprising unanimity.

Whose testimony shall we take first? **Judges** ought to be good witnesses; their observation should have been ample, and their judicial habit of mind should insure conservative statement. As long ago as 1670, Sir Matthew Hale, the great chief-justice of England, thus recorded himself with reference to a term of twenty years:

THE CAUSE OF CRIME.

" I have found that if the murders and manslaughters, the burglaries and robberies, the riots and tumults, the adulteries, fornications, rapes, and other enormities that have happened in that time, were divided into *five* parts, *four* of them have been the issues and product of excessive drinking."

Just 202 years later, Judge Allison, in a speech delivered in Philadelphia, thus declared:

"In our criminal courts we can trace four fifths of the crimes that are committed to the influence of rum. There is not one case in twenty where a man is tried for his life in which rum is not the direct or indirect cause of the murder."

Thus two men of high judicial positions in two countries, two full centuries apart, give in almost the same identical testimony. Between them, and since the evidence of Judge Allison in 1872, scores of other jurists have gone upon record in similar terms.

State boards of charities, police boards, and other organizations of such kind may well be trusted in evidence. In the annual report for 1874 of the Board of Police Justices of New York City, that Board referred to intoxication and said:

> "We are fully satisfied that it is the one great leading cause which renders the existence of our police courts necessary."

The Massachusetts State Board of Charities has in like manner recorded its findings in successive annual reports. OFFICIAL TESTIMONY. In that for 1867, speaking of the aggregate returns of convicts, it said:

> "About two thirds are set down as intemperate, but this number is known to be too small. Probably more than 80 per cent. come within this class, intemperance being the chief occasion of crime, as it is of pauperism, and (in a less degree) of insanity."

In 1869 the same Board, referring to the same evil, again declared:

> "The proportion of crime traceable to this great vice must be set down, as heretofore, at not less than four fifths."

Prison Inspectors should be competent witnesses. Frederick Hill, long inspector of prisons in England, and a recognized high authority in all matters of penal science, has written thus:

> "I am within the truth when I state, as the result of extensive and minute inquiry, that in four cases out of five, when an offense has been committed, intoxicating drink has been one of the causes."

The inspectors of the Massachusetts State Prison, in their report for 1868, agreed in saying of the convicts there maintained:

"About four fifths of the number committed the crimes for which they were sentenced either directly or indirectly by the use of intoxicating drinks."

Thus, with surprising, or at least striking, unanimity, testify those whose daily observation and official duty qualify them to know the facts. When other men, seeking the facts only, and willing to publish them, however they run, collate evidence and tabulate the same, these experts are amply fortified.

We have room but for one citation of **tabulated evidence** thus furnished. "The Political Prohibitionist" for MUNICIPAL 1887 gave a table, compiled with great care STATISTICS. from the police statistics of fifty-eight cities in the United States, showing the total number of arrests in those cities for 1886, and the proportion of arrests for drunkenness, disorderly conduct, etc. Of course the figures were official, and were not supplied in the special interest of Political Economy or of Reform, by the police authorities. These 58 cities represented 17 States, and their total population was upwards of 6,000,000, or full one tenth the entire population of all the States.

The total of arrests was 304,279, and the percentage of arrests due to Drink averaged about 66⅓ per cent. The lowest percentage was 30, and the highest an even 100. The largest number of population to one saloon was in Waltham, Mass., 1,824; the smallest number in Lafayette, Ind., 89. The largest population to one arrest for drunkenness, etc., was in Poughkeepsie, 615, with a $95 license fee; the smallest in New Haven, 22, with a $200 license fee.

Accepting this percentage from police statistics, rather than the four fifths estimated and declared by other authorities, we should materially reduce the waste chargeable to the Liquor Traffic on the ground covered by this chapter. We are fairly justified, we may assume, in fixing the percentage at 75, and holding **the Liquor Traffic accountable for three fourths of the expense incurred by the State on account of crime,** and the arrest and punishment of those who violate law. We may as fairly charge the Liquor Traffic with a like proportion, at least, of the cost of pauperism, idiocy, and insanity.

PERCENTAGE FROM THE SALOONS.

Agreeing, then, upon this percentage, we are ready now in summing up the awful waste for which the Liquor Traffic must answer every year, to group the figures already shown, or to make from these such other figures as this proportion should yield. But we must first establish the **net loss and waste that are chargeable to the Liquor Traffic** on the percentage basis fixed above.

We found that the annual cost for maintenance of 67,000 paupers is $6,700,000. Three fourths of that, or 75 per cent., will be $5,025,000.

We estimated the total cost of almshouses at $17,600,000. It is fair, certainly, to charge the annual interest at 6 per cent. upon three-fourths of this as annual waste or loss—$792,000.

Three fourths of the cost of the care and support of other "incapables" will be $39,450,000 each year; and the annual interest upon three fourths of the building cost of asylums, etc., is $5,941,500.

NET CHARGE TO THE LIQUOR TRAFFIC.

Three fourths of the annual cost of maintaining prisoners is $10,500,000, and three fourths of the estimated costs of prisons, reformatories, etc., would be $300,000,000, interest upon which latter sum, at 6 per cent., is $18,000,000 every year.

Taking $60,000,000 as the annual cost of arrests, three fourths of this is $45,000,000.

WASTE IN CARE AND SUPPORT. 113

Thus upon this three fourths basis we have obtained these net figures, but we have not included *all* that might fairly be grouped under the head of "Care and Support." In outdoor relief, of those rendered needy by Drink, we could sum up a large item additional; and in the extra cost of courts, etc., for the trial of murder cases and other fruits of the Liquor Traffic, we might find still another item. But we pass these, and conclude our chapters on Consumption and Waste with the following

RECAPITULATION OF LOSS

ANNUALLY DUE TO THE LIQUOR TRAFFIC.

IN PRODUCTION.

Primary products	$134,721,554
Wages in producing these	67,360,500
Secondary products (liquor)	718,795,894
Wages in producing these	9,000,000

OF PRODUCTIVE TIME.

Ten per cent. of the 6,000,000 drinkers	60,000,000
One half time 60,000 drunkards	18,000,000
Three fourths time of 137,000 paupers and prisoners	61,650,000
One fourth time of 263,000 other "incapables"	39,450,000
Full time of 500,000 handlers and sellers of liquor	300,000,000

OF PRODUCTIVE LIFE.

By premature deaths	563,500,000
By premature deaths of insane and idiotic	209,083,500
By manhood investment unrealized upon	120,000,000
By such investment wasted in such way among the "incapables"	13,150,000

IN CARE AND SUPPORT.

Of paupers, three fourths	5,025,000
Interest on three quarters cost almshouses	792,000
Of other "incapables"	39,450,000
Interest on three quarters cost asylums	5,941,500
Of prisoners	10,500,000
Interest on three quarters cost of prisons, reformatories, etc	18,000,000
Cost of arrests, three quarters	45,000,000
	$2,439,419,948

Now if, as Ruskin says, Political Economy regulates the acts and habits of a society or State, "with reference to the means of its maintenance," precisely as domestic economy regulates the acts and habits of a household, with this awful waste an awful, indisputable, appalling national fact, what shall Political Economy do?

If Politics be the Science of Government—as nobody denies—*Political* Economy seeks, and must seek, the prudence, the well-being, the economic administration and conduct of the Government, through the proper and equitable conduct of the governed,—through true production, legitimate consumption, prohibition of Waste and the provident care of Wealth.

We will next consider the relation to these, and to the Liquor Traffic, of Authority and Human Life.

CHAPTER XIV.

RELATION OF AUTHORITY AND THE INDIVIDUAL.

WHAT is the relation of Authority and of human life to Production and Wealth, to Consumption and Waste?
Essentially—
A SELFISH RELATION, yet purely a philosophic relation, that should be also philanthropic, humanitarian.

Life produces, that it may live. It seeks wealth, that it may live more comfortably, more luxuriously. It re-
THE MOTIVE quires protection, defense, development,
OF PRODUCTION. that comfort and luxury may be safely enjoyed, and that the measure of their enjoyment may reach its maximum.

Authority is my name for the State. It is organized society. It is human life in the logical relations growing
THE SOVEREIGN out of human life. It is the concrete power
ELEMENT. necessary, whether in crude forms of semi-civilization, or the more elaborate forms of social exaltation, wherever men group together for common good or a common purpose. It is the sovereign element in man, everywhere recognized as needful in some manifestation, everywhere exercised in some degree, and as intimately related to all that a man does, for the welfare or the harm of society, of the State, as to the man himself.

The State must live. Authority must be perpetuated.
AUTHORITY How, and upon what? By and upon Pro-
IS THE STATE. duction and Wealth. On Want it would die, in the horrors of anarchy. On unproductive Labor it could not thrive or be long maintained. So Authority

makes rules—legislates—declares what may, must, and must not be—with regard to Labor and for the conservation of Capital. It has a vital interest in their product. It has a selfish relation to all production and all consumption. Its own perpetuity depends upon both.

When Adam Smith, the founder of Political Economy, first defined it, he recognized this, for he said the science proposed two objects—"to put the people in the way of procuring for themselves an ample subsistence, and to furnish the State with a revenue sufficient for the public service."

Two things are necessary, then, to the State—**Human Life, and Financial Revenue.** The second can come only from the first. It can come in best measure only from the best conditions of the first. Authority, therefore—the State—is directly, and selfishly, and always, interested in preserving life and in improving the conditions of labor, in bringing Production to its best, Consumption to its minimum consistent with the best development of the producer, Waste to its minimum absolute, and Wealth to the highest level of human good.

<small>LIFE AND REVENUE.</small>

Please observe with care how closely this function of Authority tallies with that definition of Political Economy which we accepted at the outset, and on which we based our first analysis, declaring it to be "the science which determines what laws men ought to adopt in order that they may, with the least possible exertion, procure the greatest abundance of things useful for the satisfaction of their wants; may distribute them justly, and consume them rationally."

Remember also the further statement of De Laveleye that "Political Economy and law underlie one another"; and recall our early conclusion, even more irresistible now as the logic of all this, "that whenever any element or influence enters life and the State to paralyze energy, to decrease production, to render distribution unfair, to impair credit, to pervert desire, to banish the spirit of thrift, and to destroy capital, Political Economy should find some law to eliminate that element or influence, and to protect life and the State from its baleful effects."

So Political Economy has to do with legislation, because legislation is only the adoption of rules, by Author- **POLITICAL** ity, for the better possibilities of life; and **ECONOMY'S IDEAL.** because **Political Economy,** as De Laveleye says, "**seeks an ideal, the same as moral science, law, or politics.**"

Its ideal can come only through ideal life; it can be reasonably sought only through honest effort to improve life and exalt the State.

Again says De Laveleye:

"Political Economy should never forget that material wealth is a means and not an end; the condition of moral and intellectual progress, not the end of life."

And so, while the relation of which we are now treating is a selfish one, on the part of Authority there is *underlying the selfishness* **an idealizing necessity.** Man shall be made better that the State may be made surer. The best laws that can contribute to his betterment are demanded by the State. The best surroundings that can be insured for his productive comfort are essential to the State. The source of all revenue, the cause of all wealth, the prime factor in all relations determining value, he is the final end and aim of all Political Economy, he is its subject and object in one.

"We are, in fact," says Judge Pitman (in "Alcohol and the State"), "all under a sort of betterment law, and whenever society determines that any policy improves the value of property and the comfort of life, the individual, GENERAL even though he dissents, must contribute BETTERMENT LAW. his share. It is one of the necessary conditions of government, and one on which, in the long run, the happiness of every one depends."

There are political economists who oppose this betterment idea; who will acknowledge no relation between Authority and the moral and material progress of man; who will even say, with Herbert Spencer, that "Government is essentially immoral"; who will oppose all State provision for the poor and all sanitary regulation by the State; who will even insist that the State has no right to educate—that education at public expense is a public wrong. But these economists are few, and on a rigid analysis of their views and utterances they would nearly dwindle down to Spencer himself—with a residuum of doubt about Spencer! The best, and the best known, writers on Economy, as a rule, while they may variously refer to it, admit the Betterment Law, and some of them really cite proof of its existence or necessity.

Even John Stuart Mill, who would limit the powers of Authority not less than Spencer, in some respects has MILL ON THE recognized the general bad results flowing ROMAN EMPIRE. from the failure to recognize or enforce this general Betterment Idea, and has thus recorded his testimony:

"When inequality of wealth once commences in a community not constantly engaged in repairing by industry the injuries of fortune, its advances are gigantic; the great masses of wealth swallow up the smaller. The Roman Empire ultimately became covered with the vast landed possessions of a comparatively few families, for whose luxury, and still more for whose ostentation, the most costly products were raised, while the cultivators of the soil were slaves, or small tenants in a nearly servile condition. From this time the wealth of the Empire progressively declined. In the beginning, the public revenues and the resources of rich individuals sufficed at least to cover Italy with splendid edifices, public and private, but at length so dwindled under the enervating influences of misgovernment that what remained was not sufficient to keep those edifices from decay."

The **Roman revenues** failed of maintaining the power of the Roman Empire, and the Empire gave way because the average development and betterment of human life was made impossible. Authority, in its relation to human life, to Production and Wealth, to the perpetuity of the State, did not realize the idealizing necessity.

Writing of those **Turkish provinces,** once the richest which the Roman Empire knew, Dr. Lennep, a reputable traveler, used language that De Laveleye quotes as follows:

DECADENCE UNDER TURKISH RULE.

" The populations of these provinces, capable in themselves of great progress, are stifled in a general atmosphere of malversation and decay. Beggars are everywhere; from top to bottom of the social scale there is mendicity, theft, and extortion. Little work is done at present, and there will be less in the future. Commerce is degenerating into peddling, banking into mere usury; every undertaking is a fraud; politics are an intrigue, and the system of police sheer brigandage. The fields are deserted, the forests devastated, mineral riches neglected, and the roads, bridges, and all public works falling into ruin."

Authority, in Turkish robes and fez, saw no idealizing necessity, and scorned the General Betterment idea.

Now, if such results could come from such cause, under imperialism, how much more should the cause be dreaded and guarded against under a republican form of government, where **the sovereign citizen is the unit of Authority!** By him, as the average unit, must the concrete character of Authority be judged, must the fruits of government be determined. Through him, if at all, must the perpetuity of government be guaranteed.

THE CITIZEN UNIT OF GOVERNMENT.

What he is, the State must be. What Authority becomes in his own person, government will develop in its organic form. It is idle for Spencer to say that "as civilization advances does government decay." In a republic this would be impossible. **In a republic, civilization advances only by and through the individual.** It is the uplift of the unit that elevates the whole aggregation.

In his "Thoughts on Government," Mr. Arthur Helps thus declares:

"It is the opinion of some people, but, as I contend, a wrong and delusive opinion, that as civilization advances there will be less and less need of government. I maintain that, on the contrary, there will be more and more need."

Judge Pitman quotes Mr. Helps and agrees with him, and after saying that "the causes for this are not difficult to understand" records himself in these words:

HUMAN SOLIDARITY.

"In the first place, as one of the results of modern civilization, men are brought closer together in every way, and their relations multiplied in number and complexity, so that, as Professor Huxley observes, the action of one man has more influence over another, and it becomes 'less possible for one to do a wrong thing without interfering more or less with the freedom of his fellows.'

"Then, again, a closer study of the laws of human solidarity has shown how the well-being of all depends on the well-being and well-doing of each; while a better acquaintance with the moral and physical laws of the universe has revealed kinds of injury and damage unnoticed by former generations. . . .

"Simultaneously with this, there has grown up under the educating influence of Christianity a tenderer sympathy for the weak, a stronger sense of human brotherhood. And when to these causes we add the historic fact that in all civilized countries the *people* have been steadily, if slowly, 'coming to power,' it is not strange that legislation has been growing more philanthropic, and government more paternal."

Government is a fact. There is no land where Labor has its chance, and where Civilization fruits itself, where this fact is not found. As Judge Pitman tersely puts it:

"Men are born under government as they are born into society. They have the power of withdrawal from either; but if they remain and accept the advantages, they must pay the price."

What are the advantages in this Republic of ours?

Production in peace, amid conditions generally favorable; consumption adequate to call for a reasonable surplus from the producers; and possibilities, under the General Betterment Law, of legitimate demand equal to every possible supply, if Waste be wisely guarded against, and legitimate consumption be insured.

ADVANTAGES AND PRICE OF CITIZENSHIP.

What is the price?

Honest obedience to law; a cheerful acquiescence in that desire for human betterment which, however selfishly founded, rises to and is inspired by a genuine ideal; a ready recognition of concrete Authority as having natural jurisdiction over everything within the State which can or may work it good or ill.

In the body social, **every man yields a measure of his liberty to other men.** Bring two men together, and you divide by two the personal liberty of each. Multiply these by twenty, and you bring about the necessity for politics—you make possible and needful Political Economy.

And in the body politic every man yields a measure of his liberty to that Authority which is the body politic incarnate—the sovereign element in man crystallized. He is no more a law unto himself alone. He no longer legislates—makes rules—merely for himself. Every conclusion of his own will, if allowed

MAN IN THE MASS.

to stand, becomes an enactment for his fellow. *If it injure the other man*, that man has equal right to enact some conclusion to *his* injury.

So in self-defense, it follows, *he must consider the other man*. In self-defense he must legislate for his fellow. In self-defense he must permit his fellow to legislate for him. In self-defense, out of a wise and worthy selfishness, he must, and he does, yield up a portion of that personal liberty for which he now and then so heroically contends.

<small>THE OTHER MAN.</small>

In its final analysis, and carried to its legitimate end, all law is but crystallized, organic self-defense for the individual man, wherein, for his own protection, he **sets over himself certain metes and bounds.**

Whenever and wherever and however he organizes Authority, then and there and thus he establishes the relation of that Authority and of human life under it through which, or for which, or by which, it is exercised —a relation of mutual self-surrender, selfishly inspired it may be, patriotically maintained it should be, for the good of all.

And yet it is as true, in another sense, that law is not for the individual man, but for Society. Alone he never organizes Authority. It is the product of contact.

For himself alone it is never needed. *Its necessity comes in with the other man.*

Moral rights they both retain when they enter the same neighborhood; but these must be fenced about with legal limitations. Self-defense requires it, as we have said; but Authority—the State—has a higher duty than to defend units, to protect the property of units.

<small>MORAL RIGHTS AND LEGAL LIMITATIONS.</small>

Says the Bill of Rights in the Constitution of Massachusetts:

"Government is instituted for the common good; for the protection, safety, prosperity, and happiness of the people; and not for the profit, honor, or private interest of any one man, family, or class of men.

Instituted for *the common good*, drawing a revenue for its support from *the common goods*, Political Economy demands that Government, Authority, in all its legislation, shall recognize and foster **the best interests of all the people**—shall encourage no vices or ills for the sake of a revenue, but *in every manner possible shall exalt and purify the State.*

This means moral betterment—the uplift of the nation through individual character, the upward steady trend of national life through individual elevation. Lecky emphasizes this, in "A History of European Morals," when, speaking of a nation and its enduring quality, he says:

"Its foundation is laid in pure domestic life; in commercial integrity; in a high standard of moral worth and of public spirit; in simple habits; in courage, uprightness, and a certain soundness and moderation of judgment which spring quite as much from character as from intellect. If you would form a wise judgment of the future of a nation, *observe carefully whether these forces are increasing or decaying.*"

CHAPTER XV.

SOVEREIGN RELATION OF AUTHORITY.

WHAT is the relation of Authority to the Liquor Traffic? Historically and confessedly, **a Sovereign Relation.** By which we mean that Government, whether embodied in some imperial Cæsar or in some personification of popu-
GOVERNMENT lar will, is **the recognized master** of the
MASTERSHIP. Liquor Traffic; that this Traffic is a confessedly fit subject of governmental mastership; that through the natural self-assertion of politico-economic law, even before Political Economy was formulated into a science, this mastery was in some form or to some degree maintained; that the Traffic has always in some form or degree admitted such mastery; and that any mastery, any right of control, means absolute and unreserved sovereignty, the right of absolute rulership.

Some theorists oppose any sovereignty of this kind. Mill stands at the head of these, and is the most quoted
SOCIETY AND writer among them. In his famous essay on
TRADE. "Liberty" he defines what he considers **the true functions of Government,** and the principle that should determine legislation; and while analysis of his principle yields "self-protection," and while he concedes the exercise of power "over any member of a civilized community" "to prevent harm to others," he does not admit the sovereignty we claim. He denies it, but only after certain other admissions that are marked, and that, together with these concessions made, put him in serious logical straits. In one of these he says:

"Trade is a social act. Whoever undertakes to sell any description of goods to the public does what affects the interest of other persons, and of society in general; and thus his conduct, in principle, comes within the jurisdiction of society."

And speaking with more particularity of reference, on another page he says:

"The interest, however, of these dealers in promoting intemperance is a real evil, and justifies the State in imposing restrictions and requiring guarantees, which but for that justification would be infringements of legitimate liberty."

And in another chapter, on the "Limits to the Authority of Society over the Individual," there seems a concession **LEGITIMATE LIBERTY.** not less damaging to his logic or helpful to ours in these words:

"Whenever, in short, there is a definite damage, or a definite risk of damage, either to an individual or to the public, the case is taken out of this province of liberty and placed in that of morality or law."

As to what Mill can mean by the word "definite," in this connection, Judge Pitman, with true judicial carefulness, thus remarks:

"Surely it is the evident *quantum*, and not the exactness with which the estimate of damage can be made, that gives society occasion to interfere. . . . It is a truism to say that no business or pursuit known to civilized life inflicts greater damage or exposes society to greater risks than the traffic in question. It is not 'definite' simply because it is too great to be calculable; it is fearfully indefinite, but it is a fixed fact in the past and morally certain in the future."

The most friendly analysis of Mr. Mill's position, and of the whole argument in behalf of Personal Liberty, can **GOVERNMENT AND THE INDIVIDUAL.** show only that **Government has no right to interfere with an individual's acts until they infringe on some other individual's rights,** and this infringement of rights is precisely what the Liquor Traffic stands charged with before the bar of Patriotic Public Opinion, by the advocate of Applied Political Economy; and in evidence against it can be arrayed an endless procession of witnesses from factory, jail, poorhouse, courthouse, work-bench, and store.

The logic of Mr. Mill makes directly against the liquor-dealer, and as directly, irrefutably, in favor of that sovereignty which we have claimed for the State. Let one more quotation from his essay on "Liberty" suffice to prove this:

<small>MILL AND THE LIQUOR TRAFFIC.</small>

"For such actions as are prejudicial to the interests of others the individual is accountable, and may be subjected to either social or legal punishments, if society is of opinion that the one or the other is requisite for its protection."

To "be subjected" means a possible state of subjectivity, and that were impossible except for the existence of an actual sovereignty which might assert itself.

"Punishments" imply power and right to punish. **Social organization means law and penalties.** And such organization must be. As President Woolsey says in his "Political Science":

"The individual could make nothing of himself or of his rights, except in society; society unorganized could make no progress, could have no security, no recognized rights, no order, no settled industry, no motive for forethought, no hope for the future.

"The need of such an institution as the State, the physical provision for its existence, the fact that it has appeared everywhere in the world, unless in a few most degraded tribes, shows that it is in a manner necessary; and if necessary, natural; and if natural, divine. It is as natural as rights are, and as society is, and is the bond of both. It is the means for all the highest ends of man and society."

<small>NEED OF THE STATE.</small>

Then the State is, must be, and ought to be, truly and wisely sovereign. **The individual rights of man must yield to the political and economic sovereignty of** the State. Prof. Lindley M. Keasbey thus amplifies and enforces this thought:

" In economic as in political liberty the sovereign power sets the final bounds. So long as the supreme authority lay in the hands of despots, of feudal lords, or even of the absolute monarchs, this domain of economic freedom was, it is true, unnecessarily contracted, and its boundaries arbitrary. Nowadays, however, since the people themselves have become the State, the case is different. Under the constitutional system the people as an organic unit allot to themselves in severalty a definite sphere of industrial action, and place their government over the same to guard its boundaries. If one individual should then entrench upon the economic rights of another, these same governmental authorities will interfere. If, on the other hand, any organ itself should endeavor to overstep the power delegated to it by the sovereign State and encroach upon the field of individual autonomy, the system of checks and balances in the modern constitution will operate to redress the wrong. Or, finally, if it become the prevailing opinion among the people that **the domain of individual economic liberty** thus laid down by them has in the course of time become too narrow or too extended to serve the best interests of their organic life, they may in their capacity as sovereign State, by amendment of their Constitution, reconstruct the boundaries of industrial freedom to suit these changed conditions. In any case, it is the State which remains supreme : individuals, as such, simply carry on their several economic activities under its control and at its pleasure."

<small>THE STATE
THE SOVEREIGN.</small>

Professor Keasbey also asserts

" That from beginning to end, in inception as well as development, the sovereign State has always been, is now, and in all probability will ever remain economic as well as political in character ; . . . that the final source of political and economic power must in the very nature of things be one and the same ; that our modern national States, in other words, are the economic sovereigns of the age, and that no individual industrial transaction can be begun, carried on, or completed without the express or implied consent of one of these supreme authorities."

The sovereign relationship of the State to the Liquor Traffic clearly follows this line of reasoning, and is logically demonstrated by the attitude of the one toward the other for lo! these many centuries. That attitude has been either of Prohibition, Partial Restraint, Tax, or Regulation, whatever the form of Government, whatever the condition of the governed, whatever the age of the world. That attitude came of Authority, and of Authority absolute. Deferring until another lesson such analysis as we may be able to make of the nature of License, the more modern and popular form of regulation, we will now merely repeat that its genesis was Authority, and will show who exercised it and why.

THE STATE'S ATTITUDE.

"Render unto Cæsar the things that are Cæsar's." Cæsar was king. The king must have his tribute-money. So License at the beginning was not the License of to-day. It was neither permission nor restraint; it was an assessment, a levy, a tax, a demand for tribute.

GENESIS OF LICENSE.

But though not even partial restraint, it had its origin and source in a power which might restrain altogether— the power of Government, put in exercise for the good of the governed; a power which had again and again prohibited the Liquor Traffic absolutely; which had made India a Prohibition country 3,000 years before Prohibition was heard of in America; which had caused the total destruction of the vineyards in China, root and branch, 1,100 years before Christ; which had crushed out liquor-sellers in Scotland with the extremest rigor of imperial law before our second century ended; which had been manifest in Scotland and England, many times and in many ways, before the beginnings of License.

POWER OF RESTRAINT.

There were some curious things about those beginnings. As has been said, the first license was a tax. So far as we can learn, Scotland—home of cakes and ale—began the modern system of *regulating* Intemperance by **laws controlling the sale** of Liquor.

PROHIBITION IN HISTORY.

Nearly all previous attempts at regulation (and they can scarcely be numbered) had been aimed at the *drinker*, not the seller. A Chinese edict had ordered that the people who drank should be put to death. One of Rome's early enactments had forbidden women to drink even the juice of the grape; and early annals do say that those old Romans kissed their wives with more than affectionate frequency, to find out whether they had been violating this law!

In Burmah, at one time, intoxication had been visited with the death penalty. A monastic law of St. Gildas had said that "if any monk, through drinking too freely," got "thick of speech," so that he could not "join in the psalmody," he was to be "deprived of his supper." And another canonical law, in the Irish Church, had said: "If a priest gets drunk *through inadvertence*, he must do penance seven days; if *through carelessness*, fifteen; if *through contempt*, forty." A deacon or a monk had been obliged to do penance four weeks for the like offense, but a poor subdeacon could get inadvertently, carelessly, or contemptuously drunk any time and atone for it in three days!

It is not easy to tell just when began the new regulation system, with reference to the seller rather than to the drinker; it was back of the twelfth century. But we know who paid most of the early taxes or license fees. As before, at the beginning of a great evil, "the woman" did it! Scotch matrons brewed the Scotch ale and paid the Scotch license fee of four-pence annually, which authorized them to brew. Any could brew who chose; any could sell who brewed for sale; but all who brewed must pay. None was then forbidden or restrained.

<small>SCOTCH WOMEN BREWERS.</small>

Government did not then require a certificate of good character, signed by several freeholders,—doubtless all the Scotch women had good characters,—although governmental authority fenced the license round with curious limitations. None could carry her brews into another town and sell them; none could sell who had not brewed especially for sale, and every brew must have been previously "tasted" by a public "taster," sworn to impartiality. All public **officials were forbidden to brew and sell**; and all who received license were compelled to brew from year's end to year's end, for said the law:

"What woman that will brew ale to sell, shall brew all the year thro', after the custom of the town. And if she does not, she shall be suspended of her office by the space of a year and a day."

So it appears that license at the outset did more than demand a tribute; it conferred some privilege, and carried EARLY FEATURES with it an "office" (and it is generally fa-OF REGULATION. vored now by those who want office); and as the insignia of that office, it was further decreed that "each brewer shall put her ale wand outside her house at her window or above her door, that it may be visible to all men." Failing to do this, she must pay a fine of fourpence. And in selling, moreover, she must fill her measure brim full of ale, and a public visitor was appointed by law to see that she so filled it and did not cheat with froth! It may be, after all, that those good Scotch women had some tricks about them.

This **Regulation System** cannot easily be traced through its early centuries, but barring a bit of the tenth REGULATION century,—when King Edgar made it more FOR REVENUE. prohibitive than regulative by putting down all alehouses except one in each borough or small town,— it seems clear that the system existed rather to insure revenue than to check intemperance, that royalty was anxious to promote drinking rather than to stop it, for the price of ale was regulated by royal decree, and made, as now it strikes us, ridiculously low. By statute, in 1272, English brewers were ordered to sell two gallons for one penny in cities, and about twice as much for the same sum in the country.

Three hundred years later there are spasmodic efforts to make the system more restrictive, but regulation goes on, with the natural results, until by and by Shakespeare makes Iago say: "In England they are most potent for potting. Your Dane, your German, and your swag-bellied Hollander, are nothing to your English"; and another writer declares: "We seem to be steeped in liquors. We drink as if we were nothing but sponges, or had tunnels in our mouths."

And still the Regulation continues, varying in restrictiveness through two more centuries, growing more and more specific, on the whole, and less and less efficient, as distillation becomes more common and the public appetite for ale grows into general thirst for gin, until a common sign among ginsellers in London is "Drunk for a penny, dead drunk for two-pence, clean straw for nothing."

Then comes **High-License Regulation,** to stay the awful flood, in the form of a Parliamentary measure car-

EARLY HIGH LICENSE.

ried in 1736, imposing twenty shillings a gallon duty on all spirituous liquors (ale not being then regarded as spirituous), and making the retail license fee £50 a year; but riots follow, and smuggling, and an immense clandestine trade; the traffic will not regulate; the revenue must be increased; the duties are lowered, the license fees reduced, consumption multiplies, and the national habit of gin-drinking becomes, according to Lecky, the master-curse of English life, to which most of the crime and an immense proportion of the misery of the nation may be ascribed.

In this running *historical review of License*, we have seen its evolution under the rulership of Authority, through **THE LOGIC OF LICENSE.** centuries of submission to that Authority. And to-day the logic of License declares that **the smallest right of License can be conferred only by Authority which has the largest possible right to withhold.** To confer a little means the right, the power, to withhold much, to withhold all.

It is the good of the governed which all Authority must keep in mind. There exists no Authority, to permit or to **THE FUNCTION OF GOVERNMENT.** forbid, which is not based upon this principle. Representative or autocratic, the power of Government has but one legitimate function—to conserve the common weal; to insure the greatest good to the greatest number; to bring Production under the healthiest conditions; and to insure the smallest possible minimum of waste. Brought to bear in behalf of any industry, or system, which is inimical to the many, however profitable to a few—which multiplies non-producers, and increases waste, and burdens productive labor—it is a power misapplied, a function misdirected, perverted, and abused.

CHAPTER XVI.

THE NATURE OF LICENSE.

The sovereign relation of Authority to the Liquor Traffic is imperatively and fundamentally essential to the broad and beneficent application of Political Economy.

Historically, a relation of actual rulership has been shown. Submission to that rulership, through many centuries, ought long since to have established the fact of it, and to have been its world-wide recognition and confession by the Liquor Traffic. Through logic, through law, through historic fact, the kind, the character, the degree, of that rulership should be to-day beyond question, in any Government of any form.

<small>SUBMISSION BY THE LIQUOR TRAFFIC.</small>

And yet to-day the Liquor Traffic looks Authority boldly in the face and says:

"You may control me—a little; you may limit me—a little; you are my nominal sovereign, and I am your nominal subject, but I have rights which you can not overstep, I have powers which you can not coerce: respect them and I obey (if I please), deny them and I rebel."

It behooves us, then, to meet such declaration with further study of the relationship we have been considering, and in the light of what Authority must seek —**the good of the governed.** In seeking that good, Authority must seek and determine what is injurious or ill. Admit, once, that Authority cannot restrain or coerce the injurious thing which it has found, and you recognize a greater than Government, you ac-

<small>AUTHORITY TO RESTRAIN.</small>

knowledge a power superior to the State. Your Authority becomes a king in cap and bells, a clown swaying the scepter.

Now, since License has been so many centuries submitted to by the Liquor Traffic, let us examine the nature of License, having seen its origin. That origin was in Authority,—this no man will dispute. From whence does it now derive existence, and by what is it perpetuated? Authority. *By whom is this Authority exercised, and What is its nature?*

These are questions of importance, deserving thoughtful answer.

You have a Board of Excise in your town, or a Court in your county. It grants or refuses license. Does the authority referred to rest in that Court or that Board? A Legislature enacted the law under which Board and Court were chosen. Did this authority inhere in that Legislature?

SOURCE OF AUTHORITY.

No! Back of the Court, back of excisemen, back of legislators, this authority is found. It sits upon no throne. It wears no royal or courtly robes. "WE THE PEOPLE" wield it. "WE THE PEOPLE" are responsible for it. "WE THE PEOPLE" should know thoroughly its nature, and intelligently bear ourselves in its use. Now, as to its nature, let us see.

License is defined by the Standard Dictionary as: "1. Authority or liberty given to do or forbear an act; an expression of consent. 2. A written or printed certificate of a legal permit or license to do anything that would be otherwise unlawful or forbidden."

LICENSE DEFINED.

"To license," Webster affirms, is "to permit by grant of authority; to remove from legal restraint by a grant of permission; to authorize to act in a particular character."

Which definitions clearly imply: Restraint—Authority;

authority to restrain; authority to permit, by grant or certificate, which may also be refused; authorization to act, by authority which might forbid; permission for, authorization of, that which, by the authority granting it, was before forbidden and restrained.

"To permit *by grant;*" "to remove from legal restraint *by a grant.*"

Grants were once kingly concessions. *A grant*, in name and in fact, implied sovereign authority. So far as *the nature* of authority is concerned, "WE THE PEOPLE" are all kings. We delegate, we distribute, our authority, but its essence, its quality, remains unchanged. So far as it applies, in any degree, it is absolute. For its proper application we are responsible; its character we did not create and we cannot change. It must be sovereign, or it must cease to be.

The license certificate which hangs on the wall of any saloon is *a grant.* It confers an actual, indefeasible right, **THE GRANT** as actually and indefeasibly as if signed **OF AUTHORITY.** by a king. The authority which gave it, or authorized the giving of it, was as actual and absolute as a king's. It would be worth nothing to the holder were not this true. The holder has paid for it a fixed price, and unless the value rests on authority final, full and competent to fix that price, and to protect the payer of it in the right for which he pays—unless the grant is indefeasible and kingly in its nature—the holder has been swindled.

Either authority is absolute to confer the grant, or it takes money under false pretenses. "WE THE PEOPLE" **WE** have a right to withhold the grant altogether, **THE PEOPLE.** or we have no right to demand its price. That price is paid for a concession ours to make, or we are but footpads on the highway of trade, practising robbery under plea of the law.

There are many advocates of License who concede its origin in Authority, but who deny its essentially permissive character, asserting that the purpose of a License law is restraint, although denying the right of Prohibition. They even claim for the word License two meanings—**to permit,** and **to restrain**; and they plant themselves on the second of these, with utter disregard of the logic in the case.

If there be any difference between permission and restraint, surely the broader this difference the narrower is the margin between restraint and prohibition. If to restrain and to permit are essentially different, to prohibit and to restrain must be essentially identical. To prohibit, therefore, cannot be wrong while to restrain is right.

<small>PERMISSION AND RESTRAINT.</small>

But while two things are implied in the word License or by its accepted definitions, only one thing is designated by the word itself—*permission.* For when you "permit," by grant of authority which might refuse, do you *forbid?* When you "authorize," do you *condemn?* When you "remove from legal restraint," do you legally restrain?

There is a sense in which License may and must have two meanings—one meaning for the man who *gets* the license, and by it is *authorized to act;* and another meaning for the man who *doesn't* get it, and is *forbidden to act.* But he may and should insist, this man without a license, that the same sovereign power which denies him had equal right to *deny the other man.*

The law of License does not establish the partial prohibition implied by it and possible under it. That partial prohibition was, before, complete and absolute Prohibition. License, in the law, merely advertises and proves that such entire Prohibition did previously exist. License merely says

<small>PROHIBITION ANTERIOR TO LICENSE.</small>

that before, in the law or in the very constitution of things, Prohibition *was*.

These logical deductions from the law and the nature of License, though formulated by this writer some years ago, have recently been reenforced by the highest possible judicial decisions. In 1890 the Supreme Court of the United States made this very positive deliverance:

NO RIGHT IN THE CITIZEN. "There is no inherent right in a citizen to sell intoxicating liquors by retail; it is not a privilege of a citizen of a State or a citizen of the United States."

And **a profound general principle** was laid down by that Court, in close connection with this, limiting the powers of authority, in these words:

"No legislature can bargain away the public health or the public morals. The people themselves cannot do it, much less their servants. Government is organized with a view to their preservation, and cannot divest itself of the power to provide for them."

So that "WE THE PEOPLE," composing this republican form of Government, cannot shift responsibility for public morals and the public health; we cannot delegate even that our legislative representatives may bargain them away.

NO LEGISLATIVE RIGHT.

Three years earlier than this indeed **supreme utterance** of our highest judicial body, the Supreme Court, in 1887, thus declared of the Liquor Traffic:

THE COURT ON THE TRAFFIC. "Nor can we ignore the fact, established by statistics accessible to every one, that the disorder, pauperism, and crime prevalent in the country are, in large measure, directly traceable to this evil, nor can it be said that government interferes with or impairs any one's constitutional rights of liberty or property when it determines that the manufacture and sale of intoxicating drinks for general use as a beverage are or may become hurtful to society and to every member of it, and is therefore a business in which no one may lawfully engage."

Long before this Chief-Justice Taney had said:

"I see nothing in the Constitution of the United States to prevent it from regulating or restraining the traffic, or from prohibiting it altogether."

Associate Justice McLean, of the same Supreme Court, had said:

"The necessity of license presupposes a prohibition of the right to sell, as to those who have no license. . . . If the foreign article be injurious to the health or morals of the community, a State may, in the exercise of that great and conservative police power which lies at the foundation of its prosperity, *prohibit* the sale of it. . . . By preserving, as far as possible, the health, the safety, and the moral energies of society, its prosperity is advanced."

Justice Catron had said:

"I admit as inevitable that if the State has the power of restraint by licenses to any extent, she has the discretionary power to judge of its limit, and may go to the length of *prohibiting* sales altogether."

JUDICIARY ON PROHIBITION.

After admitting the "misery, pauperism, and crime which have their origin in the use and abuse of ardent spirits," and the right and power of "that Authority," the State, to correct the evils thereof, Justice Grier had said:

"If a loss of revenue should accrue to the United States from a diminished consumption of ardent spirits, she will be a gainer a thousand-fold in the health, wealth, and happiness of the people."

We have space for but one further citation, and this is from Judge Harrington, Chief-Justice of Delaware:

"We have seen no adjudged case which denies the power of a State in the exercise of its sovereignty to regulate the traffic in liquor for restraint as well as for revenue, and, **as a police measure**, to restrict or *prohibit* the sale of liquor as injurious to public morals or dangerous to public peace. The subjection of private property, in the mode of its enjoyment, to the public good, and its subordination to general rights liable to be injured by its unrestricted use, is a principle lying at the foundations of government. It is a condition of the social state, the price of its enjoyment entering into the very structure of organized society, existing by necessity for its preservation."

Thus judicial interpretation as a unit, and the very logic of License itself, lead us inevitably to accept the sovereignty of the State over the Liquor Traffic. Thus License declares, with positive and unflinching emphasis, that Prohibition is right, legitimate, and just.

For what is it in the License system that any temperance man, any Political Economist, approves? The Prohibition principle. What makes License anywhere, even in theory, restrictive? The Prohibition principle. On what is License founded? The Prohibition principle. What can make the License system of any benefit to the State, beyond free trade and legitimate taxation thereon?

THE PROHIBITION PRINCIPLE.

Only the Prohibition principle as applied therein, though always and everywhere antagonized thereby.

Yet Prohibition has been opposed on the plea that it would violate organic law. Whereas, if Prohibition does infract that organic law, count the round week a unit, and every Sunday-closing statute infracts the law in proportion as one day is to seven, or one-seventh is to one; or count 100 men a unit, license one and prohibit 99, and you infract the organic law in the same proportion as 99 to 1.

PROHIBITION VERSUS LICENSE.

Based on the Prohibition principle—based on full and absolute authority to restrain—if Prohibition be unconstitutional, **License cannot successfully claim constitutionality;** and if it be *not* legitimately based on that principle, and if it be *not* legitimately the grant of authority on which that principle rests, though so antagonistic to both, then License is essentially and commercially a fraud.

But is License constitutional? If anything more than a fraud, it is based on the previous *fact* of Prohibition, and that fact rested on the *principle* of Prohibition. If *this principle of* **Prohibition is constitutional,** then is not *the fact of* **License unconstitutional**? Does it not follow that License is either a legal fraud or an illegal unconstitutionality?

LICENSE UNCONSTITUTIONAL.

It directly antagonizes the only principle on which it can be directly sustained. Apart from that principle, it cannot stand. Declare Prohibition unconstitutional, and you sweep License from the statute-books. Admit Prohibition to be in harmony with organic law, and you must impeach License for infracting that law. You can never license what was never prohibited. You can never constitutionally prohibit what is right. You can never constitutionally license what is constitutionally wrong.

What is a Constitution?

The embodied spirit of a Nation or State; the groundwork of government, to be less metaphysical in definition; in the language of another, "the agreement and arrangement of the people in the State, as to mutual rights and obligations." It is the supreme expression of popular authority. What the Constitution may say depends only on what the true purposes of popular government may be—"a government of the people, by the people, and for the people." These purposes are thus set forth with comprehensive clearness in our National Constitution:

GROUNDWORK OF GOVERNMENT.

"To establish justice, insure domestic tranquillity, provide for the common defense, *promote the general welfare*, and secure the blessings of liberty to ourselves and our posterity."

Says the Constitution of Pennsylvania:

"All power is inherent in the people, and all free governments are founded on their authority and instituted for *their peace, safety, and happiness.*"

Says the Constitution of New York:

CONSTITUTIONAL DECLARATIONS.
"We the people of the State of New York, grateful to God for our freedom, in order to enjoy its blessings do ordain," etc.

And back of these constitutional utterances we find the Declaration of Independence, our one **ultimate expression of human liberty,** with its deliberate and solemn enunciations " that all men are created equal; that they are endowed by their Creator with certain inalienable rights; that among these are life, liberty, and *the pursuit of happiness."*

The safety, the peace, the morality, the welfare and happiness of a people, of a State, should and do form the

AIM AND OBJECT OF GOVERNMENT.
true aim and object of Government; should and do underlie the Constitution of every State and of the entire Union of States.

Because and only because this is true, the Liquor Traffic may be and has been prohibited; the sovereign power of the State has been put forth against it. And the reasons which have made Prohibition right and constitutional ever, anywhere, are the very reasons which make License wrong and unconstitutional now and everywhere, if the spirit of organic law is properly considered and understood.

An important decision by the Kentucky Court of Appeals (Commonwealth vs. Douglas) runs along this line, asserts the true functions of government, declares what are the supports of the State, and sets forth the logical limitations of Authority. It says:

" When we consider that honesty, morality, religion, and education are the main pillars of the State, and for the protection and promotion of which government was instituted among men, it at once strikes the mind that the Government, through its agents, cannot throw off these trust duties by selling, bartering, or giving them away. The preservation of the trust is essential to the happiness and welfare of the beneficiaries, which the trustees have no power to sell or give away. If it be conceded that the State can give, sell, and barter any one of them, it follows that it can thus surrender its control of all, and convert the State into dens of bawdy-houses, gambling-shops, and other places of vice and demoralization, provided the grantees pay for the privileges and thus deprive the State of its power to repeal the grants and all control of the subjects as far as the grantees are concerned; and the trust duty of protecting and fostering the honesty, health, and morals and good order of the State would be cast to the winds, and vice and crime would triumph in their stead. Now, it seems to us that the essential principles of self-preservation forbid that the Commonwealth should possess a power so revolting because destructive of the main pillars of government."

Against the principle of Prohibition, as applied to the Liquor Traffic, no court of last resort has ever yet declared. Under a **Constitution to promote popular safety,** to insure domestic peace, to enhance the general happiness, and to conserve the common welfare, no statute for the peril of the people, for the disturbance of peace, for the promotion of misery and the bane of a vast multitude, can be legitimate. Every License Law should begin with these words:

[LICENSE PROP. ERLY ENTITLED.]

"An Act entitled 'An Act to promote misery among men, to disturb the peace of the State, to injure the general welfare, to increase taxation, and to imperil our common interests.'"

Thus rightly entitled, the highest court would promptly declare against it. Against such an open avowal of antagonism to the Constitution, the Constitution's most eminent defenders would rise in righteous indignation, and wipe it out.

CHAPTER XVII.

DUTY OF AUTHORITY.

WE come now to consider the fourth and final Grand Division of our theme:

The Duty of Authority toward the Liquor Traffic, in view of these relations and of the momentous interests they involve.

What are these momentous, these enormous, interests?

THE INTERESTS INVOLVED. In a general and broad way, and to a considerable extent, they have been referred to and discussed. In further analysis and final summary, they may be broadly classified as

Financial,
Moral, and
Political.

It seems necessary that we devote some further space to the

Financial Interests Involved.

We have already considered these, at length, from the **Cost Side of the Liquor Traffic;** they require candid consideration from the **Income Side of that Traffic.**

The duty of Authority toward the Liquor Traffic has been long and widely measured from this Income side.

THE INCOME SIDE. License of that Traffic has been long and unceasingly urged because of the revenue it should and does yield. No other pleas have been anywhere so potent in its behalf.

"The State must live!" has been a long, far cry. It has been heard and repeated by statesmen, by politicians, by taxpayers, by Christian citizens, who saw only the revenue side of the Liquor Traffic, and who did not consider the cost side. They have looked at the income as with a microscope; their search for the cost has been telescopic.

As an organized body, **the State must live by Taxation.** The machinery of the State must be kept in motion by the power of Revenue. Revenue must come from the public domain, or from private property, from individual effort. When drawn from private resources, it is the result of Taxation. And then, as De Laveleye has declared, "it is the price paid by the citizens for the blessings of social order."

SUPPORT FOR THE STATE.

In the language of Montesquieu:

TAXATION DEFINED.
"The revenue of the State is a portion of his wealth sacrificed by each citizen in order to gain security for the rest, or the means of enjoying it more agreeably."

De Laveleye further says that—

"When in exchange for the tax a government gives neither security nor comfort, the tax is mere robbery."

Does it not follow that, when the security is incomplete, and the comfort inadequate, the tax is robbery to a certain extent? Do not partial comfort and security alone prove partial robbery? If I, a citizen, pay for security not afforded me, has not my money been taken upon a false pretense? Has Authority any right thus to take my tax, my **payment for security and comfort,** and then accept a payment, a tax, from any other man for any business that discounts the security and comfort for which I pay? When he pays for that function of government which insures to him protection in the calling he selects, and profit in pursuit of it, and such comfort as may satisfy his taste, have I not equal right to

RETURN FOR THE TRIBUTE.

equal protection in the calling of my choice, in the comfort which my taste approves?

If he pay a special tax on a special business, is it not for the special purpose that in such business he may have a special privilege? Has Authority any right to grant any man any special privilege, to the cost of my security and my comfort?

In his chapter on the General Principles of Taxation, John Stuart Mill declares:

<small>MILL ON TAXATION.</small> "The ends of government are as comprehensive as those of the social union. They consist of all the good, and all the immunity from evil, which the existence of government can be made, either directly or indirectly, to bestow."

When I pay, then, for the support of government, I give tribute, I sacrifice of my possessions, that **the best ends of government** may be mine; I contribute to the maintenance of government that I may receive from it the greatest possible good, and may be insured by it the largest possible immunity from ill. Has Authority any right to recognize, to foster, to protect, upon any terms of payment, as of license or tax, any bad business or industry, any evil or wrong, from which I cannot be guaranteed that immunity for which I pay?

Says De Laveleye: "Taxes ought never to be raised <small>IMMORAL SOURCES OF TAXATION.</small> from immoral sources, such as lotteries and gambling-houses."

Why? Because they are **evils from which the moral, tax-paying citizen pays to be defended.** But does he need, or desire, greater immunity from these than from the average saloon? Does not the latter provoke more public disorder, more public crime, and more private and public waste, than the gambling-house? Is not the saloon a worse corrupter of morals than the lottery? Does not the greater always include the less? and does not the average saloon to-day include the lottery or gambling feature in some form? is it not the gambler's home or headquarters?

Taxation of the Liquor Traffic, in discharge of Authority's duty, is argued for, or based upon, or excused on account of, two claims alone—

Revenue,

Regulation.

These claims are seldom divorced in fact, though often separated in appearance. And the pleas for them, the THE REGULATION arguments in their behalf, are so intermixed CLAIM. and involved with the pleas for License itself, which forms the real basis of all Regulation, and under which all Revenue is derived, that the three terms are nearly synonymous, and can scarcely be considered apart.

It is urged by some that a License law treats the Liquor Traffic as if it had not previously existed, and had never been prohibited; as if it had never before been considered by Authority; as if it were a legitimate kind of business, proper in community, and a proper source of revenue.

But if so, we may fairly ask, why license it? And then the answer comes:

"We do not license it. The word is a misnomer, or misapplied. The license law, so-called, is but *a law of regulation*. Its effect is partly prohibitive; but all men have equal opportunities under it, if they will meet the conditions equally imposed on all."

If we ask what these conditions are, we are answered:

"They must pay into the public treasury a fee, or a tax. LICENSE CONSID- Having paid this (and being duly vouched ERED AS A TAX. for as of good moral character), any man may sell liquor."

Those who urge loudest this **payment of a tax**, and

who make least of the License feature, or deny it entirely, quote Mill to us and say:

"Among luxuries of general consumption, taxation should by preference attach itself to stimulants, because these, though in themselves as legitimate indulgences as any others, are more liable than most others to be used in excess, so that the check to consumption naturally arising from taxation is, on the whole, better applied to them than to other things."

In return, we may quote Wayland, one of the earliest and best writers on Economy in this country, who says:

"In most countries it is now adopted as a rule of indirect taxation that those commodities, such as intoxicating liquors, the consumption of which is regarded as injurious, shall be most heavily taxed.

"Experience has shown," he continues, "that the consumption of such articles is not materially diminished by the tax. As a check on immorality, the measure is therefore of little avail; but as a source of revenue, it is found to yield large results."

The results, as will be shown, are large only in the positive, and not in the comparative, sense. But they are **THE REVENUE MAGNIFIED.** large enough to make the Income side of this question appear far larger than it comparatively is, because near enough to be magnified unduly out of proportion. You can hold a silver dollar so close to the eye that it will eclipse the full moon in the heavens, or the church across the street. Men look in such magnifying fashion at the Revenue from the manufacture and sale of liquor.

Government must be supported, they remind us, and **the burdens of government** must be borne. And in the language of an eminent statesman (James G. Blaine), they assert: "It is better to tax whisky than farms, and homesteads, and shops."

But when we tax whisky, by whom is the tax paid?

The farms, and homesteads, and shops.

When we charge the whisky-seller a license fee, of any amount, by whom is the fee paid? The farms, and homesteads, and shops. Who pays to Government the ninety cents or one dollar a gallon Government tax imposed on all the whisky legitimately produced and sold? The drinker, not the seller.

<small>WHO PAYS THE TAX?</small>

It is true that the seller must pay before he can sell, and that in paying the national tax he does not nominally pay for a license, but buys a revenue permit; but *he merely advances the money which the drinker pays back to him, with usury;* and calling the National License fee only a tax does not change its nature.

Mr. David A. Wells, an economist whose words carry much weight with American thinkers, in an article in *The Forum*, has thus forcibly declared:

"If the prosecution of any trade or occupation, or the manufacture and use of any product, constitutes an evil of sufficient magnitude to call for adverse legislation, let the State proceed against it directly, courageously, and with determination. To impose taxes upon an evil in any degree short of its prohibition is in effect to recognize and license it. To demand a portion of the gains of a person practising fraud may be an effectual method for putting an end to his knavery by making his practise unprofitable, but it would be, all the same, a very poor way for a State to adopt as a means for suppressing fraud."

When they were trying once in Ohio to get rid of the License odium attaching to a liquor law in that State, and proclaimed it a High-Tax Law, Senator Sherman very truly said:

<small>THE LIQUOR TRAFFIC DIFFERENTIATED.</small>

" I cannot see how you can have a tax law without its operating as a license law. A license is a legal grant. A tax on a trade or occupation implies a permission to follow that trade or occupation. *We do not tax a crime.* We prohibit and punish it. We do not share in the profits of a larceny, but by a tax we do share in the profit of liquor-selling, and therefore allow or license it."

"We do not tax a crime," says Mr. Sherman. And Bouvier, a distinguished French definer, declares license permission to do that which without such permission *would be a crime.*"

<small>LICENSE VERSUS TAX.</small>

What would make it so?

The original Prohibition implied, which every license law presupposes and admits.

By what right could Prohibition so apply to any occupation or industry as to make it, under any circumstances, criminal?

Only by the right of Authority's discrimination against it, because in its character and effects it differs from all classes of legitimate industry or occupation.

If we do not admit that the Liquor Traffic differs entirely from all other kinds of traffic in its nature and consequences, we must claim that it has been and is now grossly ill-treated and wronged. If it does not differ sufficiently to justify Prohibition, it is unjustly the subject of License or of disproportionate tax. It is either a victim of governmental tyranny, or it is by nature a criminal thing in government.

What is a crime?

A violation of law. And the **Liquor Traffic, licensed or unlicensed, taxed or untaxed, violates the unwritten laws of trade,** of commercial reciprocity, of the general welfare, and the written statutes of the State. *It cannot be lawful, according to the spirit and purpose of law* and the nature and character of the Traffic itself.

<small>TAXING OR LICENSING CRIME.</small> To license it, therefore, is to license a crime; to tax it, according to Senator Sherman, is both to tax *and* to license a crime.

The Liquor Traffic is a crime against morality and good Government, for it violates every written and unwritten law of both. To tax it in support of Government is to license the crime by which good Government is made impossible.

To license a crime is criminal. It follows, therefore, that they by whose authority crime is licensed are themselves criminal, and the tax they receive for the crime they license does not condone the crime they commit.

This seems in farthest analysis the logic of the License question; and it may appear to others unduly severe. But if it be logic, we are not responsible for the severity of its application.

THE ULTIMATE LOGIC.

Is the revenue from this Traffic sufficient to mollify the wound which logic makes? Political Economy is not supposed to deal with conscience, but with figures and facts; and so it asks, after learning what the Liquor Traffic costs, **what does the Traffic pay?**

REVENUE FROM THE TRAFFIC. For the year ending June 30, 1893, the revenues collected by our General Government from the Liquor Traffic were:

From distilled liquors.................	$94,712,938.16
From malt liquors....................	32,527,423.84
Total............................	$127,240,362.00

This total was in excess of the total for the year preceding by $5,892,925.58.

It sounds like a large sum to realize from one source, and that through **Indirect Taxation,** which the people are not supposed to feel. But the people pay it, through the special tax collectors whom they appoint by License to gather it in, otherwise known as liquor-sellers; and they pay, along with it, many times as much more of Indirect Taxes directly caused by this Indirect Taxation, that is, after all, so direct.

Direct Taxation is favored by Economists. By this term they mean the raising of a revenue directly from the business, trade, occupation or industry, rather than from any product thereof; in other words, they prefer that the man shall pay who produces or sells, rather than the product produced or sold. So **License is upheld as one form of Direct Taxation**; and the Income Tax is urged as another form. And from License of the Liquor Traffic comes a large revenue, no doubt, that must be added to the sum already shown in determining what that Traffic pays. How much does this direct tax upon that Traffic yield?

<small>DIRECT AND INDIRECT TAXATION.</small>

The same figures which gave us the revenue from the per-gallon taxation on liquors produced in this country for the year ending June 30, 1893,—the Report of the Commissioner of Internal Revenue for that year—gave the total number of dealers in all liquors as 243,609. This report does not show the local tax, being city or State License fee imposed on or derived from each of these. Many of them were druggists and State agents, legally engaged in dispensing liquors in Prohibition States and counties for medicinal and mechanical purposes, and they paid small fees—$30 being the smallest.

<small>TAX-PAYING LIQUOR-DEALERS.</small>

Many others, as in Omaha and elsewhere throughout Nebraska, paid large fees—ranging from $500 to $1,000 each. It is impossible to determine the exact average, but we may fairly accept the estimate of a Liquor authority.

Mr. Gallus Thomann, manager of the Literary Bureau of the United States Liquor-Dealers' Association, who is quite widely accepted by the liquor men as a statistician on their side, in a pamphlet entitled "The Nation's Drink-Bill Economically Considered," estimates the average license fee at $200.

<small>ANNUAL RECEIPTS FROM THE TRAFFIC.</small>

Accepting this estimate, and multiplying the number of dealers by the amount of license revenue derived from each, we have—

Direct revenue from liquor-dealers............	$48,721,800
Add to this the per-gallon revenue from all liquors...........................	127,240,362
And the total is.....................	$175,962,162

which the liquor traffic pays per year.

We found its yearly cost to be..............	$2,453,969,948
Deduct its yearly revenue..................	175,962,162
And the balance of its cost against revenue stands at.......................	$2,278,007,786

From its Income side, then, and considering the financial interests involved, it is clear enough that Authority's duty toward the Liquor Traffic does not demand its perpetuation for sake of the revenue it may yield.

CHAPTER XVIII.

AUTHORITY'S DUTY FURTHER CONSIDERED.

FROM advocating License as **a measure of Taxation,** pure and simple (assuming that it can possibly be considered simple or pure), the friends of License shift readily to urging its claims as **a Measure of Regulation,** and insist upon **the Duty of Authority to Regulate** what they assert it has not the right or the power to suppress.

AUTHORITY AND REGULATION.

That Regulation may be more effective, they have come, with much unanimity and plausibility, to plead for *High* License, reenforcing their claims for it, as a measure of Regulation, with further claim as to its revenue-producing power.

Upon the Regulation side four claims are made for High License in determining Authority's duty toward the Liquor Traffic:

CLAIMS FOR HIGH LICENSE.

1. *It will reduce the number of saloons.*
2. By this reduction, *it will wipe out the low dives.*
3. In this way *it will make more respectable the saloons that remain* and insure a more respectable and law-abiding class of saloon-keepers.
4. *It will reduce the amount of liquor drank, and the waste and crime resulting therefrom.*

Upon the Revenue side one claim is urged, viz.:

It will compel the Traffic to pay its way.

Considering the last claim first, only a few figures are needed to show that it is untrue. There were in 1893 243,609 liquor-dealers of all kinds in this country, counting in druggists, and State

FROM THE REVENUE SIDE.

agents in Prohibition States; and many men in those States who took out United States permits, but could not secure local or State license, were promptly arrested by State authorities, and did not continue business. A liberal estimate of those who were then and would now be actual dealers, and who might be expected to pay any license, would be 200,000. If the first claim on the Regulative side be true, this number would greatly diminish under general High License.

But suppose the number continues at 200,000, and suppose the extremely *high* fee of $1,000 be exacted of each, the result is a revenue of but $200,000,000 a year,—not one fifth the direct cost of the Liquor Traffic yearly—not one twelfth its total cost. So, under High License, the Traffic could not pay its way.

As to the Regulative claims, they stand analysis little, if any, better.

Are the number of saloons reduced by it? No doubt in some places and cases; not in all; not in most.

By a sworn statement of Mr. W. D. Christy, city clerk of Des Moines, Iowa, it appears that in 1871 the license fee in that city was $150 a year, and under it there were twelve saloons; that next year they increased the fee one third, making it $200, and the saloons doubled, reaching 25; that until 1880 the fee remained at $200, and the saloons ran up to 39; that the fee was then raised to $250, and ten more saloons were added that year; and that in 1882, as low High License had not checked the increase of saloons, they lifted the fee to $1,000, and that sixty saloons took out license the first quarter!

REGULATIVE CLAIMS CONSIDERED.

There was no proportionate increase in population.

The leading daily paper in Des Moines, *The Iowa State Register*, had this to say in testimony:

"High License, we have been unceasingly told by the anti-Prohibition people and press, will decrease the number of saloons and kill off the low doggeries. In Des Moines the license has just been advanced from $250 to $1,000, and eleven more saloons have taken out the high license than took out the low. Will some of the evangelists of High License as the only practical temperance measure kindly explain this? Especially how can it be explained by the river cities in Iowa, where $250 is called a high license? These river papers said if Des Moines would adopt High License it would show good sense and actual temperance, and that such High License would reduce the number of saloons here to ten or twelve 'respectable concerns,' in which drunkards would be made in a polite and genteel way. Des Moines has followed this advice, and tried the experiment of High License for the State, which they would not try for themselves, and made the license $1,000, or four times as high as they recommended—to the result of what? To the result of adding eleven licensed saloons to its previous number, and therefore to the result of proving that as a temperance method High License is a snare, a delusion, and a cheat."

[sidenote: HIGH LICENSE IN IOWA]

So spake a political organ, with no radical sympathies in favor of Prohibition, but in a State of known Temperance character, where **the High-License experiment** could find as favorable conditions as anywhere would exist. St. Louis tried High License, and the Rev. Dr. William G. Eliot, Chancellor of Washington University, there located, thus declared:

[sidenote: HIGH LICENSE IN MISSOURI]

"The highest license exacted, and the strictest vigilance of police philanthropists, have not succeeded in reducing the number of dramshops, the amount of liquor consumed, the number of unlicensed liquor-sellers, or the fearful results in poverty, misery, and crime."

Other cities and towns could be cited to prove that High License does not always decrease the number of saloons, but instances could be given where it has actually or apparently done this—Chicago at one time, Minneapolis at another, and Philadelphia, under the Brooks Law, more recently.

But if we concede that as a rule the number of saloons be reduced, will that make the Duty of Authority more plain in behalf of Regulation? Remember that *Authority is the State*, and **the State must act according to the laws and principles of Political Economy.**

Political Economy must consider **the Traffic**, its volume, its character, its Financial, Moral, and Political effects, not merely or chiefly the number of places where it is carried on. A more important question than the numerical effect of High License upon Saloons is this—

THE VOLUME OF DRINK.

Has it lessened the volume of the Liquor Traffic, or beneficially altered its character, or appreciably improved its effects?

The effects of a stream should fairly measure its volume. High License was inaugurated, in so far as this country and recent centuries go, in Nebraska, where sincere temperance men secured its adoption as *a Restrictive* law. John B. Finch drafted it, or labored to obtain its enactment by the Legislature, and bitterly repented his work before he died. It demonstrated the unwisdom of it, the untruth of all material claims in behalf of it.

The inmates of the Nebraska Penitentiary, under High License, increased from 128 in 1879 to 345 in 1889—a gain of 167 per cent. in ten years.

EFFECTS UNDER HIGH LICENSE.

If any two or three of the claims made for High License are well-founded, the *effects* must have been clearly shown in Nebraska outside the penitentiary, and they could be determined only by comparison. While Nebraska has had High License, or during the latter portion of the time, Kansas has had Prohibition; and High License, it may be granted, has been the better enforced. The two States lie side by side in the fertile West, with Nebraska, as a whole, the more fertile and therefore possibly somewhat superior. They offer the fairest

FACTS IN COMPARISON.

comparison possible of two systems, as in force in two States.

By the brewers' reports for the several States for a period of several years, it appears that in 1887 there were 108,756 barrels of beer sold in Nebraska, and 16,488 sold in Kansas; and that in 1892 there were 138,035 barrels sold in Nebraska and only 1,643 in Kansas.

The assessed valuation of taxable wealth in Nebraska in 1880 was $90,000,000; in 1889 it was $182,000,000. **ASSESSED VALUATION OF PROPERTY.** Kansas in 1880 had an assessed valuation of $160,000,000, and in 1889 of $360,000,000. The increase in Nebraska was $92,000,000, under High License; in Kansas, under Prohibition not so well enforced, $200,000,000.

In 1880 the per capita wealth in Nebraska was in round numbers $200; in Kansas it was $161. In 1890 *it had decreased to $174 in Nebraska, and increased to $203 in Kansas.*

In 1891 there were 3,780 miles of railway operated in Nebraska, and 9,759 in Kansas. The average attendance at the public schools that year was in Nebraska 146,315, and in Kansas, 246,102. **FURTHER FACTS COMPARED.** There were paid to the teachers that year in Nebraska $2,194,288, and in Kansas, $3,033,761.

Thus it will be seen that **individual wealth decreased under High License** and increased under Prohibition, and that public education, the safeguard of republican institutions, was better cared for where the License policy did not prevail.

Illinois adopted High License. The claims for it were there as elsewhere: it was to check intemperance, to diminish crime, to decrease pauperism. After two years of its trial, questions were sent out to each of the 102 county jails and almshouses of the State, to find the precise number of prisoners in jail and of paupers in the almshouses during the last six months of 1882 under low license, and of 1884 under high.

According to reports that followed, from but forty-two jails, the **increase in criminals,** in as many counties, **HIGH LICENSE** was from 975 in 1882 to 1,032 in 1884; while **IN ILLINOIS.** the inmates of the State's northern penitentiary increased from 304 to 377—or nearly 25 per cent. A like increase was reported from the southern.

In the almshouses of these 42 counties there were but 1,574 inmates in 1882, against 2,257 in 1884—a gain of over 40 per cent. in two years; while Cook County (Chicago) increased its 860 paupers to 1,398—a gain of over 60 per cent.

Edwards County, without a saloon for 30 years, reported no occasion for its almshouse, even, until 1884, when High License gave it 35 inmates within six months.

Seven States have maintained a High-License policy since 1887, and some of these inaugurated such policy **HIGH LICENSE IN** prior to that time. Four of these are very **OTHER STATES.** populous commonwealths—Illinois, Massachusetts, Michigan, and Pennsylvania; and if High License did largely decrease the volume of liquor consumed in those States, there would be a sensible diminution of the total consumed in all the States.

As a matter of fact, the **increase of liquor consumption** in this country for the year 1893 over the year 1892, counting only the liquors here produced and on which revenue was paid, was 88,937,182 gallons. It appears indisputable, therefore, judging alike from figures and effects, that the volume of the Liquor Traffic has not at all decreased as a result of High License.

Has the increase of tariff on the Liquor, or of tax on the seller, improved the character of either, or made the Traffic more respectable, its influence less demoralizing?

In another form we have put this question before, and have partially answered it. Further answer, briefly, **CHARACTER OF THE TRAFFIC** may not be amiss; and again we must judge a cause and its character by its effects, and again we must go for the effects of liquor to those who keep the **records of crime and arrests**. Again comparison is necessary.

And in a comparison of the police reports for 1888 of 41 High-License cities of the United States, with 38 **COMPARISON OF ARRESTS.** representative low-license cities, it is shown that the arrests for drunkenness and disorderly conduct in the 41 High-License cities were one for every 39 of the population, while similar arrests in the 38 low-license cities numbered one for every 39.7 of population—a slight balance in favor of the low-license side.

In the **High-License cities**, with an average license fee of $665 for each saloon, it appears that of the total arrests for that year (1888) 56.4 were for drunkenness and disorderly conduct; and that in the 38 low license cities, with an average license fee of $122 for each saloon, but 52.9 per cent. of the total arrests were for such cause.

Here are some comparative figures with reference to particular towns, as reported in the New York *Voice*:

In 1878 Rockford, Ill., had 23 saloons paying an annual license fee of $250 each, with 150 arrests for drunkenness and disorderly conduct. In 1886 the same city had 26 saloons paying an annual license fee of $600 each, with 305 arrests for drunkenness and disorderly conduct.

In 1885 Los Angeles, Cal., saloons paid an annual license of $120 each, and there were 702 arrests for drunkenness. In 1888 the license fee was $600, with 1,428 arrests for drunkenness.

In 1883 Joliet, Ill., saloons paid $50 license, and there were 271 arrests for drunkenness. In 1888 the license was $1,000, and there were 965 arrests for drunkenness.

In 1885 Lowell, Mass., saloons paid $50 to $300 for license, and arrests for drunkenness numbered 1,683. In 1888 the license fee was $150 to $600, and arrests for drunkenness numbered 3,041.

In 1885 Salem, Mass., was under $150 license, and arrests for drunkenness were 796. In 1888 Salem was under $750 license, and arrests for drunkenness were 1,162.

In 1885 Detroit, Mich., was under $300 license, and had 3,593 arrests for drunkenness. In 1888 Detroit was under $500 license, and had 3,815 arrests for drunkenness.

In 1885 Grand Rapids, Mich., saloons paid $300 license, and arrests for drunkenness were 510. In 1888 the saloons paid $510 license, and arrests for drunkenness had increased to 722.

In 1886 Minneapolis saloons paid $500 license, and there were 350 of them, with 1,839 arrests for drunkenness. In 1889 the license fee was $1,000, with 244 saloons and 2,558 arrests for drunkenness.

In 1887 St. Paul, Minn., saloons paid a license fee of $100 each ; there were 700 saloons in the city, and 2,494 arrests for drunkenness. In 1889 the license fee was $1,000, with 386 saloons and 2,394 arrests for drunkenness.

It is evident from these figures, and from many more which could be cited, that the High-License saloon, if not quite so numerous in some places as was its predecessor, produces the same results in even a greater degree. Its character cannot have improved.

Clearly, then, we must conclude that neither upon its Regulative, nor Restrictive, nor its Revenue side, is the **AUTHORITY AND HIGH LICENSE.** High-License saloon deserving of more considerate treatment from Authority than its predecessor received *or was worthy to receive*. It shows Authority no more deference, no more respect, than did its predecessor. It does not make more law-abiding and respectable the man who sells.

Why should it? How could it? He has paid tribute to Authority, in a large amount, for a special purpose—to make money. **The larger the tribute, or bonus, which Authority demands** from him, **the larger the premium which Authority in effect offers** him **to violate morality and break law.**

He must and he will get that bonus back, in defiance

of Authority. He does get it back. He does break the law. He sells to minors. He sells to drunkards. He sells on Sunday. He sells to whomsoever will buy, whenever the buyer wills. And however fine and respectable in appearance his place may be, it cannot be respectable in fact, for no place can be respectable which does not respect law and conserve morality.

RECOVERING THE BONUS.

In it young manhood is invited to become *particeps criminis* in the violation of law, and the common regard of citizenship for law and order is weakened, neutralized, debased. In it, more than in the low dive or doggery so much condemned, the body social, the body politic, is saturated with contempt for law's enforcement, for the fundamental forces of the State.

And the low dive openly violates law, and continues existence, because the place of High License must secretly violate law to live. The *theory* was that the man who should pay a large bonus for the privilege of liquor-selling would himself make sure that no man should sell who did not pay. The *fact* is that he dare not thus attempt to defend himself in his special privilege, because himself so open to attack as a violator of law.

BREEDING CONTEMPT FOR LAW.

Fact, philosophy, and human nature are all against this theory. Exact of any man a large bonus for any privilege, and he will strive to get his bonus back,—that's *philosophy*. After he has paid for his privilege, if the business covered by it be of a doubtful character, he will even do doubtful things to insure the bonus,—that's *human nature*. Paying $500 or $1,000 for a chance to make money *selling liquor*, he will break every law that stands between him and profit,—that's *fact*.

PHILOSOPHY, HUMAN NATURE, AND FACT.

11

Mr. P. A. Burdick once told me, in illustration of this fact, a little story about a town of some 3,000 people up in Wisconsin. A kinsman of his was mayor of the town, and told the story to him.

The State had adopted limited High License, and in the little town referred to the fee was raised from $50 to $250. There were five saloons in the town when the change was made, and the people believed it would wipe them all out.

"I didn't believe one of the five saloon-keepers could or would put up the larger fee," said the mayor, in telling of it. "But to my great surprise all the five men came up and laid down their $250 a-piece, and demanded License; and with them came two more. So we had seven applications in place of five; but one of the new men was of such notoriously bad character that we refused him, and licensed only six.

A WISCONSIN ILLUSTRATION.

"After a while," he continued, "one of the six men licensed, in a casual conversation with me, incidentally remarked that the seventh man was regularly selling without a license. I asked him why he did not make complaint against him and have him shut up."

What answer do you think the mayor received?

"I can't afford it," frankly answered this man.

"You can't afford it?" asked the mayor, in surprise, "why not?"

"Why, don't you know," asked the man in turn, "that not one of us six men who paid for license is obeying the law? The man who didn't pay knows it. Suppose I complain against him, and you shut him up this week on my complaint? *Next week you may shut me up on his complaint.* He has paid nothing and can afford to take some risk. I have paid in hard money, and I can't afford to lose it; I must get my money back."

"And that opened my eyes," declared the mayor, "on the High-License business."

It follows, as inevitably as fate, that **any Regulative system as to the Liquor Traffic weakens and finally paralyzes every power to regulate.**

The more legal the Liquor Traffic is in form, the less legal it is apt, if not certain, to become in fact. The more illegal it is permitted to remain, the more its illegality dominates public sentiment and common respect for law.

CHAPTER XIX.

HARMONY OF MORAL AND POLITICAL FORCES.

THE duty of Authority toward the Liquor Traffic should not and cannot be determined by consideration alone of the financial interests involved. There must also be careful and sufficient consideration of the **moral interests involved.**

Recall what has been said of **an Idealizing Necessity.** Remember that Man must be made better, that the State SOCIETY AND may be made surer. Consider what Man is ITS FORCES. to the State, and what Morality is to Man.

The State is but organized Society. And these four things are true:

1. Society is composed of three factors—its Organized Moral Forces, its Organized Political Forces, and the Individual Man.
2. The maintenance of Society, in any safe and enduring form, demands absolute harmony between its Organized Moral and Organized Political Forces.
3. This absolutely essential harmony between Society's Organized Moral and Organized Political Forces must come through Society's third factor, the Individual Man.
4. This absolutely essential harmony becomes absolutely impossible when the Organized Political Forces of Society create, maintain, and foster any system of law, or business, or politics, the ultimate of which is the demoralization of Man, the sole harmonizing agent.

What are the Organized Moral Forces of Society? Primarily they are three:

First—**The Home.** It is the unit of social organism —the smallest organization known to Society. In it moral impulses have their earliest beginnings. From it go forth the influences that determine civilization, mold communities, and shape the State. The State can rise no higher, in its culture and its character, than its average Home.

<small>ORGANIZED MORAL FORCES.</small>

The Home is and must be a moral organization. Demoralize the Home, and you distintegrate the foundations of the State. It is because of this accepted fact that marriage laws exist, and that polygamy is made a crime. Through all the centuries Authority has guarded and shielded the sanctity and purity of the Home. The faithful devotion of one man to one woman, and their mutual care, as husband and wife, of the children committed to their love and keeping, form *the moral foundation of the State*—the strong pillars upon which must rest the superstructure of social and political security.

<small>MORAL FOUNDATIONS.</small>

Second—**The School.** It supplements the Home. It is the higher or larger form of social organization, wherein and whereby the work of the Home is developed, the teachings of the Home are taken up and carried forward, in mental growth and moral progress, to the upbuilding of character in Manhood and Womanhood, the refinement of Citizenship, and the beneficent advantage of the State.

And the school must be a moral organization; it must remain a moral force. Such it would and must remain, even could and should you eliminate from every course of study in every school every text-book with a distinctively moral intent. Public education must and will be a moral agency while the civilized

<small>MORAL AGENCIES.</small>

State endures. It is a moral and political necessity in a government like our own.

Third—**The Church,** the highest form of moral organization known to men. In it the best impulses and teachings of the Home, and the noblest and purest unfoldings of the School, find their sweetest and ripest fruitage, their development nearest approaching the divine. In it are focalized the strongest moral incentives, the noblest social sympathies and ambitions, the truest aspirations of the Citizen, the supreme devotion and loyalty of the Christian Patriot.

<small>MORAL FRUITAGE.</small>

From it resounds throughout the State a call and a command which the School must hear and the Home must heed—the loftiest utterance which can summon Christian citizenship to social and political duty—

"Render, therefore, unto Cæsar the things that are Cæsar's, and unto God the things that are God's."

And thus are taught and commanded, in close and inseparable connection, the supreme function of Citizenship in the State, the supreme requirement of Morality in the Citizen. Thus the Church enjoins upon every Citizen his duty to God and Government. To fit him for the complete discharge of that duty these three organized moral forces of society are a necessity, and for his best benefit they should be always at their best and under the best possible conditions.

<small>SUPREME FUNCTION OF CITIZENSHIP.</small>

There are **secondary moral forces**—organizations of many kinds; but these we have named are the primary and important. There they stand—universal, distinct, positive, all-important—the Home, and the School, and the Church.

The Organized Political Forces are many, but they are uniformly included in or controlled by the form of organization known as a **Political Party**, and their ultimate expression is and inevitably must be **Law**.

ORGANIZED POLITICAL FORCES. How shall we determine whether a Political Force is in harmony with Moral Forces? **By the Law it enacts and administers the policy of administration it proposes and proclaims.**

How shall we judge of a Law or a Policy?

TEST OF A LAW OR POLICY. **By its effect upon the Home, and the School, and the Church.**

How shall the Duty of Authority toward the Liquor Traffic be determined, in view of the Moral Interests involved, as between Suppression and Regulation?

By the effect upon the Home, and the School, and the Church, of the Licensed or Unlicensed Saloon.

Does the Saloon—the Liquor Traffic—make more comfortable, and secure, and happy, and helpful, and blessed, and beneficent, the Home? Is the Home's atmosphere made sweeter and more inspiring in which to grow up a new generation for the perpetuity of the State?

Does the Saloon make easier and surer the work of the School? Is education more general the more numerous are the Licensed Saloons, the more extensive the Liquor Traffic?

THE SALOON AND MORAL FORCES.

Is the Saloon an ally of the Church, a helper in its effort for the redemption of man from sin, for his full and free development in Christian citizenship?

If so, then there is harmony between these moral forces and those political forces which maintain the Saloon system, the Liquor Traffic, through a policy of License or Taxation. But what say the careful observers, the Christian patriots, and the students of Sociology? Judging from their evidence, what are the facts?

Listen first to Judge Pitman, as he touches upon this topic in "Alcohol and the State":

"Let us look into contrasted homes, where the only variable element is the drinking habit of the head. The full wages of the temperate man bring from year to year better food, better clothing, and better shelter. Improved sanitary arrangements tell on the health of father, wife, and children. The house becomes more and more a home. The passer-by notices the vines that cluster about the doorway, and the little flowers that peep through the windows. Upon the inside walls the picture speaks of a dawning taste, and the piano or some simpler musical instrument shows that the daughter is adding a charm and refinement to the family circle. Books and periodicals show the surplus dollar. Every influence is elevating.

<small>CONTRASTED HOMES.</small>

"Introduce the element of drinking and you reverse the picture. Year by year the physical comforts of the house lessen. The tenement must narrow to the means, and locate itself in noisome surroundings. The wife first pinches herself in food and clothing, but the time soon comes when the children, too, must suffer. The scanty clothing becomes ragged. The Church and the school know the children no longer. No flowers of beauty adorn, no sound of music cheers, such a dwelling. The fire goes out upon the hearth, and the light of hope fades from the heart. Soon the very form of a family is broken up, and public charity cares for the scattered fragments. An American home has been blotted out.

"Now, it is not with the private misery that we are here concerned, but with the effect upon the State. If the chief interest of the State is in the character of its citizens, then no agency is more destructive to its interests than the dramshop, because the dramshop is the great enemy of the home; and it is the character of the home which is not only the test, but the efficient factor in an advancing or a falling civilization."

"The tenement must narrow to the means," declares Judge Pitman. We may add that **comfort and character will conform to the tenement**, in a large measure; and all will be determined very largely by the surroundings. There cannot be physical health in a habitation set where all the atmosphere is pestilential; there cannot be moral health where prevails a pestilence of immorality.

<small>DRINK IN HOME AND NEIGHBORHOOD.</small>

Speaking of beershops and their effect upon their surroundings, an English Archdeacon (Garbitt) some years ago declared:

"A large experience tells me that when a neighborhood is visited by this scourge no organization, no zeal, no piety, however devoted, no personal labors, however apostolic, will avail to effect any solid amelioration."

Surround the Home with saloons, and the Home atmosphere will smell of beer and whisky. **What the children breathe into their childhood the men and the women will by and by maintain or become.**

In their fifth annual report the Board of State Charities of Massachusetts said this:

"Poverty and vice are what the poor man buys with his poisoned liquor; sickness, beastliness, laziness, and pollution are what the State gives in exchange for the license money which the dramseller filches from the lean purse of the day laborer and the half-grown lad and hands over, sullied with shame, to the high-salaried official who receives it."

What the poor man buys, and what from the State he receives, directly in themselves or indirectly in their effects, are brought into his Home and curse it. "Beastliness, laziness, and pollution" can come of nothing that benefits and blesses the Home.

<small>WHAT THE DRINKER BUYS.</small>

Says Dr. Sumner Stebbins, in an essay on "The Fruits of the Liquor Traffic":

"We have laws to shield children from abuse, but a license law nullifies them all. The State should be their guardian, but it scourges them with fathers made heartless and cruel in Government dramshops."

Abuse of the children, pollution of their young lives, beastliness that endangers their moral and physical welfare, can come of nothing friendly to the Home, and do come universally from the Liquor Traffic.

<small>DRINK AND CHILDHOOD.</small>

The report of a committee appointed to inquire in regard to the **Idiots** of Massachusetts showed that **eleven twelfths** of this pitiable class were **born of intemperate parents.** There can be no sadder visible testimony to the unfriendly effect of Liquor in the Home than imbecility in the childhood that should bless and brighten it. And as one writer says:

"Back of all the visible ravages of Intemperance, and deeper than all these, there lies a field of devastation which has never been fully explored, and can never be more than partially reported. It is the wasted realm of the social affections, the violated sanctuary of domestic peace."

There should be sufficient proof of the direct and immediate harmful effect of the Saloon upon the School, in the one limitation imposed upon the Saloon by almost every License Law, viz., that no Saloon shall be within a given distance of any School. Surely if the Saloon were a benefit to Education, it could not be too near the school-house. Has a law ever been heard of which decreed how many hundred feet apart should be the Church and the Home, or the Home and the School?

If the Saloon be bad for the School 200 feet from a school-house door, how much better can it be one mile **SALOON AND SCHOOL.** away? **Any hindrance to Public Education is a curse to the Republic.** Poverty is a hindrance. The Saloon causes poverty. The Saloon keeps children out of school, that they may assist in the support of poverty-smitten drinking parents and themselves.

In the Sixth Annual Report (for 1875) of the Massachusetts Bureau of Statistics of Labor it was declared, among other conclusions:

"That fathers rely, or are forced to depend, upon their children for from *one quarter to one third* of the family earnings;"

and the same high and reliable authority said

"That children *under fifteen years of age* supply, by their labor, from *one eighth to one sixth* of the total family earnings."

If the children are in the factory, they cannot be at the school.

Mr. Philbrick, long Superintendent of Schools in Boston, emphatically affirmed:

"The liquor-shops and the schools are, in all respects, antagonistic to each other."

It is this often-declared, this widely-confessed, this patent, this potent antagonism, which inspired the enactment of compulsory temperance education laws in 37 States of our Union prior to 1894. The passage of these laws was **everywhere opposed by saloon men**, who have nowhere been conspicuous as friends of the Public School system.

<small>COMPULSORY TEMPERANCE EDUCATION.</small>

Are they the friends of the Church?

Says Judge Pitman:

"The Liquor Traffic and the Sabbath are in natural enmity. It is no chance association which leads to the cry, 'Down with Sunday Laws and the Liquor Laws,' in so many parts of our country. The Traffic wants the day."

The foe of the Sabbath cannot be the friend of the church.

In 1888 the Maine Conference of the M. E. Church, among other strong utterances, said this:

"It needs no argument of ours to show that the liquor traffic and its inevitable conduit, the drinking saloon, are the most gigantic and formidable foes of our Christian civilization; the sworn, bitter, and persistent enemy of the Gospel of Christ; * * * the personification of almost all evil, paralyzing the right arm of the church."

<small>THE SALOON AND THE CHURCH.</small>

In the same year the North Nebraska Conference adopted radical resolutions—

"recognizing the liquor traffic as the greatest foe of the church, the home, and the government."

The General Conference of Seventh-Day Baptists, held in 1891, thus declared:

"The liquor traffic is the unrelenting enemy of righteousness and purity, of Christ, the Church, and Humanity."

The Universalists, in Biennial Session at Worcester the same year, said:

"The Home, the State, and the Church are confronted by no foe to their peace and prosperity so great as is the drink habit."

The American Baptist Home Mission Society, in session at Chicago in 1890, adopted striking resolutions declaring of the liquor traffic—

"that it has no defensible right to exist, that it can never be reformed, and that it stands condemned by its unrighteous fruits as a thing un-Christian, un-American and perilous utterly to every interest of life;"

Preceding this utterance by a preamble which declared that traffic—

"An enemy of satanic and appalling force, menacing the purity of the Christian Church, the virtue of society, and the safety of government."

The Congregationalists, in Triennial Council at Minneapolis in 1892, thus affirmed:

"The ultimate aim of all Christian effort should be the entire suppression of the open saloon or tippling-house."

The General Synod of the Reformed Church, in its Eighty-eighth Annual Meeting, at Asbury Park, thus

CHURCH TESTIMONIES.

"Resolved, That we hold the saloon to be an institution responsible for a large part of the wrecked bodies, diseased minds, and lost souls of our fellow men. We lay to its account ruined and dissevered families, neglected children, broken fortunes, and blighted hopes. We charge to the saloon enormous burdens of taxation, the absorption of the wages of the wage-earners, and the transfering of the burden of their support to the self-supporting members of the community."

The General Assembly of the Presbyterian Church, in its 104th Annual Meeting, in a long series of Resolutions declared—

"That this Assembly regards the Saloon, licensed or unlicensed, as a curse to the land, inimical to our free institutions, and a constant jeopardy to the present and lasting peace and happiness of all members of the home, and, furthermore, loyalty to Christ and His Church should constrain every Christian citizen to be earnestly zealous in securing the removal of the traffic."

In 1892, the General Conference of the Methodist Episcopal Church, in session at Omaha, reiterated the utterance of its Episcopal Address in 1888, as follows:

"The liquor traffic is so pernicious in all its bearings, so inimical to the interests of honest trade, so repugnant to the moral sense, so injurious to the peace and order of society, so hurtful to the home, to the church, and to the body politic, and so utterly antagonistic to all that is precious in life, that the only proper attitude toward it, for Christians, is that of relentless hostility. **It can never be legalized without sin.**"

The same year, at its annual gathering in Philadelphia, the Baptist Young People's Union of North America declared:

A CLOUD OF WITNESSES.

"The liquor traffic is the prolific source of crime, poverty and woe, the foe of humanity, a menace to our civilization, and a great obstacle to the progress of Christianity."

The 62d General Assembly of the Cumberland Presbyterian Church, in session at Memphis, thus affirmed:

"Positive prohibition of the sale or manufacture of intoxicants is the *only consistent position for the church* to take upon this question, and to that end our prayers and our votes shall concur."

The 33d General Assembly of the United Presbyterian Church, after re-affirming an utterance of that body in 1889,

"that any form of license-taxation of the liquor traffic is unscriptural in principle and contrary to good government," went on with most emphatic plainness to assert that

" partizan friendship for the saloon must be accepted as hostility to the Church, the home, and all that is valuable to society; that no party is worthy the support of Christian men that fails to antagonize the saloon."

The Annual Meeting of the Christian Endeavor Societies, in Minneapolis, with some 12,000 delegates in attendance, representing one million membership, adopted the following:

"Since the liquor traffic is the implacable enemy of righteousness and purity, of Christ and the Church—

"*Resolved*, That we condemn intemperance in every form: that we stand for total abstinence, for the suppression of the saloon, and the annihilation of the power of the whisky ring in the politics of this nation."

And thus are our questions answered as to the **effects of the saloon, the Liquor Traffic, upon the Home, the School, and the Church.** A large volume of similar answers could be cited. The unanimity with which all bodies of Christian citizens testify in this regard is most significant. Millions of God-loving men and women cannot be mistaken in this their public testimony.

CHAPTER XX.

LOCAL OPTION ANALYZED.

IN such further consideration as appears necessary of the Moral Interests Involved in determining Authority's Duty toward the Liquor Traffic, we must analyze one attitude which has been widely and ably urged on Authority, under the term **Local Option**.

It came as a new Regulative phrase or fact, to fit the old Economic thought or law of Supply and Demand. It came in recognition of mere local authority, as of the county or town, under general State legislation; it has been broadened to meet the boundaries of a Commonwealth, under special legislative acts for Constitutional Amendment.

<small>AN OLD ECONOMIC LAW.</small>

Within its narrower limitations it has had the longer test, and has, on the whole, been the more successful. In this narrower way it seems to have been first applied in Great Britain, through the influence if not the dominating power, in certain small areas, of large land-owners; and it was there applied as the fact for which here the name has come to stand synonymous—*Local Suppression*.

As far back as 1760 John Wesley found one of these areas in Ireland; and several of them have existed there during the present century—are a beneficent fact now. Bessbrook is one, with its industrial town of Saltaire. Tyrone County is another, with 61 square miles, and 10,000 people, but no public-houses, as the local term is, and no policeman.

<small>EARLY LOCAL SUPPRESSION.</small>

According to *The Edinburgh Review* for January, 1873, there were at that time in England and Scotland 89 estates upon which the liquor traffic was suppressed; the **option to suppress** being exercised by their owners. Since that year, near Newcastle-on-Tyne, and along the Mersey near Liverpool, the option to exclude the dramshop has been exercised with extensive effect by landlords and people.

<small>LANDLORD SUPPRESSION.</small>

In this country Local Option fairly began, **by counties,** in Georgia, in 1833; spread over New England from 1835 to 1840; and has made extensive progress territorially since the War in many States—notably Pennsylvania, Indiana, Kentucky, North Carolina, Georgia, Mississippi, Alabama, and Maryland. In the broader application of it, **by States,** through popular votes upon a Prohibitory Constitutional Amendment, it began in Kansas in 1880, where such Amendment continues; has been successfully tried since in Maine and Rhode Island and the Dakotas; was declared unconstitutionally attempted in Iowa; and has failed of carrying State Prohibition in Massachusetts, Connecticut, New Hampshire, Michigan, Tennessee, Pennsylvania, West Virginia, Washington, Ohio, and Texas.

<small>LOCAL OPTION BY COUNTIES.</small>

Upon **the face** of it, Local Option seems a fair and proper thing: it allows the will and wish of The People to rule as to the Liquor Traffic.

As to **the fact** of it, great good may have been accomplished—has been, beyond all question—in many cases, by the choice which has resulted over more or less extended areas. Local Suppression, through Local Option or the exercise of it, has been for longer or shorter periods a great local benefit.

<small>LOGIC OF LOCAL OPTION.</small>

As to **the principle** of it—what will analysis reveal? What conclusions appear inevitable, in **the light of analysis ?**

These:

1st. That to concede men anywhere the right to say that License may be, is to concede that somewhere License may be right, or that somewhere men may of right permit a wrong.

2d. That to concede the right anywhere to permit a wrong is everywhere to imperil the right itself, and make the wrong everywhere more powerful.

3d. That to concede the right of License anywhere is to admit that nowhere can it be wrong; and

4th. That to admit the right of License everywhere is to surrender everywhere our final and supreme argument against it.

"There is no inherent right in a citizen to sell intoxicating liquor," says the Supreme Court.

If there is no inherent right in the citizen to sell, is there not inherent wrong in the sale? Would not the citizen have such inherent right, if there were not such inherent wrong? If there be such inherent wrong in the sale, what right have any number of men to say that anywhere the citizen may sell?

<small>WRONG IN THE SALE.</small>

It has been urged that there is a majority right in this matter, and that what a majority of the people want, in any locality, the majority must have and the minority cannot refuse. The claim is dangerous; the logic of it would imperil society, might ruin the State. **There must be for the State a moral standard, upon which Law may rest, and against which the will even of a majority may not array itself.**

<small>A MORAL STANDARD FOR THE STATE.</small>

Never should it be conceded that a minority of the whole State, though it be a majority in some narrow area thereof, may reject this moral standard at will.

In his calm, judicial fashion Judge Pitman puts the case as follows:

"The State is the nominal unit of sovereignty, and it is opposite to sound theories of government to transfer to local fractions the decision of a question of such general and far-reaching importance as the policy to be pursued toward the liquor traffic. * * * If the drink traffic is indeed the destroyer of national wealth, the clog that drags down labor, the poisoner of the public health, the enemy of the home, the feeder of pauperism, the stimulant of crime, the foe of Christian civilization, and degenerator of the race, then the State clearly owes to each community of its citizens its best wisdom and its most persistent energy in the repression of such a traffic, and it may not rightfully or even prudently abandon the virtuous, or for that matter the vicious, citizen anywhere to the rule of a debased locality."

THE UNIT OF SOVEREIGNTY.

Suppose it were decided to set loose, in a given county of some Commonwealth, a thousand thieves and murderers from some great prison or penitentiary. They might then form a majority of the voting population there. Would it be right and wise to let them formulate their own code of criminal law? Yet that is the theory of Local Option.

RIGHTS OF MAJORITIES.

In the settlement of Moral Right vs. Wrong, majorities never have counted; the majority wish of localities, or sections, has never been a final arbiter.

Abraham Lincoln, in one of his early speeches concerning another great question, thus declared:

"Whoever desires the prevention of the spread of slavery and the nationalization of that institution yields all when he yields to any policy that either recognizes slavery as being right or as being an indifferent thing. Nothing will make you successful but setting up a policy which shall treat the thing as being wrong."

When Slavery was a fact, every slaveholder was a Local Optionist. He stood for the will and wish of a majority in every slave State. But great masses of men who now favor Local Option as to the Liquor Traffic did not stand with him then, and would not accept a local or sectional settlement of that question.

FORMER LOCAL OPTIONISTS.

Why? **Because of the moral issues involved,** and the moral, political, and economic interests of the whole nation, which were at stake. Interests far greater and more momentous are dependent on the proper discharge of Authority's duty toward the Liquor Traffic. If a majority-right in a whole State did not remove the moral and political wrong of slavery, how can a majority-right in a single county or town of a State remove the wrong of License?

A good minister once remarked that Local Option meant: "God save the country; the devil may take the towns!"

It is in the towns—the cities—that immoral sentiment focalizes and festers and breeds. From the social cancers which these must remain while infected and afflicted with License, flows out **the virus of liquor-poisoned social and political life,** to infest the country at large. As well might we expect pure blood and perfect health in a person with gangrene eating away at his vitals, as to expect a healthy social and political condition in the State that permits the Saloon cancer to thrive at the centers of population because a majority there elect that it may.

CENTERS OF IMMORAL SENTIMENT.

Local Option has done much good, let us admit this; it has wrought great evil, let us not deny that. Its immediate effects have been more marked in many cases than its lasting benefits. Under it, where Prohibition has been a narrow, local fact, the popular voice has often gone against Prohibition as a broad State policy.

It is said that every Local-Option county in Texas went for liquor when Texas voted upon a Constitutional Amendment for Prohibition. The broader option to suppress the Liquor Traffic has been voted down, because the narrower attempt at suppression failed, largely through its narrowness and the in-

WHAT LOCAL OPTION DOES.

fluences closely surrounding and neutralizing its effects. No State which had experimented with narrow Local-Option methods has carried State Prohibition by Constitutional Amendment.

Local Option does at least six things:

1. It draws an imaginary line, difficult of continued recognition, between local policies, while it effaces the positive line of a broad principle.
2. It appropriates to fractional parts of a State the power of decision as to a matter directly and vitally and inevitably affecting the whole.
3. It breaks the educational force and influence of law, and wastes the moral significance of popular choice between Right and Wrong.
4. It blunts the popular conscience, makes more difficult the administration of justice, and weakens public sentiment in Law's behalf.
5. It concedes to popular will the right to provide for satisfaction of a popular want, to the general waste and loss, and without regard for the general welfare.
6. It permits and invites independence and antagonism of moral and political standards between closely related parts of a moral and political whole.

As to the **moral and financial effect of Local Option,** some very plain words are said in the "Cyclopedia of Temperance and Prohibition," by Prof. H. A. Scomp, of Oxford, Ga., whose residence in a State where Local Option has produced its best results must have qualified him to speak as well of it as any one can or should. Among other things he remarks:

"Local Option, like license, makes revenues local, but expenses general. County or Town A votes 'For the Sale,' levies its license fees, collects its police fines, and monopolizes its private chain-gang of rock-pile labor; while its heavy criminal docket, pauperage, almshouses, and the fearful residuum of increased depravity and immorality, which always follow the traffic, are thrown like an incubus upon the State and county at large.

"As license naturally shifts to the crowded communities, its revenues flow to the towns. To purchase popular indulgence, these fees are commonly decreed to schools and benevolent purposes. Thus it has happened, especially in the South, that nearly all the well-supported public schools are in license towns, and depend chiefly upon the liquor revenue for sustenance. As a consequence, thousands of families of our most substantial rural population are annually drawn into these towns to enjoy the benefits of the schools, and the children are brought face to face with the saloons, and grow up under their baleful influence. Thus the system operates to degenerate the people, to crowd the towns, and to depopulate and pauperize the country.

EFFECTS OF LOCAL OPTION.

"Local selfishness is therefore engendered and fostered. What cares Town A for the sword and fire it sends through the adjacent territory while it revels in its revenues?"

Two facts appear significant:

1. The friends of Prohibition prefer Local Option to the ordinary methods of license, as a rule, and uniformly work for the best fruits of it, as opportunity is presented.
2. The friends of Liquor prefer Local Option to Prohibition, and favor the first in all cases when the second is a probable alternative.

To forbid all possibility of such an alternative, liquor men have widely advocated Local Option as a method, while they have opposed Local Prohibition as a result. More and more **as a method** Temperance advocates are opposing Local Option, while they steadily labor, when the method offers, to secure Local Prohibition **as a result.**

MEN AND METHODS CONTRASTED.

That both classes of men favor the method, under certain conditions, is evidence that it counts more or less as a compromise. To borrow a live term from a dead issue,

Local Option is the "Squatter Sovereignty" of the Saloon. And as a minister once remarked of the "Missouri Com-

THE NEW SQUATTER SOVEREIGNTY. promise," when Slavery was the living issue, "in a compromise the devil always gets the best of the bargain."

Said Stephen A. Douglas in 1857:

"If Kansas wants a Slave-State constitution, she has a right to it; if she wants a Free-State constitution, she has a right to it. It is none of my business which way the slave clause is decided."

But Abraham Lincoln answered:

"He (Douglas) contends that whatever community wants slaves has a right to have them. So they have *if it is not a wrong*. But *if it is a wrong*, he cannot say a *people have a right to do a wrong*."

Douglas was a Local Optionist; Lincoln was not. Lincoln did not believe slaveholding could be right in

LINCOLN AND DOUGLAS. Kentucky and wrong in Kansas. He foresaw how, by immigration and the subtle extension of slaveholding influence across the Missouri border, the popular sentiment from a Slave State should cover and dominate free territory.

What he foresaw then as to Slavery, in its permeating and infecting power, every small and large Prohibition area realizes to-day as to the Saloon. There was no effort made to capture free territory before 1860 that is not matched now to extend Saloon power over no-saloon towns, and counties, and States.

The law of Supply and Demand is not left normal and healthy, as **a genuine economic law.** The Supply is

SUPPLY AND DEMAND. carried in, smuggled in, forced in, that the Demand may follow. Liquor-dealers' associations establish saloons where there is no immediate call for them, and run them by hired agents, at a loss, for months at a time, that they may **create a Demand.** It is a common way of propagating liquor sentiment, of securing License privilege indefinitely, of winning what the Traffic wants and for what it is eager to pay. To this end, the finest locations are selected, and the most elegant appointments are procured. It is like growing liquor sentiment in a luxurious hothouse, where flowers of pleasure bloom, and the perfumes of delight are seductively sweet, and those who pass the place, or who may venture in, hear delicious music, and also, if they listen carefully, may hear this egotistic, aristocratic

HOTHOUSE LIQUOR SENTIMENT.

SONG OF THE DECANTER.

I am proud of the place where I glisten to-day!
Here it is that men come who have money to pay—
Not the low, the degraded, the wretched and vile,
But the rich who their leisure would swiftly beguile.
I invite the young men, who have homes that are pure,
To leave mothers and sisters whose love would allure,
And I offer to each a delight and a boon,—
In the joys of a gilded High-License Saloon.

I would never be seen in a lowlier place,
For I come of a haughty aristocrat race;
I was born in a castle, 'mid silver and gold;
I have glittered for princes and kings that were bold;
I have poured out my treasure for daintiest lips,
And am always at hand when the queenliest sips;
In my presence are beauty, from midnight till noon,
And the pleasure that fills a High-License Saloon.

I can fool the wise preachers with glitter and pride,
Till the Scripture they preach they have often denied;
" *Look not on the wine!*" is the Bible command,
But they look upon me, and with dalliance bland
I beguile them to sip till its praise they declare,
And its curse by their Scripture they piously share;
And their name and their fame, I am sure, very soon
Will be mine to maintain the High-License Saloon.

Look around me and say, Are the men who come here
Of the class whom society rightly should fear?
By their manners refined, and their elegant dress,
You must know that position and purse they possess.
For the drunkards and thieves you must go to the slum,
Where they swill and they guzzle their beer and their rum;
He is crazy, indeed, as the craziest loon,
Who compares the low slum with the gilded Saloon.

Let the dive be condemned, while around me I bring
Politicians and preachers the praises to sing
Of High License, to-day! Does it matter to me
That so long as *this* is, the low places must be?
Men go down, I admit, in the scale of desire,
Who their appetites feed, not lift steadily higher;
To the slums let them go, if they must and they will,
While around me are pride and hypocrisy still!

I would never young men by my radiance win
To the ruin of love and the riot of sin;
Let me tempt them alone to the pleasures that lie
Where the streams of delight flow in melody by;
If they farther must go, being tempted so far,
It is they who both foolish and criminal are,
And if down, by and by, to the dive they must go,
Let them bear all the blame while they suffer the woe!

Do you say that I win to whatever is won,
Be it chill of the darkness or cheer of the sun?
Do you say that the dive is the Finis of Drink
That the drinker must find, tho' he shiver and shrink
From it now? A decanter knows better than you
What is good for the many tho' bad for a few,
And in every decanter there's only a boon
If it stands in a gilded High-License Saloon.

I've a brother who bides in the home of a priest
Whose own praises of wine have not faltered or ceased.
Do you think he would cherish a child of my race,
Give it welcome and care, and maintain it a place,

If but ruin and woe from our family came,
If we brought only sorrow and trouble and shame?
No, indeed! he would banish my kind very soon,
And as well he would ban the High-License Saloon.

Do you hint that his conscience he surely must keep
Where the lotos of liquor can lull it to sleep?
Maybe so, maybe so! but at conscience I laugh
When the preacher comes piously to me to quaff;
I have sent many like him to ruin and death
By the bane of my presence, the blight of my breath;
I will spare him, I think, thro' his life's afternoon,
For the help that he gives the High-License Saloon.

I'm a wily decanter, whatever you think,
I have won many lips to the praises of drink;
There are demons that lurk in my bosom and hiss,
But I make men believe they are angels of bliss;
There are fiends all about me no mortal can see
Till around his lost soul they are grinning in glee;
Yet they think me a blessed, beneficent boon,
The wise fools who uphold the High-License Saloon.

CHAPTER XXI.

DEMORALIZATION BY THE SALOON.

WE come, finally, to consider the **Political Interests Involved.** We come to consideration of these face to face with certain conditions:

<small>EXISTING GOVERNMENTAL CONDITIONS.</small>

1. A form of government in which the citizen is the unit of authority.
2. The existence of organized moral and political forces, which must work in harmony to perpetuate government.
3. An inherent necessity that the citizen shall be the harmonizing factor between these forces.
4. The impossibility of his being such a factor when political forces maintain any system which demoralizes him as a harmonizing agent.
5. Failure to harmonize moral and political forces because the latter maintain the demoralizing system of License.
6. Absolute hostility between these forces, as a result of this system, because of its demoralizing effect upon the individual man.

<small>EFFECT OF THE LICENSE SYSTEM.</small> Demoralization of the citizen goes on through the License System in two distinct realms of activity:

Inside the place of License;
Outside the licensed place.

In the former realm the demoralization is threefold:
Physical,

Moral, and Political.

In the latter realm it is or may be only twofold, Moral and Political, but its effects may be quite as bad upon our political interests. If a man be demoralized as to his moral instincts and his political conscience, so that he but <small>DEMORALIZATION OF CONSCIENCE.</small> dimly discerns his moral and political duty, and comes to put policy in place of a moral standard, as to things both moral and political, it might not be greatly worse for the State were he become indeed also a physical wreck.

No man can morally and politically perform all the functions of citizenship, and properly assist in perpetuating the Government, whose body is diseased by Drink, whose brain is fired by it, whose whole manhood is cursed by it. Government must live, Society must continue, the State must remain a fact, on the fruit of man's labor. **Every political interest** demands that he be a producer, not a consumer; and to this end his hands must be steady, <small>PRODUCTIVE CITIZENSHIP.</small> his brain cool, his judgment clear. **Every moral interest** demands that he be a good citizen, with ambition high and pure to assist in uplifting and preserving the moral and political character of the State; and to this end he must have a moral and political conscience, which will forever set principle above policy, and refuse any policy which antagonizes principle.

<small>HARMONIZATION OF FORCES.</small> No man can be a good citizen who does not seek always and consistently to harmonize Moral and Political Forces.

No man can harmonize these forces *inside* the saloon.

No man, by whose act the saloon exists, can harmonize these forces *outside* the saloon.

And **the saloon demoralizes more men from without than from within.**

The demoralizing influences operate chiefly *from within, through appetite and avarice; from without, through avarice and ambition.*

Inside the saloon, the man behind the bar has the avarice, and the man before the bar has the appetite.

INSIDE THE SALOON.
The joint exercise of both demoralizes both men. The man behind the bar may seldom drink (it is said that some barkeepers are total abstainers); but though he be always sober, he is a demoralized citizen: *he cannot be a harmonizing factor* between moral and political forces.

Outside the saloon, the man who favors it has avarice or ambition, and is actuated by one or the other—or both. The saloon's revenue appeals to his avarice—through its rental, which is a part of his income, or through its contribution to the revenues of the State. It appeals to his ambition—through the political influences which focalize in it and ramify from it, by which he wishes to profit, or to benefit the party which may some day profit or honor him.

OUTSIDE THE SALOON.
He cannot harmonize moral and political forces, even though he never sets foot in a saloon, and rarely or never puts its cup of poison to his lips.

It is to the man *outside* of the saloon that the man *inside*, and behind the bar of it, owes his place and his profits. The man outside is vastly more numerous, has a much higher average of respectability, wields a greater influence in the average community. Upon his respectability and influence, *plus* his avarice and ambition, the man inside depends for his business future.

Every Local-Option contest, whether of the narrow town or county sort, or of the broad State Amendment order, has been determined by the man outside the saloon, who rarely or never steps

THE MAN OUTSIDE.

within it, but who has or has not been demoralized by it. If he has *not* been, he gave success to No-License, or Prohibition by Amendment. If he *has* been, he gave to the same its defeat.

The greater his influence and respectability, the more widely he has been recognized for his moral character and eminence of professional standing, the more weight has been given by his demoralized manhood to the saloon side.

In Michigan he was very eminent; his character appeared without blemish; he spoke from a high place, and his voice was heard throughout the State in the Amendment campaign there in 1887. He spoke from a platform in Detroit, and his speech was sown broadcast throughout every Michigan county.

"Carry the Amendment," was the burden of it, "and we shall lose $250,000 revenue every year from the saloons of Detroit alone."

IN MICHIGAN.

And by this revenue cry the Amendment was killed. As Miss Frances E. Willard afterward remarked, the Amendment "died of High License." By the **Tax Law of Michigan,** this man outside the saloon had been demoralized. In other States and contests a similar demoralizing influence has produced similar results.

In Texas, the same year, when the Amendment campaign came on, the liquor champions called a State meeting and solicited the attendance, as the call said, of "all who have not yet lost faith in the Church, the home, and the school; patriots who revere the grandeur of our great State; all who believe the people of Texas are a religious people; all Christian people." They counted, surely enough, upon the demoralization of the man outside the saloon,—even inside the Church.

IN TEXAS.

With his aid the Amendment was beaten there,—with

his aid, supplemented by the alliance of political leaders, the saloon support of the press, and large money contributions from the liquor organizations outside the State. One political leader refused his alliance with others against the Amendment in these words:

"In every community," wrote United States Senator Reagan, "we find men once honored and respected reduced to poverty, wretchedness, and dishonor, spending their money and time in drinking-saloons, wives weighed down in grief and sorrow and want, and heart-broken and helpless children growing up in ignorance, beggary, and vice, because husbands and fathers have been made drunkards and vagabonds by patronizing the drinking-saloons. Millions of dollars are invested in this business of making men drunkards and in producing the desolation and ruin of women and children, which, if employed in agricultural, manufacturing, or commercial pursuits, and directed by the talents and time wasted in these drinking-houses, would add untold millions to the aggregate wealth of the State, and make as many thousands of happy families as are now made miserable because this money and time are given to the selling and drinking of intoxicating liquors. In view of these facts, with all respect to the meeting at Austin and its committee, I must express my regret that any effort has been made to make a party question of it, and especially do I regret that Democrats should seek to identify that great and grand historic party with the fortunes and fate of whisky-shops, drunkards, and criminals."

A SENATOR ON THE SALOON.

Local Option and political combination killed the Amendment in Texas by over 90,000 majority.

In Tennessee the same year, during the Amendment campaign there, the man outside the saloon was appealed to in very unusual fashion by men inside the prison. Four hundred convicts in the State penitentiary signed this petition:

To the voters of the State of Tennessee :—
In all ages in the history of mankind crises, reformations, and revolutions have been the direct result of practical experiences by the human family.

DEMORALIZATION BY THE SALOON. 191

TENNESSEE CONVICTS' PETITION. One of these experiences has taught the people of the State of Tennessee that their prisons are filled, their poorhouses occupied, and their paupers created by the direct influences of that soul-destroying demon, whisky. We, the inmates of the State penitentiary, knowing by observation and convinced by undeniable facts that liquor is the cause of all the misery we endure, of all the hardships and privations we subject those to dependent upon us, do hereby most earnestly ask that the voters of this great State may seriously consider the question before them and give their aid in word and deed to the cause of Prohibition.

We do not say that every prisoner in the State is a habitual drunkard. We do not claim that every criminal act was perpetrated under the influence of whisky; but we fearlessly assert that three fourths within these walls can trace their downfall directly or indirectly to that cause.

Wearing the garb of disgrace, being dishonored and counted unworthy to mingle with the people of our State, we yet have the same devotion to our mothers, the same affection for our sisters; and for their sake and for the sake of our children, we appeal to you to unite as one man and free the State from a curse created by the hands of men, discountenanced by the law of God.

But the majority in Tennessee against the Amendment was 27,693. Under a **Four-Mile Law**, the Liquor Traffic had concentrated its cancerous poison in the cities and towns, and had thence injected that poison through all the moral, commercial, and political circulation of the State.

Pennsylvania gave a majority against a Prohibition Amendment in 1889 of 188,027. The Brooks High-License law, with its large revenues to Philadelphia, Pittsburg, and Allegheny, had been for two years demoralizing the citizenship in those cities and infecting citizenship throughout the State. In Pennsylvania the man outside the saloon whose demoralization by it was the most marked, and the most immorally fruitful, was the **newspaper editor and publisher**.

DEMORALIZATION OF THE PRESS.

General H. W. Palmer, chairman of the Amendment Committee, who had been Attorney-General of the State by Republican election, declared that "the defeat of the Prohibition Amendment in Pennsylvania was occasioned by the combined villainy of the Republican and Democratic machines, using every practise known to corrupt politics"; and after asserting that the newspapers prostituted themselves in the most shameless fashion, he went on to say:

GENERAL PALMER'S TESTIMONY.

" I do not complain because they have opposed Prohibition, but because they have permitted the saloons to use their columns for the most shameful purposes—for systematically deceiving the people. They have printed bogus despatches, and unhesitatingly used what they knew was bogus matter in a way to mislead even newspaper men. If their editors deny this charge, they deliberately write themselves down liars. They have printed articles manufactured right here in Philadelphia under the guise of honest despatches from Des Moines, Topeka, Atchison, and other places in Prohibition States, giving what pretended to be facts and figures, and asserting the failure of prohibitory laws and the havoc wrought by them.

" These despatches have been printed in the ordinary way in the news columns, without any marks to distinguish them as paid matter; yet they have been paid for from the rum funds at so much per line; and this disgraceful work has been going on all over the State right along from the beginning of the campaign.

" We have sent to the Prohibition cities and obtained from the highest authorities the most conclusive denials of the statements made in the bogus 'despatches.' These denials we have carried to the newspapers that printed the false assertions, hoping that motives of decency and fairness would persuade the editors to make corrections. But their charge for doing justice was 50 cents a line, with the condition that each correction should appear with an advertising-mark—****.

" Money, money, was what the newspapers greedily clamored for. I know of one daily paper in this city that stood ready to sell itself to the Prohibitionists for $10,000. ' Pay us $10,000 and we are yours; otherwise we go in for rum and all it is worth in dollars and cents.' "

The newspapers in turn demoralized the reading masses. One H. P. Crowell, manager of the **liquor funds and forces** in that Pennsylvania campaign, afterward made a free statement of how the demoralizing work was done. Asked how the newspapers were handled, he said:

"We bought them by paying down so much cash. I visited the editors in person, or had some good man do so, and arranged to pay each paper for its support a certain amount of money. Throughout the State we paid weekly papers from $50 to $500 to publish such matter as we might furnish, either news or editorial, but the city daily papers we had to pay from $1,000 to $4,000. . . . It was understood with most all of the papers that we would furnish the matter, and so we employed a man to write for us and prepare articles for publication, which would be furnished to the papers to be printed as news or editorial matter, as we might direct. The most effective matter we could get up in the influencing of votes was that Prohibition did not prohibit, and the revenue, taxation, and how Prohibition would hurt the farmers. We would have these articles printed in different papers, and then buy thousands of copies of the paper and send them to the farmers. If you work the farmers on the tax question, you can catch them every time."

<small>ANOTHER WITNESS.</small>

In other words, you can **demoralize the farmer** with a false claim that the Liquor Traffic makes a market for the products of his farm, and yields a revenue which decreases his taxes. He is outside the saloon, but he perpetuates it for supposed financial reasons.

A whole volume of equally emphatic testimony could be given to show how by bribery, by deceit, by lying, by open and outrageous fraud, by sickening corruption, the demoralization of manhood is carried on whenever danger seems imminent to the saloon, and indeed all the time, to insure its perpetuity. What we have cited refers alone to special effort, periodically put forth, and the fruit of that. It were easy to furnish witnesses in large number showing how our political interests are involved in the every-day course of affairs by the demoralizing power of drink.

<small>DEMORALIZATION OF MANHOOD.</small>

Inside and outside the saloon, its constant effects are seen, demonstrated through the drinker and the nondrinking saloon ally. How far these effects reach out, how widespread may be and are their baneful influences, few people realize and understand.

A competent witness in regard to this may be called now, in one newspaper that surely was not in the pay of any demoralizing agent when these words were uttered by it:

"Who can fail to see," said the New York *Tribune*, "that the strenuous efforts of all the better elements of the nation after higher things in religion, in education, in politics, in social and domestic life, are continually checked and aborted by the debasing influence of drink in its myriad manifestations. An ignorant suffrage is bad enough, but it may be mended. But ignorance steeped in whisky is a diabolical prescription for poisoning free government, and education does not defend us against the drink evil. When we have done our best for our boys, and they set out to take a part in the government of their country, they find that the entrance to politics is through the door of the saloon, and that the men who in our great cities wield the largest political influence are those whose connection with the bottle is the closest."

THE TRIBUNE TESTIFIES.

"For it is at the bar of the saloon," continued *The Tribune*, speaking more boldly than the party organ as a rule is willing to speak—

"that the voters meet to consider their course, to receive instructions from their leaders, and to drink away the intelligence that should have showed them the humiliation of their position; and throughout our politics this malign and brutalizing influence is felt. From the caucus to the convention, from the State Legislature to Congress, the power and presence of drink are manifest. The reform measures which wisdom and patriotism demand must be submitted to the allies and stipendiaries of those whose whole existence is pledged against every civilizing agency, and for whom national purification means extinction and death."

If, then, national purification "means extinction and death" for the saloon, Authority's plain duty is to declare always for more than the saloon's regulation.

REGULATION IS PERPETUATION.

These five propositions are indisputable:

1. **We cannot regulate that which we do not perpetuate.**
2. We should not perpetuate that which renders national purification impossible.
3. We cannot regulate in any wholesome or helpful fashion an interest that regulates the manner and the degree of our regulation.
4. *We cannot regulate by mere moral forces that which thrives by political power.*
5. We cannot rob the Liquor Traffic of political power by political perpetuation.

The friend of the saloon is the enemy of society. The supporter of the saloon system is the foe of true morals, of pure politics, of economic government. Whoever indorses the saloon system, by supporting license and regulation, which tend logically to protect and perpetuate it—publican, priest, or party—is hostile to Home, the foe of material welfare, unfriendly to Production and Wealth, an ally of Consumption and Waste, and wantonly betrays the best form of government known to man.

A LOGICAL INDICTMENT.

CHAPTER XXII.

DISLOYALTY OF THE LIQUOR TRAFFIC.

IN the light of all that has gone before, these conclusions appear to be inevitable and irresistible:

<small>A LOYAL DUTY.</small>
1. That it is the Duty of Authority to prohibit and absolutely to suppress the Liquor Traffic (meaning the manufacture and sale of intoxicating liquors for beverage use).
2. That such traffic is disloyal to Government, the organized enemy of law, and a growing menace to Authority.
3. That self-preservation demands of Authority the full discharge of its Duty in regard thereto.
4. That such discharge of Duty can be only by and through the establishment and enforcement of a policy of Prohibition as broad as Authority's bounds.

The highest loyalty to Government is impossible with men who in business and political alliance are out of harmony with moral forces.

<small>LOYALTY DEFINED.</small> What is Loyalty? According to the Standard Dictionary: "The quality or state of being loyal. Devoted allegiance to a government or chief."

"The state or quality of being loyal," says Webster; with quoted explanation that Loyalty, "being derived from the French word *Loi*, properly expresses that fidelity which one owes according to law."

Loyal is defined by the Standard as "bearing true allegiance to constituted authority."

To be loyal, says Webster, is **"to be devoted to the**

maintenance of law; to be disposed to uphold the lawful authority."

The Liquor Traffic is defiant of law, and in open or secret rebellion against authority. It has been a law-breaker since first it came to know the real restraint of law. From the beginning of License and Regulation it has been the same.

"Thou shalt not sell to a minor," says the State to the saloon; and regularly a large percentage of the liquor sold is bought by young men under legal age.

"Thou shalt not sell to an habitual drunkard," says the State to the saloon; and regularly the habitual drunkards <small>DEFIANCE OF LAW.</small> reel up before the bar and obtain the liquor illegally dealt out to them.

"Thou shalt not sell upon the Sabbath day," says the State to the saloon; and regularly the saloon's back door is ajar, if the front door be not squarely open, and the Sunday profits of the saloon are not less, and are often more, than those upon the other six days of the week.

Loud and frequent outcry has been made against Prohibition, in the claim that "Prohibition does not prohibit"; <small>PROOF OF DISLOYALTY.</small> and so far as the claim be true, it is in direct evidence that the Liquor Traffic is *not* "devoted to the maintenance of law." As the claim is urged more loudly by the liquor-sellers than by any other class, it must be accepted as their own confession or boast of disloyalty.

So far as Prohibition is or has been anywhere a failure, such failure is due directly to the lawbreaking spirit of the Liquor Traffic, and to its open or secret organization to defy law, to dominate the State.

The President of the New York State Liquor-Dealers' Association testified with boastfulness, in 1894, before a senatorial investigating committee, that there is "hardly a liquor-dealer in the State of New York, from Buffalo to Montauk Point," who does not habitually violate the law **AS TO THE SUNDAY LAW.** against selling liquor on Sunday; that he is himself such an habitual lawbreaker. Whoever will violate law as to one feature of it will hold the whole law in contempt. Whoever considers and demonstrates himself above and superior to any law has weakened the force and effect of all law.

Any business that dare and does assert its independence of or superiority to any law is a detriment, a danger, to the State.

Such a business the Liquor Traffic long has been in this country. Its independence of law has grown more and **REBELLION AGAINST LAW.** more marked and emphatic year by year; its open and organized rebellion against law has become more and more defiant.

To this rebellion every Law and Order League instituted has been a witness; of such rebellion the courts furnish endless record; and in startling further testimony are the numerous murders of good men, in different places, by the Liquor Traffic's assassins, because of loyal efforts to secure the enforcement of law.

But the disloyal spirit of the Liquor Traffic is not shown merely in its own direct assertion of lawlessness, it is farther evinced by the effects of drink upon others than liquor-sellers—upon those who but for the Liquor Traffic would not be lawbreakers.

Law suffers, through organized sentiment and effort against it, from three other sources:

    The Striker,
    The Communist,
    The Anarchist.

Each of these finds inspiration in or about the saloon. When they had Prohibition in Atlanta, the Atlanta *Con-*

stitution, speaking of the results of it as compared with liquor-selling days prior thereto, among other significant testimony remarked:

<small>DRINK AND STRIKES.</small>

> "Contractors say their men do better work, and on Saturday evenings, when they receive their week's wages, spend the same for flour, hams, dry-goods, or other necessary things for their families. Thus they are in better spirits, have more hope, and *are not inclined to strike* and growl about higher wages."

"*Not inclined to strike!*"
What is a strike?
It may be, it sometimes is, a needed and proper protest of Labor against the injustice of Capital. In a "History of Strikes in America," by Arthur A. Freeman, published in *The Engineering Magazine,* it is declared that "of late nearly every great strike may justly be said to have been an attack on the whole system of private property and competitive industry"; and Mr. Freeman declares that "for this radical change of attitude on the part of the laboring masses legislation is chiefly responsible."

<small>FORMER OBJECT OF STRIKES.</small>

He blames the Government for its method of legal interference with strikes; he seems not to consider their **chief cause and inspiration,** the saloon. He thinks they have changed character and purpose, and seeks to show how, but not altogether why, as he goes on to say:

> "While it is true, on the one hand, that since 1886 the labor organizations have lost considerable ground, and that to-day even the most powerful unions find it impossible to enforce their demands by means of great strikes and 'tie-ups,' it is also true that the dangers and evils of collisions between employers and workmen are greater now than they ever were. The old trade-unionist had no sympathy whatever with state socialistic notions and was careful to disavow his responsibility for revolutionary attacks on the fundamental principles of industrial society. He merely insisted on what seemed to him 'a fair day's wage for a fair

day's work,' and repudiated the radical program of expropriation and abolition of private enterprise. He had no quarrel with free competi-
THE NEW UNIONISM. tion, property, profits, or the right of the employer to be his own master. He claimed the right to strike, to boycott, and to act in concert with his fellows; but he did not theoretically go any greater length. He occasionally resorted to violence, but this was done in the heat and excitement of struggle, and no justification was ever attempted of any destruction of property or interference with liberty. To-day, however, a totally different spirit pervades and controls the world of organized labor. The 'new unionism' has virtually espoused the state socialistic doctrine that free competition and private enterprise are incompatible with the interests of labor, and strikes are regarded as the preliminary encounters which hasten the inevitable final conflict between capital and labor. The attitude of the Homestead strikers and their socialist sympathizers in and out of Congress is still fresh in the public mind. Every failure, defeat, and disappointment necessarily tends to drive the workmen into more and more extreme positions. The more desperate the situation the greater the danger of violence and reckless disregard of bounds set by law."

Whatever legitimate necessity may once have existed for strikes, and however their character may have changed **INSPIRATION OF STRIKES.** since, the fact stands that now, in seven cases out of ten, a strike is but the half-drunken, largely brutish, thoroughly lawless and reckless offspring of a beer-barrel. The new sympathy of "the old trade-unionist" with foreign "socialistic notions" and "revolutionary attacks on the fundamental principles of industrial society," was born before or behind the bar of a beer saloon. Its father was a beer-selling communist or anarchist. It is the illegitimate child of our foreignized American Liquor Traffic.

Cooperation has been urged as a cure for strikes, and in settlement of all difference between Labor and Capital. **COOPERATION AND STRIKES.** There is much to recommend it, and its benefits have been great. But it seldom has a fair chance; it never can have, in any broad fashion, while the saloon system exists. Leave the saloons, maintain any law that permits them, and "cooperation" is but a child's cry in a tempest. There can be no true cooperation, with the best fruits of it, where Labor supports the saloons. Any attempt at cooperation while they continue partners in social privilege is like the colored man's partnership: "When we began business togedder," he said, "I put in all de capital, and de udder man all de experience. Now I has de experience, and he's done got all de capital."

The saloons are getting the capital, and sober society has the experience. When the laborer's surplus goes over a bar, cooperation for him is a failure. His most costly tribute to the barkeeper inspires the strike and leads to bloodshed.

When the great **Buffalo railroad strike** was on, in 1893, and the militia was ordered and kept there in large force, one daily telegraphic report said:

<small>BEER AT BUFFALO.</small> "All day the strikers have been pouring down beer and whisky in the saloons around the Lehigh yards, and bloody times are expected before to-morrow."

And they were bloody, with burning cars and consuming freight to make the night more terrible. A friend of mine, the daughter of Gen. Clinton B. Fisk, was en route to bury her husband by her father's side in Michigan, and spent that night in such terror as she will never forget, with the demons of carnage and outlawry on every hand, herself in doubt through long and awful hours whether she would ever get away from the Buffalo freight yards, with her coffined companion in the baggage car ahead.

" *Not inclined to strike!* "

<small>WAGES AND DRINK AT HOMESTEAD.</small> No, sober men are not, as a rule. The testimony at Homestead, Pa., during the fearful strike there in 1892, was that the men who had been receiving highest wages had really saved

the least money. Why? *The more pay the more money spent in saloons.*

The man who saves money, though his wages be small, is rarely a striker and seldom a communist.

Said Tramp No. 1, in a reputed conversation between two of the tramp class:

"I say, Bill, what is communism!"

Said Tramp No. 2:

"I'll explain it to you. I've got an empty bottle, and you've got a dime. I let you have the bottle. You buy a dime's worth of whisky and put it in the bottle, and I drink it out, and then pound you on the head with the empty bottle."

[margin: TRAMPS ON COMMUNISM.]

It is the **empty bottle**, or the **empty purse**, that makes the **communist**, the **anarchist**.

One of the latter sort made a confession at Pittsburg, while the Homestead troubles were at their worst, just after one anarchist had shot Mr. Frick, and the papers were teeming with the talk of his kind. This one was very honest, for he had been converted to better ways. He said:

"I was an anarchist because I loved beer. I loved beer because I was an anarchist. . . . My wife loved me and ours, but I loved my anarchy and my beer. She went to work. She washed clothes to support me and my anarchy. I abused the capitalist for making me poor and making my wife work. I drank beer and abused men of money. Finally, when I was unable to make an impression upon the capitalist, I transferred my abuse to my wife. The impression made upon her was worth considering. One day I did consider it. I became a Salvationist and stopped abusing my wife. I also stopped abusing capitalists, who didn't care for my abuse, and stopped drinking beer."

[margin: ANARCHISM AND BEER.]

Whenever and wherever the anarchist and his crimes are traced back to their common source and his, there is found a saloon. The connection of saloons in Chicago with the Haymarket murders there committed by a gang of anarchists is well known to all who read the current reports of that lurid time. Said one paper:

> "The saloon played a very disreputable role in the **Chicago riots.** Reports say that the men who had money spent it in getting drinks for themselves and friends, and soon they were fighting drunk. The anarchists went forth from saloons to make their incendiary harangues, and they slunk away into saloons when charged on by the police. August Spies and Michael Schwab were arrested in a room over a saloon, where they printed their anarchist paper, and in the same room were found the forms of type from which incendiary handbills were printed.
>
> "The **Milwaukee riots** were also fomented by anarchists, who were aided in no slight degree by the saloons. Large numbers of the rioters were striking employees of breweries, and the objective point of the mob at each of its wild demonstrations was either a brewery or one of the immense beer-gardens of the city."

SALOONS AND ANARCHISTS.

In six years, from 1881 to 1886, inclusive, according to "The History of Strikes," by Mr. Freeman, 22,304 establishments were involved in strikes, while 2,214 had lockouts, and the total number of employees involved was 1,323,203. The loss to the strikers was $51,814,732; and to the workmen locked out $8,157,717; while the loss to employers through strikes was $30,701,553, and through lockouts $3,462,261, making a total loss to labor and capital on this account of $94,136,263. And for this loss the saloon system was mainly responsible, as also for the indirect losses attendant through resulting crime and its cost.

THE COST OF STRIKES.

With the saloon closed in the neighborhood of great industries, great strikes would be the exception, and great outrages, wanton destruction of property, would not characterize any strike. **Lawlessness is the natural fruit of the open saloon.** Open defiance of law stalks brazenly abroad through the saloon's open door, while conspiracies against law and order brood and breed within.

Not content with its open defiance of law outside, and its secret conspiracies against law within, the saloon **POLITICAL POWER IN OUR CITIES.** boldly organizes for the legislative dethronement of every law that antagonizes it, and through bribery in caucus and convention and bulldozing at the polls, forces its way into Legislature and Congress, sits by proxy in the seat of executive power, and rules in its own behalf.

New York, Chicago, Cincinnati, Philadelphia, Boston, and St. Louis—our six great cities—dominate the politics of this country, and are themselves dominated by the saloon.

In 1884 Mr. Robert Graham, secretary of the (Episcopal) Church Temperance Society, found that of 1,002 political conventions and primaries held in New York City alone, that year, 633 were held in saloons and 96 in places but one door removed from saloons.

Earlier than this by six years Wendell Phillips had thus forcibly declared:

"New York ruled by drunkards is proof of the despotism of the dramshop—men whom murderers serve that they may escape, and because they have escaped, the gallows, rule that city. The ribald crew which holds them up could neither stifle its own conscience nor rally its retinue but for the help of the grogshop. **PHILLIPS ON CITY RULE.** A like testimony comes from the history of our other great cities. State laws are defied in their streets; and by means of the dramshop and the gilded saloons of fashionable hotels, their ballot-box is in the hands of the criminal classes—of men who avowedly and systematically defy the laws. Indeed, this is the case in Boston."

Mr. Joseph Cook, New England's greatest oracle since Mr. Phillips died, more recently, speaking of the Liquor Traffic, said this: **DANGER TO THE REPUBLIC.**

"There is now no doubt in candid minds that its influence is the greatest political danger to the Republic, not only in municipal but also in State and national politics. The severe but simple truth is that the most urgent question in American politics for some time to come will be, Shall our chief robbers become our chief rulers?"

Even our national humorists appear to have comprehended the political situation, and the Traffic as a chief factor therein. "Bill Nye," in a burlesque "History of the United States," speaking of the hour when Columbus discovered America, thus ironically remarks:

"A saloon was at once started, and the first step thus taken toward the foundation of a republic. From that one little timid saloon, with its family entrance, has sprung the magnificent and majestic machine which, lubricated with spoils and driven by wind, gives to every American to-day the right to live under a Government selected for him by men who make that their business."

The **New York City Reform Club** is a non-partizan body of business and professional men, organized to watch legislative and municipal affairs and to work for the reformation thereof. In 1891 it made this deliberate utterance:

"The City Reform Club is not interested for or against the liquor traffic as such. It is not concerned with the effect of the traffic upon the individual, but only with the influence of the liquor-dealer upon the politics and the government of this city directly and through his influence in State politics. The club observes that that influence is constantly exerted against the interests of the people and on the side of corruption, and it now sees in the liquor-dealers' bill of this year the amazing spectacle of an organized business seeking to subvert for private gain the fundamental principles of our law. The club sees, further, that this business has acquired by constant vigilance, unremitting effort, and large expenditures enormous power in the politics of this State. In their efforts the liquor-dealers are united without regard to party. They care nothing for political principles. Their united strength is used only for private gain. The evil has reached a stage at which it can be considered without reference to the question of the natural right of a man to engage in the liquor trade, or of the right of the State to restrict that trade, and of the amount of injury or benefit resulting from it. The most beneficent

CITY REFORM
CLUB'S
TESTIMONY.

business, organized as the liquor trade is organized in this State, exerting the same power with voters, politicians, and legislators, and showing the same determination to attain its private ends by any means and at any cost to the people, would be such an enemy to the State as to excite the open hostility of all patriotic citizens. It would show itself to be such an enemy as must be put down, and it would force upon the people the question whether it ought not to be suppressed before it could further usurp the executive and legislative functions of government."

All that was thus said of the Traffic in New York pertains to it elsewhere. But the Liquor Traffic is the lawless child of law. The law by which it is begotten comes of a License Policy, for which the citizen is or is not responsible. That License Policy, formulated in law, leads directly and inevitably to law-breaking and the defiance of law; it breeds and broods law-breakers; it is the hothouse of political disloyalty. Sincere and absolute devotion to law, on the part of the citizen, should lead him to refuse any support to a policy which ultimates in open rebellion or in secret conspiracy against law.

CHAPTER XXIII.

NEED AND EFFECTS OF PROHIBITION.

The perpetuation of the Republic demands absolute harmony between its organized Moral and Political Forces. Such harmony is absolutely impossible when any influence exists and seeks to dominate the politics and government of city and State, which, in the language of the New York City Reform Club, "is constantly exerted against the interests of the people and on the side of corruption."

<small>MORAL AND POLITICAL FORCES.</small>

The political power of the Liquor Traffic centers in our cities. There it consorts with every other influence that is corrupt. There it gives to political methods their character, and determines political leadership. And it has been estimated that in A. D. 1900 the cities of this country, above a population of 8,000 each, will comprise the dominant voting majority of the United States.

Remember that harmony between Moral and Political Forces must and can come only through the unit of the State—the citizen, the individual man. Remember that he is more or less the creature of his environment; that his nature, his tendencies, his attributes, will be determined by the air he breathes, the law he obeys, the mental and moral life of which he forms a part. Remember that in our cities congregate the worst elements of our own nationality, and to them are flocking the worst elements from nationalities over the sea.

<small>CITY CONTROL OF THE STATE.</small>

Upon the **city standards of morality and law**, as fixed securely within the next half-century, will depend the problem of popular government. Within the cities, as outside, the standard of law must not be lower than the standard of morals; and that both may be maintained at the same high and imperative level, both must rest upon a solid foundation of *principle*.

What is a principle?

A fixed, unchanging and unalterable, moral, physical, mathematical, political, or economic law.

According to the Standard Dictionary:

" A source or cause from which a thing proceeds ; a power that acts continuously or uniformly ; a permanent or fundamental cause that naturally or necessarily produces certain results."

Accepting these definitions of principle, admitting that the law of the legislator must be based upon principle, it UNIFORMITY follows that the attitude of authority toward OF LAW. the Liquor Traffic must be uniform wherever authority extends; must be uniform, and fixed, and reliable; must be the same to-day as last year, not variable and changing with the seasons or with shifting public sentiment; must be the same in Mississippi as in Massachusetts, in New York as in Nebraska, in California as in Connecticut—the same all over our broad nation, from year's end to year's end, whatever party controls government and administers political affairs.

There is no reason, that can stand the test of logic and philosophy or of sound politics, why one State should deal SOME differently with the Liquor Traffic from any GOVERNING other State; why one town or one county PRINCIPLE. should be more or less lenient with it than the neighboring county or town. Morally, industrially, and politically, from one border-line of our great nation to its opposite boundary, "we be brethren." What hurts one, harms all.

No State, no county, no town, can be a law merely unto itself. Some governing principle carries, as to every great question of government, from Maine to Mexico. Deny that principle thus should govern, and you deny the possibility, even the need, of government. Admit mere individual sentiment, or will, or habit, or necessity, to be sovereign, and government is a sham, anarchy is a fact.

In *Freiheit*, the organ of anarchistic teachings in New York, appeared not long since a summary of the **creed and aspiration of the anarchist,** in which were the following words:

<blockquote>
"To be an anarchist means to be a man who acts in accordance with his own personal rights and duties. We do not wish to be any one's slave, any one's master. We wish to be free from the control of the State ; we will have no masters. To make the existence of a government needless, we deny the need of moral laws. There is no immorality where there is no teaching of morals."
</blockquote>

<small>MORALS AND LAW.</small>

There must be teaching of morals where there are moral laws. There will be immorality where the laws are immoral. Laws are sure to be immoral where based on mere public sentiment or private appetite instead of fixed and enduring principle.

Truly and wisely declares Dr. John Bascom, former president of Wisconsin State University, writing in the "Cyclopedia of Temperance and Prohibition":

<blockquote>
"Civil law is itself a moral agent, and a most primary and efficient one. We are using it in all the relations of life to secure the conditions and give the motives of morality: to express the moral temper of the community. A moral conflict is all-embracing. We enter it from every side. We bring to it the sweet words of affection and the strong hands of resistance.

" Let law be immoral, and the society it encloses will be immoral. Nothing alone—indeed, not even law—can make men moral. We need
</blockquote>

<small>LAW A MORAL AGENT.</small>

all influences, individual and collective, persuasive and mandatory, to compass this great end. Give us moral forces, in their integrity and entirety, as they flow through each mind singly, and all minds in their conjoint civic action."

Said Judge Sprague, a generation gone by, before a committee of the Massachusetts Legislature:

"It is a profound observation that the morality of no people can be maintained above the morality of their laws. Their institutions are an index of their sentiments. Reason, observation, and history all teach this. While gambling-houses were licensed in Paris and New Orleans, that vice could not there be made disgraceful. . . . Where polygamy is lawful, a plurality of wives is reputable. . . . *The laws of a country may reconcile public sentiment to crimes, even the most abhorrent to our nature, to murder itself.*"

LAW AND POPULAR MORALITY.

Murder once, among a then civilized people, as I have read, was legally but a vice, and the murderer merely vicious. At length the Government recognized it as something that should be somehow restricted or regulated, and a fee was charged the murderer, of which the State demanded a share. And it was not until the State had thus indorsed the vice, by recognizing it and sharing in its awful revenue, that murder legally became a crime. Vice has its evolution always, but always under civil and moral law, and through the educative influences which moral and civil law afford.

"You do not make enough of **the educating power of law**," said a former slaveholder to me once, in Mississippi. And then he went on to explain.

"You Northern men, I mean," he added. "We know all about it down here. You came down here, you men did, a few years ago, and you said to me, you said to my neighbors, 'You shan't hold any more slaves.' We didn't like it; we didn't think you had any right to say it. There was absolutely no

EDUCATIONAL POWERS OF LAW.

public sentiment in the State to uphold you in saying it. But **the power of the Government** was behind you, and we obeyed. The law has had its effect. It has been our schoolmaster. It has educated public sentiment, until to-day you can't find three men in a thousand in all the State of Mississippi who would take their slaves back again if they could do so by a turn of the hand."

The educating power of Prohibition, as applied to the holding of slaves, had a fair chance, a thorough test. It was backed by the moral and political power of Government. Its breadth of application was ample to make the test complete. Had it applied only to a county here and there, in here and there a State, the education of public sentiment under it would have been slow, and the benefits of such education would not have been soon apparent.

<small>THE LAW OUR SCHOOLMASTER.</small>

Is it not reasonable to suppose that the educating power of Prohibition as to the Liquor Traffic would be manifestly as great, if it were given a test equally fair and complete? It has nowhere had such a test in this country. The moral and political power of government has not been behind it, over any wide area, for any long period, with any positive understanding of permanence. Town, county, and State lines, at the widest, have bounded its geographical limits. It has been *local* Prohibition mainly, where Prohibition at all, and subject to those largely nullifying influences just over boundary lines that nobody could see and many did not respect. A year, or little more, has comprised its possible term, into which, in order to overcome it at the term's end, have been crowded all possible contempt for it, and defiance of it, and litigation on its account, that so public sentiment might fail of its educational effect.

<small>PROHIBITION'S EFFECTS LIMITED.</small>

What the People did yesterday, it has been argued, or

last year, they can undo to-morrow, or five years hence, without recognition or assertion that what they did in Prohibition of the Liquor Traffic was founded on **an unchanging principle** and must abide—a principle that must everywhere apply, and must everywhere and for all the future be maintained.

And so, under Local Option, the everywhere immoral system of License has alternated, every year or two, as THE VARIABLE a rule, in the towns of New England and the POLICY. counties of the South, with the spasmodic trials of local Prohibition; and the disloyal Liquor Traffic, refusing obedience to lawful Authority, has opposed public sentiment by repeated claim of Prohibition's failure, and by all the demonstration of such claim that lawlessness and political power could achieve.

Even in areas State-wide, the *temporary* character of Prohibition, by constitutional amendment, has been insisted upon by its enemies, and more or less admitted by its friends, and the possibility of Resubmission, and a nullifying amendment, has been held up in threatening or persuasive appeal before the people of State and nation, with steady discount of the educational result on public sentiment, within and without the State, as a natural and inevitable consequence.

If in any county, or any State, the local policy of Prohibition had been superimposed by some **power from** PERMANENT **without,** peculiar and superior, and recog-POLICY ESSENTIAL. nized as Authority supreme, from which there was no appeal, would not the permanence of that policy, even within such narrow limits, have yielded broad and beneficent educational fruits?

There was no appeal from the power that prohibited forevermore the holding of slaves in Mississippi. It was a power from without. Its mandate was final and fixed.

Changing local sentiment did not affect it. Constitutional Prohibition of slaves had been written over every foot of Mississippi soil, with the iron pen of moral, social, and political sentiment outside—sentiment founded on right and justice, and which had been slowly and surely and irresistibly crystallizing into moral edicts and national law.

<small>PERMANENT PROHIBITION OF SLAVERY.</small>

This one fact is significant, and should stand as the prophecy and proof of what a widespread and uniform policy concerning the Liquor Traffic would do were it formulated into law supreme, based upon principle unchanging:

Wherever, even in areas limited, Prohibition has been made a fixed and final fact, by power within or without which was absolute, there public sentiment has gradually and surely and permanently risen to the high level of the law.

" The benefits of the law have changed from foes into warmest friends, men of the highest position: governors, senators, mayors, and leading citizens of every class, who were intensely hostile or profoundly distrustful, have been constrained to testify in unequivocal and even enthusiastic language to the great good done by Prohibition."

Volumes of testimony could be produced in proof of this. In Kansas Gov. John A. Martin, who had been an opposer of the Prohibitory Amendment, when first agitated, and a friend of the liquor-dealers when later they defied the law, in his farewell message to the State Legislature, January, 1889, made a noteworthy series of statements as to the effects of Prohibition throughout the State at large, and in the towns especially, and added:

<small>CONSTITUTIONAL PROHIBITION.</small>

" These suggestive and convincing facts appeal to the reason and the conscience of the people. They have reconciled those who doubted the success and silenced those who opposed the policy of prohibiting the liquor traffic."

J. W. Hamilton, State treasurer of Kansas in 1889, thus testified:

"It is well known to my friends that when the Prohibition question was first agitated, I was an anti-Prohibitionist. I did all in my power to defeat the Amendment. I was what they called a Glick Resubmissionist. [This being a later stage of opposition when, under Governor Glick, an effort was made to resubmit.]

"But I was mistaken then. The Prohibitory law has my indorse-

ITS EFFECTS IN KANSAS.

ment, not alone because it is the doctrine of my party but because I believe it is right. I do not see how any fair-minded man who has lived in Kansas for the past five years can be otherwise than in favor of the law."

In the year 1889 there was not a criminal case on the docket in Topeka, the capital city, with 60,000 population. So Governor Martin declared. And the same year the prosecuting attorney for the county in which Topeka is situated made the following statement:

"At one time there were 140 saloons open in Topeka; their average sales per day were not less than $30 each, which would make $4,200 spent daily for liquor. This amount came largely from the working-people; to-day there is not one dollar of that amount spent for whisky. Where does it go? It goes for food and clothing, children and wife. I know of scores of instances where families were suffering for food because their father gave his wages to the saloon-keeper. Now they are living in a cozy home of their own; they have all the necessities of life, and indeed a few luxuries; the children, who were once poverty-stricken, and living in rags, are now attending public schools, and the father will tell you he was saved by Prohibition."

In Iowa, in 1889, Gov. William Larrabee, who had been

IOWA'S TESTIMONY.

a vigorous opposer of Prohibition earlier, gave positive testimony as to its effects in that State, and said:

"The wives and mothers of the State, and especially those of small means, are almost unanimously in favor of the law. The families of laboring men now receive the benefits of the earnings that formerly went to the saloons. There is no question in my mind but what the law is doing good for the people."

These brief citations must suffice as to the **educating effect of Prohibition upon the public mind**, through its visible benefits, in the wider areas where Prohibition has come about by Authority from within—a majority of the voting class.

As to more limited areas, and the results which have followed the prohibitory exercise of power from without, only a few brief references are here permitted. Such power from without has come through corporate control of landed estates, or governmental authority superior to local.

There is in England the Artisans, Laborers, and General Dwellings' Company, which operates great estates, upon PROHIBITION which are many thousands of people, but no IN ENGLAND. dramshops. Upon one of these, known as "Shaftesbury Park," the Earl of Shaftesbury presided at its opening in 1874, and the prime minister, Lord Beaconsfield, said this:

"The experiment which you have made has succeeded, and therefore can hardly be called an experiment; but in its success is involved the triumph of the social virtues, and the character of the great body of the people."

Bessbrook and Saltaire have been cited, in Great Britain, as towns of the manufacturing sort which have shown the beneficent effects of actual Prohibition; and from such examples, even in a land of beer, have spread the influences which have freed more than 1,000 parishes in the Province of Canterbury from public houses and dramshops.

Pullman, a manufacturing suburb of Chicago, and Colorado Springs and Greeley, in Colorado, have demonstrated TOWN-BUILDING how *the power from without*, by corporate ON THE BASIS action, has effectively banished the saloon OF PROHIBITION. vice, and has brought thrift and moral elevation to those classes of community from which the saloon commonly draws its recruits and support. Pullman owes its existence and no-saloon policy to the Pullman Car Co., which founded both. Colorado Springs was founded by a corporation tributary to the Denver and Rio Grande Railway Co. The one is a wage-earners' town; the other a town of tourist visitation and health-seeking by the rich. From both the saloon has been debarred by *power from without;* and in both, and reaching far away from both, has been created and has gone out an educated Prohibition sentiment that has been widespread in its leavening effects.

One of the natural results of such influence and example is Harriman, Tenn., where a corporate *power from without* spelled Prohibition on every foot of the town site, and engraved on the city seal those descriptive, prophetic words: "*Prohibition, Peace, and Prosperity.*" It was a natural and proper thing that there, amid beautiful scenery and morally salubrious surroundings, the friends of education, morality, and good government should seek to establish the American Temperance University, at whose bidding the task was begun which led to the preparation of this book.

CHAPTER XXIV.

POLITICAL WAYS AND MEANS.

AFTER all that has gone before, these propositions may be accepted as logical:

1. A mere moral reform cannot reestablish harmony between Moral and Political Forces.
2. No moral reform can become a fact in government through Moral Forces alone.
3. Every moral reform which broadly affects the State must be made a fact in government to be effective.
4. A moral fact can be asserted and can dominate in government only through a political reform.
5. Every moral question must become political which depends for final settlement on legislation, on law, and the administration of law.

These premises being granted, certain other propositions logically follow:

1. A political reform can become a fact in government only through a political party which administers government.
2. No political party can thus establish a political reform when inside the party there is an element opposing such reform which is larger than the party's dominating majority.

What is Politics?

According to Webster, it is "the science of Government; that part of ethics which has to do with the regulation and government of a nation or State, the preservation of its safety, peace, and prosperity; the defense of its existence and rights against foreign control or conquest, the augmentation of its strength and resources, and the protection of its citizens, in their rights, with the preservation and improvement of their morals."

The Standard Dictionary thus defines it:

"*Politics*, the branch of civics that treats of the principles of civil government and the conduct of State affairs; the administration of public affairs in the interest of the peace, prosperity, and safety of the State; statecraft; political science; in a wide sense, embracing the *science of government and civil polity*."

Politics, then, relates to the Governing Authority and **RELATION OF POLITICS.** to those who are governed by it; to the State and to the unit of the State, the individual citizen.

With Politics every citizen has to do, and Politics has to do with all citizens individually.

As was declared once by Chief-Justice Story:

" The American Republic above all others demands from every citizen increasing vigilance and exertion, since we have deliberately dispensed with every guard against danger and ruin except the intelligence and virtue of the people themselves."

It follows that Politics, in our Republic, has particularly to do with private and public morals, and must always **POLITICS AND MORAL QUESTIONS.** deal with moral questions affecting citizenship and the State. **Within the purview of Politics must come every moral question which affects man in his relation to Government.** The intelligence and virtue of the people themselves, on which our Government rests, will forever demand this while our form of Government remains.

To this fact are due all Sunday laws, all marriage laws, and all other laws establishing by legal statute a moral standard among men. Politics and morals, moral questions and political reforms, can be divorced only to the peril and ruin of the State.

What is a Political Party?

According to Webster:

"One of the parts into which a people is divided on questions of public concern."

According to the Standard Dictionary:

"Any one of two or more bodies of people contending for antagonistic or rival opinions or policies in a community or society; especially one of the opposing political organizations striving for supremacy in a State."

POLITICAL PARTY DEFINED. According to Gladstone: "An instrument for attaining great ends."

According to Edmund Burke:

"A body of men joined together for the purpose of promoting, by their joint endeavors, the national interest upon some particular principle in which they are all agreed."

Of these definitions that of Burke is the best, or most widely accepted by writers on Politics. It very closely tallies with, and may have inspired, what Lieber says in "Political Ethics," viz.:

"By a Political Party we understand a number of citizens who, for some period and not momentarily, act in unison respecting some principle, interest, or measure, by lawful means, keeping therefore within the bounds of the fundamental law, and for the real or sincerely supposed good of the commonwealth."

Both Lieber and Burke would **ground a Political Party on principle**; and both dictionary definitions **BASIS AND PURPOSE OF A PARTY.** imply the same. We can scarcely conceive a real question of public concern which does not embody or is not based upon some positive principle; and surely no political organization should strive for supremacy in government upon any other basis.

One of the most famous utterances of one Political Party, in its national platform, thus declared:

"The first concern of good government is the virtue and sobriety of the people and the purity of the home."

If, then, any party upholds any policy that makes against virtue, sobriety and purity, some party may take issue with it, formulate a policy of opposition, and seek to array the major part of all the people in this policy's favor. Surely "the first concern of good government" may be the chief aim, the dominating purpose, of a Political Party loyal to good government.

A people can divide into parties only upon questions of public concern that have become moral or political issues.

What is an Issue?

According to the Standard Dictionary:

"That which has come into prominent interest or discussion."

According to Webster:

"The presentation of alternatives between which one must choose or decide."

Issues may be narrow and local, or broad and national. Under Local Option the alternatives may be saloons or no saloons, within the boundaries of a small county; but the issue is plain and explicit. Between those alternatives every man must choose or decide. So as to a State, of many counties, the issue may be equally plain, of saloons or no saloons; and all the citizens of that State may be compelled to take sides.

WHAT ARE POLITICAL ISSUES?

Political Issues are of three kinds: they are either

Issues of Principle,
Issues of Policy, or
Personal Issues.

If Personal Issues only, they must be narrow, and they

are likely to embody neither Principle nor Policy. An issue of Policy alone is not likely to be clean-cut, sharply defined, and territorially broad. An issue of Policy based upon Principle will be sharp, assertive, and as wide as the Government's bounds.

KINDS OF ISSUES.

Principle is the quality or factor in any issue which determines its breadth of recognition, application, and assertiveness.

A Principle may have narrow application, which may yet secure wide recognition and assertiveness for the issue it embodies. Thus the maintenance of saloons in the District of Columbia, or the suppression of polygamy in Utah, may become a national issue; and either may have recognition and assertion, as one has had, in the political platform of a great national political party.

PRINCIPLE AND ITS APPLICATION.

Any one party may present and assert an issue. It does not require that other parties recognize and admit the alternatives by open declaration. If one party declares against polygamy in one section and all other parties are silent about it, the Issue of Polygamy has been raised. The silence of other parties has in effect presented the alternative. It is as true in politics as in divine teachings, "He that is not for Me is against Me."

HOW ISSUES ARE PRESENTED.

When it required the assertion of a national policy to suppress the local vice mentioned (polygamy), and when one party declared for such policy, the failure of any other party to declare against it did not delay the Issue. It was presented, it was asserted, and the national policy was established.

THE ISSUE OF POLYGAMY.

A national policy becomes necessary as to any matter which requires national legislation with regard to any part of the national domain.

A National Policy must be uniform to give national satisfaction; it must apply alike to all parts of the people.

NATIONAL POLICY NEEDED. To be uniform, it must be based on a principle which can be broadly applied.

So long as any considerable portion of our national domain is under national control through territorial government, or so long as a national revenue is derived or contended for from the Liquor Taffic, so long will a National Policy be demanded as to that Traffic, so long will the question remain a political issue as to what that policy shall be.

Let one party declare against Prohibition, as hostile to personal liberty, and the Prohibition Issue is presented,

THE ISSUE OF PROHIBITION. even though all other parties are dumb with regard to it. Let one party declare for a revenue from license, and the License Issue is raised.

The Issue of Prohibition, or of License, is more squarely and emphatically presented when one party declares against Prohibition and another stands for License, and still another demands and proclaims that "the manufacture, importation, exportation, transportation, and sale of alcoholic beverages shall be made public crimes and prohibited as such."

It is impossible for any party to establish a reform of any magnitude which it has not previously recognized and asserted as an issue. **It is impossible for any man to support any party and consistently oppose or influentially disclaim its policy.**

The policy of a party is usually and properly enunciated in the party's platform. While platforms are often con-

POLICY AND PLATFORM. structed to carry votes, they should always be built upon principle. Every plank should logically match or fairly harmonize with every other. Several issues may be presented in one platform; but if a great and vital issue has been asserted—if one broad and beneficent reform be proposed, outclassing and overshadowing every other—all the planks in a platform may properly and logically refer to that issue, proclaim the need, the purpose, the philosophy, of that reform.

On the 28th of June, 1888, 1,082 delegates, representing one party of a single State, assembled at Syracuse, N. Y., with uncommon singleness of vision and spirit, adopted the following declarations:

First—The traffic in alcoholic beverages produces misery, pauperism, want, wretchedness, taxation, ruin, crime, and death; it neither begets wealth nor conserves human welfare; it is a foe to the home, a menace to the Church, and a growing peril to the State; and its total prohibition is demanded by every interest of political economy, of moral relationship, and of social life.

Second—The total prohibition of this traffic can be secured only through a policy which outlaws the traffic and refuses it all legal recognition; never by a policy of license in any form for any price.

Third—The policy of Prohibition can be applied to this traffic only through some political agency or force, and can be applied with success only through such force or agency in favor of the policy; therefore, a Prohibition Party is imperative, that the principle may have embodiment, and that the policy may be sustained through the administration of law.

Fourth—While there is and must be a national policy of some kind concerning the liquor traffic, a national party is and must be necessary to establish and maintain a national policy of Prohibition; and we reaffirm our allegiance to the National Prohibition Party; we ratify, with hearty enthusiasm, the nominations of that party for President and Vice-President of the United States, and we call upon all patriots to indorse these nominations at the polls.

Fifth—The organization of liquor men for the avowed purpose of defying law, and their repeated assertion that Prohibition laws cannot be enforced, demonstrate that the Liquor Traffic is disloyal of character, revolutionary in its methods, and of treasonable intent; and any political party that allies itself with, or does not condemn, said traffic, becomes either an active participant in, or a silent indorser of, the disloyalty and treason by it shown.

These declarations were preceded by a recognition of "God as the Supreme Ruler of men and the source of all just authority in government," and were followed by a recognition of this as "the supreme issue which this party was organized to meet and which it exists to decide," and an assertion of this as "the dominant question on which good citizens should now agree." In them appears to be embodied the essential and indisputable logic of this moral and political reform.

It is only **the Supreme Issue** which a party was organized to meet that can have its entirely loyal and most efficient service.

Any party will treat from the standpoint of expediency any question or issue regarded of secondary importance by a considerable portion of the party's membership, or as concerning which all members of the party are not agreed.

SUPREME ISSUE AND COMPROMISE.

Any question or issue thus treated by a party will be the victim of compromise, the football of party emergencies.

Every party will compromise upon every question except the supreme one which called it into being.

The whole history of **tariff legislation** is in proof of this. No party has been created, or has existed primarily and finally, to settle the tariff question. All parties have compromised concerning it since tariff legislation began. Every tariff bill passed by Congress has been an aggregation of compromises. In the first volume of his work entitled "Twenty Years in Congress," Mr. James G. Blaine said:

THE TARIFF AND COMPROMISE.

" The issues growing out of the subject of the tariff were, however, in many respects entirely distinct from the slavery question. The one (slavery) involved the highest moral considerations, the other (tariff) was governed solely by expediency."

In explaining the fact that Daniel Webster, John C. Cal-
houn, and other eminent statesmen radically
changed front on the tariff issue to suit their
constituents, Mr. Blaine added:

<small>BLAINE ON THE TARIFF.</small>

"As a whole, the record of tariff legislation, from the very origin of the Government, is a record of enlightened selfishness."

Expediency and enlightened selfishness have never yet adopted a policy, as to the tariff or the Liquor Traffic, based on a principle unyielding, of broad and beneficent application, and superior to compromise.

Two principles have been involved in all the talk about tariff all these years—**Free Trade and Protection;** but by neither one of these principles has any party been willing or able to stand without concession to the other. Expediency and selfishness have compelled parties and politicians to shift ground as to both.

<small>PRINCIPLE AND EXPEDIENCY.</small>

Professor Perry, in his "Introduction to Political Economy," upon the information of men who have served on the Ways and Means Committee at Washington, complains "that the individuals and delegations who come before that committee in behalf of new or higher protective duties, come *in the basest selfishness, without a thought or care of anybody's interests but their own.*" And he asks, with pathetic concern now for the moral element in even *his* Political Economy:

"Can a system like this, so shortsighted and greedy, so obstructive to natural and wholesome tendencies, building so little on permanent elements in man and nature, claim to be a part of the progress of the world?"

So the narrowest and most restrictive economist we have opposes Protection because it will not in his judgment conduce to *the Progress of the world.* And summarizing his arguments for Free

<small>PROGRESS OF THE WORLD.</small>

Trade, he declares in italics that it "**maximizes Products, harmonizes with Providence, means abundance, recognizes rights, is the friend of the laboring classes, defends from attack the worthiest interests.**"

If Political Economy can thus declare itself for Free Trade as between nations, or for any other policy whatever, *for reasons of this sort*, to be a consistent science, to be a science at all, *founded on principles that are unchanging and that can be uniformly applied*, it must declare for Prohibition within the State, and throughout our own nation, of all trade in alcoholic beverages, because they "are obstructive to natural and wholesome tendencies"; it must favor Prohibition because it "*maximizes products, harmonizes with Providence, means abundance, recognizes rights, is the friend of the laboring classes, and defends from attack the worthiest interests.*"

APPLIED POLITICAL ECONOMY.

And because **every Political Reform must come through a Political Party, agreed upon it, and loyal to it and responsible for it,** Political Economy may and does demand that some political party shall establish the Policy of Prohibition, as a fact in government, for the greatest good of the greatest number, for the permanent welfare of all, and for the upward progress of the world.

CHAPTER XXV.

CITIZENSHIP AND ITS DUTIES.

THE SOLE HARMONIZING AGENT. HARMONY between Moral and Political Forces, let it be said again, must come, can come only, through the individual man, the citizen, the sole harmonizing factor in the State.

One final and important question awaits answer in this concluding chapter:

How, and where, and when shall the citizen harmonize Moral and Political Forces?

In the Home, at the School, in the Church?

These are themselves the primary Moral Forces, with which Political Forces must be harmonized.

In the Reform Club, the Lodge-Room, the Law and Order League, or at the Jail, the Reformatory?

These are the secondary Moral Forces, or some of them, made necessary in large part because the primary Moral Forces have not been harmonized with by Political Forces, and have failed of doing all their natural and proper work.

In the Home, the School, or the Church, as merely a parent, a teacher, a preacher, or church member, the Citizen should exert all possible influence on behalf of morality in politics and pure government; and thus, influentially, he may and should be there a harmonizing factor, in a sense and to a degree. But—

THE ONE PLACE TO HARMONIZE. The Citizen, as a positive harmonizing agent between Moral and Political Forces, must act outside Moral Forces, but at a point so related to these and to Political Forces that his act will affect both.

There is but one point in a Republic where the citizen's act can do this—

The Ballot-Box.

There and there only can the moral quality of citizenship so assert itself as to defend and insure the moral foundations of the State. Only through the assertion of this moral quality in citizenship, through a political act, can the citizen harmonize Moral and Political Forces.

All organized Political Forces are covered by and included in the Political Party; and Law, the execution of Law, is the ultimate of all Political Force; but the Ballot-Box is the focal point of all Political Power, and **only at the Ballot-Box can Moral and Political Forces be harmonized**.

FOCAL POINT OF POLITICAL POWER.

There must every issue between parties be settled; there must every policy of the Government be determined or established. It is at the Ballot-Box that the citizen finds his supreme privilege, and meets or fails to meet his supreme responsibility.

What is his Ballot, at its best? His witness; the witness to his Citizenship. It testifies of his purpose, his principle, his character, his noblest aspirations for the State. It should testify to his profoundest political belief, his highest moral standard. To him it should be sacred; by him it should be sacredly used. To every other man it should be sacred none the less. By no man should it be bought or sold. By no combination of men should the intent or effect of it be frustrated. By all men and all parties the purity of it should be jealously guarded, the sanctity of it should be faithfully defended.

THE BALLOT'S CHARACTER.

No patriotic citizen will dispute this, but the ballot's treatment by political managers is in alarming contrast. In *The Century Magazine* for October, 1892, appeared an article by Prof. J. W. Jenks, of Cornell University, on "**Money in Practical Politics,**" which embodied many painful facts as to corruption among voters. We need quote but one paragraph:

" The proportion of voters who are subject to money influence is very great. I have had estimates given me many times by men whose knowledge is based upon experience, and I find that the localities are not very uncommon where from 10 to 35 per cent. of the voters are purchasable. In one county of New York, in which, perhaps, the Mugwump vote is larger in proportion to the total vote than in any county in the State, and in which the largest city has some 12,000 inhabitants, about 20 per cent. of the voters were purchased in 1888. . . . The evil is not confined to the cities nor to any one State. The probability is that, all things considered, in such a State as New York the farmers are as corrupt as the residents of the cities."

The same number of *The Century* gave editorial comment on this article by Professor Jenks, in which comment occurred the following illustration:

" In Rhode Island, for example, where money has been used corruptly in every election since the war, and in some before and during the war, there are known to be about 5,000 purchasable voters in a total of 57,000, or nearly 10 per cent. of the whole number. These are distributed over the State, ranging from 10 in the smaller towns to 1,000 in the cities, but in every case their names and individual prices are matters of record. . . . Prices range from $2 to $5 a head, according to demand."

Prof. J. J. McCook, of Trinity College, Hartford, Conn., conducted a remarkable investigation as to the franchise and the abuses of it, and published a noteworthy paper about this in *The Forum* for September, 1892. From private lists, furnished him by politicians, he gave tabulated statements covering twenty towns and one city in Connecticut, showing that nearly 16 per cent. of the total number of votes is venal—known by the party managers to be for sale. And referring to the testimony of those men, Professor McCook said: " It was constantly affirmed that intemperance figures very largely in the annals of vote-buying."

The Ballot must be sobriety, intelligence, character, and conscience incarnate, to give guarantee of stability and character to the State.

Conscientious and intelligent ballots are the final safeguard of republican institutions. They will be cast, as a **BALLOTS OF CONSCIENCE.** rule, for the candidates of some regularly organized party, and upon one side or the other of some recognized and well-defined issue. That they may indeed be ballots of conscience, they must be cast in a party that bases its issue on principle, and that stands for **the highest ideals in government.** That they may serve conscientious and patriotic purpose, they must be cast freely, without fear, and be registered without interference.

GARFIELD ON THE SUFFRAGE. Said Garfield in his inaugural address:

"We have no standard by which to measure the evil that may be brought upon us by ignorance and vice in the citizen when joined to corruption and fraud in the suffrage."

For ignorance and vice in the citizen, and for corruption and fraud in the suffrage, the saloon, more than any other agency, is responsible. Wholesome and effective Ballot Reform can not be had while the worst corrupter of the suffrage is perpetuated.

Suffrage frauds are manifold, but their agency, their inspiration, is uniform. More than for any other purpose they are **perpetrated in order to perpetuate the agency of their perpetration.**

To count in a candidate whom the electors have not **DEFRAUDING THE SUFFRAGE.** chosen, is fraudulent; to suppress ballots that have been cast, is fraudulent; in any way to thwart the will of the people as expressed at the ballot-box, is fraudulent; but to cheat a negro of his vote, or of his vote's intent, in Georgia or in Mississippi, is no more a fraud, no more an outrage, than to cheat a white citizen in like manner in Michigan or Ohio. **The color of the voter does not give color to the offense.** That men of one party are guilty of the offense in one State, and men of another party are guilty of it in another State, changes nothing. That hundreds of colored votes are cast and not counted in some parish of Louisiana, is no worse than that hundreds of votes are counted though never cast in some county of Michigan. Yet "a free ballot and a fair count" has become a partizan watch-cry in the North, where **Saloon frauds on the Suffrage have been heinous and shameless and past counting,** with effects beyond computation and plethoric of mischief.

When the Prohibition Amendment was declared voted down in Ohio (in 1883), its friends obtained evidence that SALOON SOURCES in over 800 polling-precincts the vote in favor OF FRAUD. of it was but counted in part, or but partly reported, or not reported at all; and the frauds thus proven were believed sufficient to have given the Amendment a majority. Men of high standing in the dominant party of that State assisted in obtaining the proof, and urged action upon it by the Legislature, but without avail. For a cause which the saloon influence had counted out at the polls, that influence allowed no redress in the halls of legislation.

When the Prohibition Amendment met a like fate in Michigan (in 1886), by only a few thousands reported as a majority against it, similar proof of frauds and outrage abounded there, the county of Gogebic alone returning, as has been stated, 700 more votes against the Amendment than there were men, women, and children in the entire county.

It is in the logic of things that a saloon system should breed corruption of the suffrage. It is inevitable that a MARKET-PLACE saloon system shall seek to perpetuate itself OF SUFFRAGE. by fraud at the ballot-box. It is a natural sequence that the saloon shall be for the ballot a market-place—a place of **commerce in citizenship**—the one foul spot in all the State where suffrages are bought and sold, where the birthright of citizenship is parted with for ignominious price.

If evidence were needed in proof of this, it could be put on record here to a painful extent. One sufficient witness will be the New York City Reform Club, referred to and quoted from before in these pages. That Club lists and publishes each year the representatives in the State Legislature elected from the city of New York. In its "Record" for 1889 was described the corrupting power of **the saloon in city politics,** as follows:

"There is about one saloon for every 35 voters. Each of these places represents a certain number of votes, the votes of hangers-on, who, for the privilege of frequenting the saloon and an occasional free drink, are at the command of the proprietor; and as each saloon serves as a center of political activity as well on election day as for weeks preceding it, the number of votes thus influenced is so increased as to be practically all powerful. The result appears in the character of the men who are sent to the Legislature. They are naturally the tools of the saloon because they are chosen by the saloon. . . .

"The further fact that there are 35,000 saloon-keepers in this State avowedly organized for the purpose of securing legislation favorable to themselves, and of preventing legislation which they deem to be unfavorable to their business interests, is too significant to be overlooked or misunderstood ; and when it is remembered that each of these saloon-keepers probably controls ten votes, at the very lowest possible estimate, it is not difficult to perceive the danger which threatens the State."

It should be earnest, honest, eloquent truth, which Whittier sings, about

THE POOR VOTER ON ELECTION DAY.

The proudest now is but my peer,
  The highest not more high;
To-day, of all the weary year,
  A king of men am I !
Alike to-day are great and small,
  The nameless and the known;
My palace is the People's Hall,
  The Ballot-Box *my* throne !

Who serves to-day upon the list
  Beside the served shall stand;
Alike the brown and wrinkled fist,
  The gloved and dainty hand ;
The rich is level with the poor,
  The weak is strong to-day ;
And sleekest broadcloth counts no more
  Than homespun frock of gray.

To-day let pomp and vain pretense
  My stubborn right abide ;
I put a plain man's common-sense
  Beside the pedant's pride ;
To-day shall simple Manhood try
  The strength of gold and land ;
The wide world has not wealth to buy
  The power in my right hand !

While there's a grief to seek redress,
  Or balance to adjust,
Where weighs our living Manhood less
  Than Mammon's vilest dust :
While there's a Right to need my vote,
  A wrong to sweep away,
Up, clouted knee and ragged coat,
  A man's a man to-day !

Yes, it ought to be truth, always, but it is not; and while the saloon system remains, perpetuated by a saloon policy in government, it never will be. It were easy to take one half of Whittier's lines and make them tell more truth, with some unpoetical additions, than they all do now under the conditions that exist. Shades of the good Quaker poet, forgive us, while we practise economy with his verse in repeated quotation:

WHITTIER REVISED.

> " The proudest now is but my peer,
>   The highest not more high;"
> In theory the thing is clear,
>   As no one will deny.
> " Alike to-day are great and small,
>   The nameless and the known ;"
> They want our votes, these fellows all,
>   They've condescending grown.
>
> " Who serves to-day upon the list
>   Beside the served shall stand,"
> And shake each brown and brawny fist
>   With greenbacks in his hand.
> " The rich is level with the poor,
>   The weak is strong to-day ;"
> Unless your candidate pays more
>   For votes, he'll lose, I say.
>
> " To-day let pomp and vain pretense
>   My stubborn right abide ;"
> I'm not quite on the party fence,
>   Nor very far one side.
> " To-day shall simple manhood try
>   The strength of gold and land ;"
> Strong arguments are those, say I,
>   You hold within your hand.
>
> " While there's a grief to seek redress,
>   Or balance to adjust,"
> I love my party none the less
>   That dear is Mammon's dust.
> " While there's a right to need my vote,
>   A wrong to sweep away,"
> I'll pull my oar in party's boat
>   So long as it will pay !

But, let us hasten to say, not every poor voter sells his vote; and the men who do sell their votes are not always poor. A great body of men cannot be bought—for money, have no price—in dollars and cents, when they will forego advocacy of certain principles, if not abandon those principles, to secure election to a paltry office: will gladly yield up individual expression, if not forswear individual belief, to please the crowd. And of this crowd a great number are bought and sold by their party prejudices, if in no baser manner; they are bought and sold by party leaders, who rely upon the strength of party ties for consummation of the sale.

The ballot must be loyal to, as it is the incarnation of, **Citizenship, Intelligence, and Conscience.** It

LOYALTY OF THE BALLOT. cannot be loyal to either and be forever loyal to party. By the very law of growth parties grow corrupt. Bad men acquire control of a victorious party, and use their power to propagate their badness. The worst elements that exist in communities are shrewdly combined by these men to operate against the good. It is the logic of politics.

But rascality seldom wins, *except as it misuses principle;* when principle rebels, and organizes rebellion in its own behalf, rascality is defeated. "When bad men conspire, good men must combine."

It has been urged that men should keep religion out of politics, and this question does not require discussion here; but there is one doctrine of religion which deserves to be taught wherever political science is studied, viz., **the free agency of man.** We should learn to realize that the party is not a secret order, held in compact by binding oaths; it is not a standing army, which must be maintained as by patriotic allegiance.

It is the veriest unreason to claim that, because parties

must be, we must jealously, religiously, under all circumstances, help to sustain our party's life, and for that purpose use our ballot only as a party tool. Upon such claim as this—upon the feeling, the habit, resulting from it—political corruption waxes and grows fat.

<small>PARTY AND THE BALLOT.</small>

In a lecture before the Society for Ethical Culture, on "Conscience in Politics" (New York, Nov. 11, 1894), Prof. Felix Adler said:

"The formation at times of a third party is the safety-valve in politics. A real political party must have the welfare of the whole people at heart, and it must hold certain principles by which it thinks to promote this welfare. Wrong partizan spirit engenders a false ethical code.

"It is right to assist in the formation of a third party, first, when the issues are unreal, vague, or obsolete; second, when the issues are real but insignificant in comparison with greater issues; third, when the issue is real, but the leader is one in whose fidelity you don't trust.

"To vote for a third-party candidate who has no chance of election is not to throw a vote away. It plants a seed for righteousness."

The Ballot's highest loyalty is to Conscience, not to party. Conscience is not a party attribute. No party has either a conscience or a soul. There is no infinitesimal part of a party to be eternally damned even when a wicked party dies.

What constitutes a party? An aggregation of men. If every party should die to-night, its component parts would be here to-morrow; there would be new parties next week. A party as such is but an intangible something which may bear tangible fruits, but the boundaries of which may be hard to find.

Somebody once damned with pointed impatience the north pole, and the polar enthusiast who provoked such profane reference complained about it bitterly to Sydney Smith.

<small>EQUATORIAL PARTY LINES.</small>

"Oh, that is nothing," comfortingly said the wit; "I

have even heard him speak disrespectfully of the equator!"

Sail the tropic seas, and you shall cross and recross the meridian without heeding it. In that broad expanse of blue no mark of division will you behold. As imaginary as lines geographical are many party lines to-day; upon the tropic seas of Politics you shall sail and seek long for an equatorial boundary between parties, which can be found, without the searchlight of Prejudice and in the simple sunlight of Truth.

The Ballot of Conscience means the best Manhood. The best manhood means the best Citizenship.

CONTRIBUTIONS TO THE COMMONWEALTH. When the State confers citizenship, it gives certain rights, privileges and guarantees. But they are not given without certain actual or implied return. They are not a free gift, which lays upon the recipient no lasting obligation. The price paid and to be paid is comprised in certain contributions to the commonwealth, in faithful care for its interests, in zealous concern for its integrity and perpetuity.

"Render, therefore, unto Cæsar the things that are Cæsar's." Every man owes tribute to God and government.

TRIBUTE TO GOD AND GOVERNMENT. He can not pay honest tribute to God, and deny to government his highest loyalty. Such highest loyalty is personified in the best manhood, approximating the noblest ideals, opposing all that degrades, assisting all that uplifts, refusing alliance with everything that corrupts, standing for Principle at all times and in all places, but supremely and always, whenever privilege and responsibility call him there, at **the Altar of the Republic, the Ballot-Box.**

There, doing his full duty, paying his full tribute of citizenship, he must guard the fruits of Production, must conserve the welfare of Labor and Capital, must assert the true attitude of Authority toward every element or agency that menaces the general good. There and always he must be loyal to the sovereignty that is within him. There and always he must "render unto Cæsar the things that are Cæsar's," so that elsewhere and always he may render "unto God the things that are God's."

CHAPTER INTERROGATORIES.

CHAPTER I.

1. How is Political Economy defined by the Dictionaries? By the Economists?
2. With what has it principally to do? To what does it relate? Where is its tap-root? What is its aim?
3. On what rests the law of the legislator?
4. What is the final definition of Political Economy adopted by this book? What are implied in this definition?
5. What was the original derivation of the term Political Economy? Who first used it?
6. Of what is all property the product?
7. To what has Political Economy the closest relation? How are Ethics and Political Economy related?
8. From what standpoint are we to study this science? What is an important factor in the problems of natural and political law?
9. What says De Laveleye about Political Economy and Law? What follows, if this be true? Who will dispute this?
10. Is there such an element or influence in the State? What should Political Economy do about it? What law meets the test?
11. How does our subject group itself? What are its grand divisions?
12. What are the minor subdivisions?

CHAPTER II.

1. On what is Production based? How many kinds of Want?
2. What is the demand of Political Economy as to Production and human life?
3. How does the gratification of a natural want affect life? How will you determine if want be unnatural?
4. What are real wants? What are false?
5. What stands between Want and Production? What said the Emperor of China?
6. What is a cause of hard times?
7. What are the prime natural wants? How are natural wants developed? What follows their development?
8. What multiplies wants? Will legitimate wants pauperize the world? Can they be too numerous?
9. How shall we denominate the present age? What of Want and Work?
10. What is Production's natural law?
11. What are the classifications of Labor?
12. How does Amasa Walker characterize Labor?
13. To what does this language directly apply?
14. What says De Laveleye about true wealth? What is false wealth?
15. What calls for alcoholic beverage?

CHAPTER III.

1. What is Productive Labor? And what is Unproductive?
2. What about the perfume, and the bottle containing it? What of the brandy bottle?
3. How is Production classified? How is Labor illustrated?
4. What determines the true productive quality of Labor? How is this illustrated?
5. How should we think of labor?
6. What is the individual man? What does aggregate labor determine?
7. What facts must be borne in mind as to labor and the laborer?
8. What of labor in its ultimate? Of the laborer on the farm? In the brewery?
9. Whence come two non-producing classes? What are they?
10. Are there non-producing classes that benefit society? What are they?
11. On what does the accumulation of wealth by a community depend? Is all non-productive labor a burden?
12. What about the player and composer? Does Paderewski rank with producers?
13. How are Manual Labor and Mind Labor compared? What of the author and the stenographer?
14. What does the inventor's mind labor make possible?

CHAPTER IV.

1. How is Labor defined? How are Labor and Ability distinguished? What is Perry's definition?
2. What exception is taken to this? How is the artist's work cited?
3. What further definitions of labor? Which is accepted as the standard?
4. How does Mill distinguish Unproductive Labor? What of the piano and the pianist?
5. Can music be used as an aid to production? What have been some of its effects?
6. Of what is Labor creative?
7. How many kinds of Utilities are there? What is the first? What the second? What the third?
8. Are Utilities any part of wealth?
9. In the production of wealth, what are essential requisites?
10. What are the requisites of Productive Labor? What are demanded of the Laborer?
11. Wnat must unite to insure Productive Labor? How are moral qualities considered? How does character weigh?
12. What of the laborer's environment? How are its conditions stated?
13. Is the Liquor Traffic friend or foe of Productive Labor?
14. What does Government owe to the laborer concerning it?

CHAPTER V.

1. How is Wealth defined? What words are preferred by some economists?
2. How is Wealth subdivided? What is Material Wealth? What Personal?
3. Whence comes Material Wealth? What are the four great natural agents?
4. How are the appropriations from Nature illustrated? What are required in the making of a coat?
5. What sang Whittier to the shoemakers?
6. Are natural agents natural wealth? Which are commonly counted so?
7. What does mineral wealth furnish? What partnership is required in production?
8. How does machinery affect labor? What was back of the machine?
9. Do mechanical devices multiply wants?
10. How does the machine affect the man?
11. What is the ratio of material and immaterial wealth?
12. How are Ignorance and Indolence related to Poverty?
13. What is Poverty?
14. What is Wealth?

CHAPTER VI.

1. How is Wealth further classified? Wherein does Individual Wealth differ from Personal Wealth?
2. What is National Wealth? How does it come?
3. What about the millionaire and his mortgage?
4. Would subdivision of a great estate increase the national wealth?
5. Of what must we take account in considering National Wealth? What does Marshall mean by the term Industry?
6. How is the creation of national wealth determined?
7. On what does the rapid accumulation of that wealth depend?
8. How must industries rank and be related? Has any one industry a right to subsist upon other industries?
9. How should legitimate industries affect each other? How does the liquor industry affect other industries?
10. What most depreciates American labor? How do politicians and scholars regard this?
11. When is the injustice done legitimate industries most marked?
12. What about the famine years in Ireland? How did suppression of the distilleries affect the people?
13. What said Oliver Wendell Holmes?
14. What is the Industrial Law of Political Economy?

CHAPTER VII.

1. What does Political Economy require concerning Wealth? Is there this proper Distribution?
2. What must be the distributing agent? By what commanded? By what paid?
3. What is Capital? What creates it?
4. On what does the growth of capital depend? By what are these mastered?
5. How comes the opportunity to save? What does this law establish?
6. How is supply affected? When will capital cease to demand labor?
7. What is Demand? On what does it depend?
8. On what depends the Standard of Living? How are two laborers compared?
9. How is Capital best employed? How would this fact affect its employment in the manufacture of liquor?
10. What proportion does Labor receive in that manufacture? How does it compare with labor's proportion in other industries?
11. What is the annual loss to Labor from the capital employed in liquor making?
12. How many persons and families would this support?
13. What other products could be annually bought with the money paid for liquor?
14. What greater home comforts would it command?

CHAPTER VIII.

1. What are the determining factors in Distribution? Do wages solve the problem?
2. What is the average family cost? And where? What the family earnings?
3. What of the farmer and artisan? What of the laborer's margin?
4. By what is this margin wiped out? How has this been demonstrated?
5. What is the annual cost of liquor to the average laboring man? Whom does he tax to pay it?
6. How did two workingmen illustrate loss and gain?
7. What did beer cost one of them each year?
8. How much was paid for tobacco and cigars?
9. How much did the lost time figure up?
10. What was the total?
11. What is the parentage of capital?
12. Under what conditions will Wages fail to equalize Wealth?
13. On what does the Prosperity of the State depend?

CHAPTER IX.

1. What do Want and Production imply? What demand does Production meet?
2. How many kinds of Consumption? And what?
3. How is wealth useful?
4. If consumption be not reproductive, what is the penalty?
5. How is reproductive consumption illustrated? What is reproductive consumption?
6. What consumption is unproductive? What is the ultimate?
7. From what is the word Consumption derived?
8. How far do reproductive uses extend? How illustrated?
9. Wherewith the farmer's product does the reproductive line finally break?
10. Is there nutriment in beer? How much?
11. What is the analysis of a pint of beer?
12. What has been the effect of Beer Legislation?
13. What is the effect of Beer Drinking? Its worst result?
14. How does chemistry testify?
15. What is Commerce? What are goods?
16. What attitude should Political Economy occupy toward sales that work harm?

CHAPTER X.

1. What is Political Economy's requirement as to Reproductive Consumption? Is such Consumption demanded to sustain a fair standard of wages?
2. What question have statesmen largely considered? And where?
3. Who was a conspicuous advocate of Protection in the Fifty-third Congress?
4. What did he say of wages? How did he say that increase of wages must come?
5. What was his testimony as to Wants and Wages? Of Consumption and Wages?
6. What two facts did he recognize?
7. How is the law of Supply and Demand illustrated in an English artisan's home?
8. Would this be true of a besodden drinker's home?
9. What will measure wages?
10. What potentiality is claimed for our people? And why?
11. Are we potentially what we should be? And why not?
12. What element in our economic problem do the statesmen ignore?
13. What is the relation of Capital and Wages? The tendency of wages? And why?
14. What means the increase in our unskilled class?
15. Why should wage-earners be multiplied?
16. How many more wage-earners could be employed if the Capital now employed in the manufacture of liquor were employed in producing useful articles?
17. How much increase would result in the Consumption of raw materials?

CHAPTER XI.

1. What subdivisions open this chapter
2. How comes Waste in Production ?
3. How is wealth denominated, as employed in Production ?
4. What is the law of Capital and Waste ?
5. What results from a large amount of Fixed Capital? What of Fixed Charges in relation to output ?
6. How does the idleness of some hands affect profits ? What was the testimony of the Messrs. Ames?
7. What of plant, output, and profit? What of Drink as affecting plants, machinery, etc. ?
8. What is the proportion of Fixed Capital to Labor in large plants, as compared with smaller ones ?
9. As the ratio of Capital to service increases, what of Labor ?
10. How do saloons affect Labor ?
11. What seems the bent of Capital ?
12. What signifies Division of Labor ? How is skill attained ?
13. What about Waste of Production ? Primary Products'? Secondary Products?
14. How may these be destroyed ? How are they most extensively wasted ?
15. What has been the aggregate waste of Secondary Product for a given period ?
16. What the annual waste of Primary Product ?
17. What should be added to the product-waste ?
18. What is the waste aggregate for twelve years, and of what items composed ?

CHAPTER XII.

1. Of what does this treat? How large is the percentage of Lost Time?
2. To what does this percentage amount in the full time of drinking laborers? To what yearly sum?
3. What percentage of drinkers are habitual drunkards?
4. What is the total of paupers and prisoners whose full time is lost? Of insane, idiotic, and otherwise defective? The total sum annually lost through them?
5. How many are engaged in liquor manufacture and sale? The sum of their time-waste annually?
6. What is every man, brought to his producing capacity? Is there a standard of productive existence?
7. Is the expectation of life affected by Drink? How much?
8. What is the loss annually of productive life? How much is Dr. Hitchcock's estimate?
9. At what age does a young man begin to return his cost? What is the cost of a boy till 21?
10. Is there a waste of Cash Capital in Manhood? How does it come?
11. What is the cash value of a man? What gave a value to the slave?
12. What total loss is shown in Manhood investment? How is it incurred?

CHAPTER XIII.

1. How shall we treat Waste in care and support?
2. What is the annual average cost of paupers? How is the cost of almshouses denominated? How much does it sum up?
3. What do the other incapables cost? And the buildings to accommodate them?
4. How much do the prisoners each cost? What do the prisons represent of dead capital?
5. What must be further included in the care and support of crime? How many annual arrests? The cost of each?
6. Is there anything productive in police effort? What are policemen? What of the courts?
7. In what proportion is the Liquor Traffic responsible for all this cost of crime? What say the Judges?
8. How do the Charity Boards testify? And the Prison Inspectors?
9. How do the percentages average of these witnesses? And of the Tabulated Evidence?
10. What is the proportion of arrests in cities chargeable to drink? The largest?
11. On what percentage of accountability by the Liquor Traffic do we fix?
12. Upon this basis what is the net cost of paupers on account of Drink? Of other incapables?
13. What the cost of prisoners and arrests? And should anything be added?
14. What is the sum total of all this Loss and Waste?
15. What, then, should Political Economy seek?

CHAPTER XIV.

1. With what question does this Chapter open? What is the answer?
2. Are other elements involved? What is the true motive of Production?
3. What term do we apply to the State? What is Authority?
4. How must the State live? On what would it die?
5. Why does Authority make laws? What said Adam Smith?
6. What two things are necessary in the State? In what, then, is Authority interested chiefly?
7. To what definitions do we return? What do they teach?
8. Why does Political Economy have to do with Legislation? What does it seek? How can its ideal come?
9. What underlies this relation of Authority? And what is demanded by the State? How does Judge Pitman declare it?
10. Is the Betterment idea conceded by all? What says Mill?
11. What illustrations are furnished?
12. What is the Unit of Authority? How must the character of Authority be judged?
13. How does Civilization advance in a republic? What of Human Solidarity?
14. What are the advantages of Citizenship? What is its price?
15. What is the social law of Personal Liberty? The law in politics?
16. In Legislation, what must be considered?
17. In final analysis, what is Law?
18. What of moral rights and legal limitations?
19. What does Political Economy demand of Government?

CHAPTER XV.

1. What is the relation of Authority to the Liquor Traffic? What does this relation mean? Is this generally acknowledged?
2. What of Mill's theory as to the true functions of Government? What admissions does he make?
3. How is he answered by Judge Pitman? What does Mill's argument show?
4. How does the logic of his position relate to the Liquor Dealer? What do punishments imply?
5. What is the meaning of social organization? What must the State be?
6. How does Prof. Keasbey treat the Sovereignty of the State? What deductions follow?
7. What has been the attitude of the State toward the Liquor Traffic for centuries?
8. What was the Genesis of License? Where did the sales-regulation of the traffic begin?
9. Had there been any previous regulation of any kind? And what?
10. When did regulation of sales commence? Who paid the first license fees? What of public officials?
11. How did the Regulation System progress? What came to be said in England?
12. When did High License appear? How high?
13. What is the logic of license?
14. What is the true function of Authority?

CHAPTER XVI.

1. For the beneficent application of Political Economy, what is fundamentally essential?
2. What has been historically shown? Yet what does the Liquor Traffic say?
3. What must Authority seek? If Authority cannot restrain the injurious thing found, what is the conclusion?
4. Who exercises Authority? What is its source?
5. What is the nature of License? How defined?
6. What do these definitions imply? What were grants?
7. What is the license certificate? What does it confer?
8. Of what nature must have been the Authority back of it? What logical conclusion follows?
9. Can License have two meanings? How and what?
10. Must there have been Prohibition before License? Does License say this?
11. What says the Supreme Court? What principle is laid down by it?
12. What is the Supreme utterance of that Court?
13. What have the Supreme Justices said?
14. What said the Chief Justice of Delaware?
15. What is the logical declaration of License? On what is it founded?
16. What can make the License System of any benefit?
17. How does License affect that Principle?
18. Can License be Constitutional, if Prohibition is not?
19. If Prohibition be Constitutional, can License be?
20. What is a Constitution? What are some Constitutional utterances?
21. Can License be Constitutional according to these?
22. How should every License Law be entitled?

CHAPTER XVII.

1. What consideration comes next? What are the interests involved?
2. What side of the Liquor Traffic must now be considered? What claim must be met?
3. How must the State live? From whence must Revenue come?
4. Of what is Revenue the result? What is Taxation?
5. What is the logic of Taxation? For what does the citizen pay? What should he receive?
6. Should Taxation come from immoral sources? Why not?
7. On what ground is Taxation of the Liquor Traffic urged? What is said for Regulation?
8. What of License, considered as a Tax? What say Mill and Wayland?
9. How is Blaine's proposition answered? Who pays the tax?
10. What said Senator Sherman in Ohio?
11. Is the Liquor Traffic essentially criminal? What is it to license a crime? What of those who license?
12. What does the Traffic pay? How does Taxation of it meet public burdens?
13. What of Direct and Indirect Taxation?
14. How much does the Traffic yield? What is the average yield for each license?
15. What are the total yearly receipts from the manufacture and sale?

CHAPTER XVIII.

1. What is urged as the most effective Regulation? What claims are made for High License?
2. How many liquor-dealers are there? Under High License, how many would probably remain?
3. At $1,000 each what would the Revenue be from these? What proportion would this bear to the Traffic's annual cost?
4. Does High License reduce the saloons? What was found in Iowa?
5. Is the volume of Drink reduced by High License? How must the State act?
6. Has High License altered the character of the Traffic? When shall we find its effects?
7. What are the facts in Nebraska and Kansas, comparatively shown?
8. How stood the taxable wealth in those two States, in 1880? In 1889?
9. Did individual wealth increase or decrease under High License? And under Prohibition?
10. What followed High License in Illinois? What were the prison reports?
11. Has the volume of liquor consumption decreased in the seven High License States?
12. How do the records of arrests for crime and disorder compare in High License and Low License cities?
13. What means the payment of a large bonus to Authority? What say Philosophy, Human Nature, and Fact?
14. Does the low dive obey the High Law? What Wisconsin illustration is given?
15. What follows as to any Regulative System?

CHAPTER XIX.

1. What further interests must be considered, in determining Authority's duty toward the Liquor Traffic? What shall we recall?
2. Of what is Society composed?
3. On what does its maintenance depend?
4. How must this harmony come?
5. When and how is it made impossible?
6. What are the organized Moral Forces of Society?
7. What is the Home? What is the School? What the Church?
8. How does the Home measure the State? What are its influences upon the State? What form the State's foundations?
9. What must the School be and remain? What of Public Education?
10. How does the Church supplement the Home and the School? What command resounds from it? What does this teach?
11. Are there other Moral Forces? What?
12. What are the Organized Political Forces, or what includes them? What is its expression?
13. How shall we determine whether a Political Force is in harmony with Moral Forces? How shall we judge of a Law or Policy?
14. How shall we determine the duty of Authority as between Suppression and Regulation?
15. What questions follow, as to the Saloon's effect on the Home, the School, and the Church?
16. What are the contrasted pictures of a Home? How are character and comfort affected?
17. What are the influences upon childhood? What does the poor man buy? What are the statistics of idiocy?
18. What proves the effect of the saloon upon the school?
19. What is a curse to the Republic? What hinders Public Education? How are the children affected?
20. What the attitude of Saloon men toward Temperance Education?
21. What are the relations of the Liquor Traffic to the Sabbath? How do the church organizations testify?
22. What utterance of them all do you consider the strongest?

17

CHAPTER XX.

1. What one attitude of Authority toward the Liquor Traffic has been urged?
2. How did Local Option come? How has it been broadened?
3. How has it been tested longest? Where was it thus first applied? And when?
4. How did it begin in this country? Since when has it widely extended, and over what territory?
5. How does it seem on the face of it? In fact? As to principle?
6. What conclusions follow analysis?
7. Is there a majority right that governs?
8. Must there be a moral standard for the State?
9. What does the State owe to each community?
10. How would the theory of Local Option apply to thieves?
11. Have majorities counted in settlement of moral questions? What of Local Option and slavery?
12. What are the centers of immoral sentiment?
13. How has Local Option affected State Prohibition?
14. What six things does Local Option do?
15. What are its Moral and Financial Effects? Where do its revenues flow? What follows?
16. What significant facts appear?
17. What course do Temperance advocates adopt?
18. What is Local Option? Where did Lincoln and Douglas stand?
19. Does the Saloon seek territorial extension? How does it operate to secure this?

CHAPTER XXI.

1. What interests are next considered?
2. What conditions confront us in their consideration?
3. How does demoralization of the Citizen go on?
4. Inside the saloon, what of it? And outside?
5. What do political and moral interests demand of the citizen?
6. What is required of the good citizen? How and where is it impossible for him to meet this requirement?
7. Where does the Saloon most widely demoralize men? How?
8. To whom does the saloon-keeper owe place? Who settles Local Option contests?
9. What were the facts in Michigan? Of what did the Amendment die?
10. How was the Amendment beaten in Texas? What was Senator Reagan's testimony?
11. Who petitioned the voters in Tennessee? What was the result?
12. What determined the result in Pennsylvania? How was the Press demoralized? Who testified about it?
13. How is the farmer demoralized? How is manhood in general demoralized?
14. What competent witness is cited? What did the *Tribune* say?
15. What five propositions logically follow?
16. What is the friend of the saloon? Of the saloon system?

CHAPTER XXII.

1. What are the conclusions that open this chapter?
2. What of the highest loyalty to Government?
3. What is Loyalty? Is the Liquor Traffic law-abiding?
4. What does it answer to the State? What proof of its disloyalty abounds?
5. Why has Prohibition failed anywhere? What says a Liquor Association's President?
6. What of a business that defies law? Is the Liquor Traffic in rebellion?
7. What effect has the Traffic on law and order? From what does Law suffer?
8. How does Prohibition affect laborers? What is a Strike?
9. What is the chief course of Strikes? Of what is a strike generally born?
10. What of Cooperation and strikes? Who gets the Capital?
11. How was the great railroad strike fed? What followed?
12. What of Wages and Drink at Homestead? Where did the wages go?
13. How did the tramp define Communism?
14. What made the anarchist? Where have his crimes originated?
15. What loss to labor did strikes involve in six years?
16. What is the fruit of saloons? What rules our great cities? Who testify?
17. What is the greatest danger to our Republic? Who says so?
18. What said the New York City Reform Club?
19. Did it witness to the truth?

CHAPTER XXIII.

1. The perpetuity of the Republic demands what? When is this impossible?
2. Where does political power focus? How is manhood affected?
3. On what does the problem of Popular Government depend?
4. On what must rest the standard of Law and Morals? What is principle?
5. What follows as to the attitude of authority? Should the State deal uniformly?
6. Are we a national unit? What carries, the nation over?
7. What is the anarchist's creed? Must morals be taught?
8. What says Dr. John Bascom of Civil Law? What said Judge Sprague?
9. What was murder once?
10. Is there educating power in Law? What historic illustration is cited?
11. What must be behind the law? Why has Prohibition's effect been limited?
12. Has the policy been fixed? What has been the effect of its variableness?
13. What of a power from without? What established Prohibition of Slavery?
14. Where has Liquor Prohibition succeeded? What testimony is offered?
15. Who testified for Kansas? What facts are given as to Topeka?
16. What Iowa witness is quoted? What does he say?
17. Where has power from without established Prohibition? What towns are in proof of its great success?

CHAPTER XXIV.

1. What are the propositions here laid down? To what do they relate?
2. How can Moral reform be made effective? What moral questions must become political?
3. What other propositions follow? How can a political reform become a fact in government?
4. What are the definitions of Politics? To what does Politics relate?
5. What must come within the purview of Politics? To what are due the Sunday and Marriage laws?
6. What is a political party? Which definition is the best?
7. On what do Burke and Lieber ground a party?
8. How may issue be taken? What is an issue? Issues are of what kinds?
9. What of Principle in an issue? How may such principle have application?
10. How may an issue be asserted? What of Polygamy?
11. When does a National Party become necessary? How must it apply?
12. How long will a national Policy be needed as to the Liquor Traffic?
13. When and how is the issue of Prohibition presented?
14. Can a party establish a reform not previously recognized as an Issue? Where is a party's policy asserted?
15. How may a platform be built?
16. How will a party treat secondary issues? What legislation affords proof? What witnesses testify?
17. What principles are involved in the Tariff? How have they been treated?
18. Why does Perry favor Free Trade? How does his language apply to Prohibition?

CHAPTER XXV.

1. How only can harmony come between Moral and Political forces? How, when, and where must the citizen act?
2. What is the one place where he can act? Should there be a moral quality in political action?
3. What is the citizen's ballot? How should it be treated? By whom?
4. What are the facts as to Ballot corruption? Who record them? What States are referred to? Do other States probably differ?
5. What must the Ballot be? How must it be cast?
6. What said President Garfield of the Citizen and the Suffrage?
7. What is chiefly responsible for this ignorance and corruption? What is the agency of suffrage frauds?
8. Does fraud on the Suffrage differ, in its quality, territorially? Does the voter's color change the crime?
9. Where have Saloon frauds on the Suffrage been perpetrated? Under what circumstances?
10. What were the facts in Ohio? In Michigan?
11. Where is it natural, inevitable, that Commerce in Citizenship shall be carried on? What testimony is recorded?
12. What should be earnest, eloquent truth?
13. How can Whittier's lines be employed?
14. Who sell their votes? How are they sold?
15. To what must the Ballot be loyal? What is the logic of Politics?
16. What religious doctrine applies? What said Prof. Adler as to party formation?
17. What is the Ballot's highest loyalty?
18. What constitutes a party? What if parties die? What of party lines?
19. What means the Ballot of Conscience? The best Manhood?
20. What does the State confer? What does it demand?
21. To whom does the Citizen owe tribute? How can it be paid?
22. Where must the Citizen stand finally for Principle?

INDEX.

Ability, 27
Additional Laborers possible, 89
Adler, Felix, 236
Ale, analyzed, 77
Allison, Judge, 109
Almshouses, cost of, 106
Altgeld, J. P., 108
Ames, the Messrs., 91
Anarchism and Beer, 202
Anarchists, Saloons and, 203
Arrests, Comparison of, 159
Artisans, the poet to the, 40
Astors, Division by the, 48
Asylums, cost of, 107
Atlanta Constitution, 198
Authority and the Individual, 115
    and High License, 160
    is the State, 115
    Relation of, 115
    Source of, 134
    Sovereign relation of, 133
    the Duty of, 143
    the grant of, 135
    to restrain, 133
Average, the Drinkers, 64
A Wisconsin Illustration, 162

Ballot-box, the, 228
    loyalty of the, 235
Ballot's character, the, 228
    of Conscience, 230
Bascom, Dr. John, 209
Beer, a Barrel of, 75
    Act of Great Britain, 77
    Anarchism and, 202
    and Tobacco, cost of, 67

Beer, drinking, 77
    no nutriment in, 76
Beer-drinking, results of, 78
    at Buffalo, 201
Betterment Law, General, 118
Blaine, James G., 147, 224
Boots and shoes, 60
Bossuet, M., 3
Bottle, the Perfume, 19
    the Brandy, 19
Boy, cost of a, 102
Brewers, English, 129
    Scotch women, 131
Brewery, Bartholomay, 21
British Medical Association, 101
Brooks High License, 191
Buffalo Railroad Strike, 201
Bunker Hill Monument, 20
Burdens of Government, 147
Burdick, P. A., 65, 162
Burke, Edmund, 219

Capacity, loss of, 98
Capital, 33, 54
    and Labor, law of, 56
    and skill, 94
    and Wages, 69, 86
    as defined by Mill, 55
    as defined by Perry, 54
    Comes, How, 55
    employment of, 57, 84
    Fixed and circulating, 90
    growth of, 55
    how best employed, 57
    in manhood, lost, 103
    Labor and, 55

Capital, other servants of, 87
  Partnership of Labor and, 42
  Saloons and, 93
  the bent of, 94
  the father of, 69
  the ratio to service, 93
  True, 69
Capital's decreasing margins, 94
  Productive power, 92
Catron, Associate Justice, 138
Character, needs and benefits of, 35
  the Laborer's, 36
Charities, State Boards of, 110
Chicago Riots, 203
China, an Emperor of, 11
  labor in, 16
  Vineyards in, 15
Christian Endeavor Societies, 174
Christy, W. D., 154
Church Temperance Society, 204
  Testimonies, 172
Citizenship, advantages and price of, 121
  and its duties, 227
  Commerce in, 232
  Productive, 187
  Supreme Function of, 166
Citizen, the, 227
  unit of Government, 119
City Control of the State, 207
  Rule, Phillips on, 204
  Standards of Morality, 207
Civilization, advances by, 120
  effects of, 13
Classes, Consuming, 22
  contrasted, 23
  Non-productive, 22
Class, the Constabulary, 23
  the Drinking, 23
Climate, 39
Clothing, 12
Coal, 61
Coat, required for, 40
Colorado Springs, Colo., 216

Comfort and Character, 168
  Standard of, 56
Commerce, 53
  a mutual benefit, 79
  mutualities in, 53
Commonwealth, Contributions to, 237
Communism, Tramps on, 202
Composer and player, 24
Compromise, Supreme Issue and, 224
  the Tariff and, 224
Congress on Economy, 81
  the Fifty-third, 81
  Twenty Years in, 224
Conscience in Politics, 236
  the ballot of, 237
Constitution defined, 140
  of New York, 141
  of Pennsylvania, 140
Consumers of Wealth, 108
Consumption and Waste, 62, 86
  and capital, 81
  character and effects of, 71
  for Enjoyment, 71
  increase of Liquor, 158
  Industrial, 71
  National, 85
  of Raw Materials, 88
  Unproductive, 72
  Unproductive and Reproductive, 71
Cook, Joseph, 204
Cost of the family, 63
Cotton Goods, 61
  of a Boy, 102
  of Beer and Tobacco, 67
Court of Appeals, Kentucky, 141
Courts and Constabulary, 108
Crime, Taxing or Licensing, 149
  the cause of, 109
Criminals, cost of, 107
  increase of, 158
Crowell, H. P., 192
Cyclopedia of Temperance, 180

INDEX.

Decanter, Song of the, 183
Defectives, time of, 99
De Laveleye, M., 3, 4, 38, 39, 52, 118, 119, 145
Demand, 56
   and supply, Law of, 55
Demoralization by the saloon, 186
   of Conscience, 187
   of manhood, 193
   of the Press, 191
Disloyalty of the Liquor Traffic, 196
   Proof of, 197
Distributing agent, 54
Distribution, better through capital, 59
   of Wealth, 62, 87
   Problem of, 54, 60
Douglas, Stephen A., 182
Drink and Childhood, 169
   and Strikes, 199
   arrests on account of, 111
   at Homestead, 201
   Habit, 99
   in Home and Neighborhood, 168
   the Volume of, 156
Dorchester, Dr., 64, 65
Drinkers, moderate, 98
Drunkards and Paupers, 99
   habitual, 98
Dunn, Rev. Dr., 77

Economy, Political, and ethics, 5
   and ethics, 5
   and National Prohibition, 6
   and the State, 6
   attitude of, 79
   Congress on, 84
   Defined by Economists, 2
   derivation and reference, 5
   Dictionary definitions, 1
   Divisions of the subject, 8
   final definition analyzed, 4
   its tap-root, 3
   Principles of, 40

Economy, source and object, 3
   Survey of, 23
   Whether abstract or applied, 2
Economic Qualities, fundamental, 35
Edison, Thomas, 26
Education, Public, 170
   compulsory Temperance, 171
Electricity, 39
English Artisan's Demands, 83
Evidence, Tabulated, 111
Exchanges, the science of, 2
Expectation of life, normal, 101
Expediency and Party, 224
   principle and, 225

Family, cost of, 63
Famine, Four years of, 51
Farmer, the, how demoralized, 193
Fernald, J. C., 102
Financial Interests involved, 143
Fisk, Gen. Clinton B., 201
Fixed Capital and Waste, 90
   Capital and Profits, 91
   Charges, 91
Food, 12
Four-mile Law, 191
Free agency of Man, 235
Freeman, Arthur A, 199, 203
Free Trade and Protection, 225
"Freiheit" on anarchistic creed, 209
Furniture, 61
Garfield, James A., 230
Gladstone, Wm. E., 219
God and Government, 237
Goods, 53
Government, aim and object of, 141
   and the individual, 125
   groundwork of, 140
   man in his relation to, 218
   the burdens of, 147
   the Citizen Unit of, 119
   the power of, 211
   the true functions of, 124

INDEX.

Government, Thoughts on, 120
Governmental conditions, 186
    mastership, 124
Graham, Robert, 204
Gregory, Dr. John M., 1

Hale, Sir Matthew, 109
Hamilton, J. W., 214
Hard Times, cause of, 11
Hargreaves, Dr., 2, 28, 57, 59, 99
Harmonization of Forces, 187
Harmonize, the one place to, 227
Harmonizing agent, the sole, 227
Harmony of Moral and Political Forces, 164
Harriman, Tenn., 216
Harrington, Chief-Justice of Delaware, 138
Helps, Arthur, 120
High License, Authority and, 160
    a Wisconsin illustration, 162
    Cities, 159
    claims for, 153
    effects under, 156
    Facts in Comparison, 156
    in Des Moines, 154
    in Illinois, 158
    in Iowa, 155
    in Missouri, 155
    in Nebraska, 156
    in other States, 158
Hill, Frederick, 110
Hitchcock, Dr., 101.
History of Strikes in America, 199, 203
Holmes, Dr. Oliver Wendell, 52
Home Comforts, greater, 61
Homes contrasted, 168
    of the poor, 64
Human Investments, losing, 105
    Life, 116
    Life, effects on, 79
    Solidarity, 120
Ideal Political Economy, 117
Idiots of Massachusetts, 170

Immoral Sentiment, Centers of, 179
Incapables, cost of, 107
Independence, Declaration of, 141
Industries, the relation of, 49
    legitimate, 50
    natural, 49
Industry, a fungus upon, 53
    and Economy, 69
    an unnatural, 50
Intelligence and sobriety, 34
    and wealth, 44
Intemperate Parents, 170
Iowa High License, 154
    State Register, 154
Ireland, famine in, 51
Issue, of Principle, 220
    of Policy, 220
    the supreme, 224
    what is an, 220
Issues, how presented, 221
    kinds of, 221
    Personal, 220
    what are political, 220

Jenks, Prof. J. W., 229
Judges, 109

Keasbey, Prof. Lindley M., 127

Labor, an imperative necessity, 10
    and capital, partnership of, 42
    and capital, the foe of, 59
    and production, character of, 18
    and sales, 28
    and the Laborer, 27
    and the Liquor Traffic, 17
    and the popular welfare, 27
    and wealth, 16
    as of the individual, 21
    average share of, 58
    classified, 16
    defined, 27
    division of, 94
    employment of, 81

INDEX.

Labor, environment of, 34
  further defined, 29
  inspirations to, 31
  in the aggregate, 21
  larger demand for, 60
  Manual and Mind, 25
  Perry's idea of, 29
  proceeds to, 57
  productive, 31
  Productive or Nonproductive, 21
  requisites of productive, 34
  self-supporting nonproductive, 24
  sodden and sober, 84
  the best interests of, 59
  the product of, 20
  true productive quality of, 21
  unreproductive and reproductive, 21
  unreproductive quality of, 18
Labor's loss from liquor, 58
  opportunities for partnership, 42
  pay from liquor, 58
  purpose and products, 18
Laborer's Environment, 36
  Foe, the, 36
  Liquor and, 87
  Time of Liquor, 98
  Time of Producing, 98
Land, 39
Larrabee, Gov. Wm., 214
Laughlin, Prof. J. K., 35, 39
Law, a Genuine Economic, 182
  a moral agent, 209
  an old economic, 175
  and popular morality, 210
  a threefold economic, 52
  Breeding contempt for, 161
  Defiance of, 197
  educational powers of, 210
  License policy and, 206
  natural and divine, 4
  of capital and labor, 56

Law of demand and supply, 55
  our schoolmaster, 211
  of supply and demand, 182
  Test of a, 167
  Uniformity of, 208
Laws and penalties, 126
  controlling the sale, 128
Lawlessness, fruit of the saloon, 203
Lecky, 123
Lennep, Dr., 119
Liberty, Legitimate, 125
  Mill on, 126
  ultimate expression of, 141
License, Authority and High, 160
  Claims for High, 153
  considered as a tax, 146
  defined, 134
  Early High, 131
  Genesis of, 128
  Prohibition anterior to, 135
  properly entitled, 142
  Right to withhold, 132
  system, effect of the, 186
  the logic of, 132
  the nature of, 133
  Unconstitutional, 140
  versus Tax, 149
Lieber and Burke, 219
Liebig, Baron, 76
Life Discounted, years of, 101
Limitations, Moral Rights and legal, 122
  Our, 7
Lincoln, Abraham, 178
  and Douglas, 182
Liquor and its laborers, 87
  consumption, increase of, 158
  production antagonizes, 59
  sentiment, hothouse, 183
  Wrong in the sale, 177
Liquor Traffic, annual receipts from, 151
  character of the, 159
  cost side of the, 143

Liquor Traffic, Differentiated, 148
  Disloyalty of, 196
  Funds and Forces, 192
  its unhappy effects, 51
  net charge to the, 112
  submission by the, 133
  the, 7, 17, 36, 53, 59, 109, 112
Living, standard of, 56
Local Option analyzed, 175-177
  and political combination, 190
  and Slavery, 178
  by counties, 176
  logic of, 176
  method and result, 181
  moral and financial effect of, 180
  the variable policy, 212
  What it does, 179
Local Optionists, former, 178
  suppression, early, 175
Loss, annual aggregate, 101
  through premature deaths, 102
  Recapitulation of, 113
Lost Capital in manhood, 103
Loyalty Defined, 196
  The Ballot's highest, 236
London Globe, 78
Loyalty of the ballot, 235

Machinery and Production, 43
Majorities, Rights of, 178
Man, Cash value of a, 104
  in his relation to Government, 218
  in the mass, 121
  the machine and the, 43
  the other, 122
Manhood Investment, 105
Mallock, W. H., 27
Manufacture, the mercury of, 56
Margin, the Massachusetts, 63
Margin, where it goes, 64
Marshall, 27, 35, 36, 48, 55
Martin, Gov. John A., 213
Massachusetts, average earnings in, 65

Massachusetts margin, 63
  Prohibitory law, 92
Mathew, Father, 64
McCook, Prof. J. J., 50, 229
McDonnell, Mr., 23
McLean, Associate Justice, 138
Metes and Bounds, 122
Michigan in, 189
  Tax Law of, 189
Mill and the Liquor Traffic, 126
Mill, John Stuart, 3, 30, 31, 33, 34, 35, 55, 118, 124, 125, 144, 145, 147
Millionaire and Mortgage, 47
Milwaukee Riots, 203
Moral Agencies, 165
  and Political Forces, Harmony of, 164
  Forces, Organized, 165
    Secondary, 166
  Foundations, 165
  Fruitage, 166
  Interest, 187
  Interests involved, 164
  Issues involved, 178
  Questions, Politics and, 218
Morals, A History of European, 123
  and Law, 209
Mortgage, Millionaire and, 47
Music, effect of, 32

Natural agents, 33, 40
Necessity, an Idealizing, 117, 164
Newcomb, 40
New York City Reform Club, 205
Nye, "Bill," 205

Officials forbidden to brew, 130
Ohio, Tax Law in, 148
"Our Penal Machinery," 108
Paderewski, 24, 30
Painter and portrait, 29
Palmer, Gen. H. W., 191
Parasite, an industrial, 51

INDEX.

Parkhurst, Rev. C. H., 3
Party and the Ballot, 236
  Basis and purpose, 219
  Lines, equatorial, 236
Paupers, care of, 106
Penalties, laws and, 126
Pennsylvania, Amendment Contest in, 192
Permission and Restraint, 136
Perpetuation of the Saloon, 194
Perry, Arthur Latham, 2, 38, 52, 54, 225
Persons and Things, 80
Phillips, Wendell, 204
Philosophy, Human Nature, and Fact, 161
Pitman, Judge, 117, 121, 177
Player and instrument, 30
Policy and Platform, 222
  essential, permanent, 212
  needed, national, 222
Political Economy, Introduction to, 225
  Ethics, 219
  Forces, organized, 167
  Interest, 187
  organization, internal, and external, 48
  Party, 167
  Party, Gladstone on, 219
  Party, what is, 219
  Power, focal point of, 228
  Power in our cities, 204
  Ways and Means, 217
Politics and Moral Questions, 218
  Conscience in, 236
  Money in Practical, 229
  relation of, 218
  saloon in city, 232
  the purview of, 218
  what is, 217
Polygamy, the issue of, 221
Popular safety, Constitution to promote, 142
Powell, Frederick, 57

Principle and its application, 221
  some governing, 208
  Unchanging, 212
Prison Inspectors, 110
Prisons and Reformatories, 99
Producer or consumer, 63
Producers, ratio of, 24
Production, Immediate, 20
  Machinery and, 43
  requisites of, 34
  the motive of, 115
  Ultimate, 20
  varied forms of, 13
Production's Total Waste, 97
Productive life, standard of, 100
  life wasted, 100
  Life, years of, 101
  Power, Capital's, 92
Products, Primary, 94
  Secondary, 94
  Waste of, 95
Profits, Fixed Charges and, 91
Prohibition, a final fact, 213
  Amendment in Ohio, 231
  in Michigan, 231
  anterior to license, 136
  at Colorado Springs, 216
  at Harriman, 216
  at Pullman, 215
  constitutional, 213
  Economics of, 102
  educating effect of, 215
  Effects in Kansas, 214.
  how limited, 211
  in Burmah, 129
  in China, 128
  in England, 215
  in History, 128
  in India, 128
  in Scotland, 128
  Iowa's Testimony, 214
  Judiciary on, 138
  need and effects of, 207
  of Slavery, permanent, 213
  Platform of, 223

Prohibition, Principle, 139
   the Issue of, 222
   Versus License, 139
Progress of the world, 225
Property, assessed valuation of, 157
Protection, Free Trade and, 225
Pullman, Ill., 215

Raw materials, Consumption of, 88
Reed, Hon. Thos. B., 81, 82, 83, 84, 85
Reform Club, New York City, 205
Reform, Political, 226
Reforms, Moral and Political, 217
Regulation and perpetuation, 195
   Authority and, 153
   early features of, 130
   early High License, 131
   for Revenue, 130
   in perpetuation, 194
   Revenue, 146
   System, 130
Relation, A Selfish, 115
   of Authority, 115
Regulative Claims considered, 154
Republic, altar of the, 238
Restraint and Permission, 136
   Moral, 23
   Power of, 128
Return for the Tribute, 144
Revenue, Financial, 116
   from the Liquor Traffic, 150
   Life and, 116
   Magnified, 147
   side, from the, 153
Right, no legislative, 137
Rights of majorities, 178
   Individual, 126
   Massachusetts Bill of, 122
   Moral, 122
Roman Empire, Mill on the, 118
   Revenues, 119
Rousseau, 15
Ruskin, John, 114

Sales, science of, 79, 80
Saloon and church, 171
   and school, 170
   frauds, 231
   the High License, 183
Saloons and Anarchists, 203
   and Capital, 93
   Percentage of expense from, 112
Say, J. B., 3
Scomp, Prof. H. A., 180
Sherman, Senator John, 148
Smith, Adam, 116
Smith, Sidney, 78
Sobriety and Intelligence, 34
   and Production, 91
Social Organization, 126
Society and its Forces, 164
   and Trade, 124
   limits to the Authority of, 125
Sovereign, the, 115
   the State the, 127
Sovereignty, the unit of, 178
   the new Squatter, 182
Spencer, Herbert, 117
Sprague, Judge, 210
Standard of Comfort, 56
   of Living, 56
State, alcoholics and the, 7
   alcohol and the, 117
   authority is the, 115
   City control of the, 207
   moral standard for the, 177
   need of the, 126
   support for the, 144
   the sovereign, 127
Story, Chief-Justice, 218
Strikes, cause and inspiration of, 199, 200
   cooperation and, 200
   drink and, 199
   former object of, 199
   the cost of, 203
Submission by the Liquor Traffic, 133

INDEX.

Suffrage, Defrauding the, 230
   frauds, 230
   Garfield on the, 230
   market-place of, 232
Suppression, Local, 175
   Landlord, 177
Supreme Court, 137
   decision, 137
   Function of Citizenship, 166

Taney, Chief-Justice, 138
Tariff and Compromise, 224
   Blaine on, 225
Taxation, a measure of, 153
   defined, 144
   Direct and Indirect, 151
   Immoral Sources of, 145
   Mill on, 145
Tax, by whom paid, 148
   License versus, 149
Taxing or licensing crime, 149
Taxpaying liquor-dealers, 151
Tennessee, Convicts Petition, 191
   Four-mile Law of, 191
Testimony, Gen. Palmer's, 192
   official, 110
Texas, in, 189
Temperance Education, compulsory, 171
Thomann, Gallus, 151
Tobacco, cost of beer and, 67
Trade, Society and, 124
Tramps on Communism, 202
Tribute, return for the, 144
   to God and Government, 237
Turkish Provinces, 119
   Rule, Decadence under, 119
The Anarchist, 197
      creed and aspiration of, 209
      Ballot, Party and, 236
      loyalty of, 235
      Bonus, Recovering, 161
      Brewers' Journal, 96
      Cave Age, 14

The Century Magazine, 229
   Church, 165
   Citizen, no right in, 137
   Communist, 197
   Drinker, what he buys, 169
   Edinburgh Review, 175
   Engineering Magazine, 199
   Forum, 50, 148, 229
   Good of the governed, 133
   Gross amount, 68
   Home, 165
   Income side, 143
   Interests involved, 143
   London Globe, 78
   Nation, political organization of, 48
   People, 135, 137
      best interests of, 123
   Political Prohibitionist, 111
   Press, Demoralization, 191
   Reproductive line, 73
   Republic, Danger to, 204
   Saloon, a Senator on, 190
      and moral Forces, 167
      Inside, 188
      Outside, 188
      Perpetuation of, 194
   School, 165
   Standard Dictionary, 1, 134
   State's Attitude, 128
      moral standard for, 177
   Striker, 197
   Tenement will conform, 168
   Tribune, New York, 194
   Ultimate Logic, 150
   Voice, 87, 159
      on Liquor and Labors, 87

Unionism, the New, 200
Utilities and wealth, 33
Utilities, Creation of, 32
   kinds of, 32

Valuation of property, assessed, 157

INDEX.

Value of a man, cash, 104
Voter, color of the, 231
   on election day, the poor, 233

Wage-earners and Wasters, 62
   and Wealth, 87
   Wages and, 82
Wages, 69
   and Drink at Homestead, 201
   and the wage-earner, 82
   and waste, 62
   and Wants, 85
   capital and, 69
   two workingmen's, 66
Walker, Amasa, 16
Want, and Labor, 10
   and Natural Law, 9
   and Production, 9
   and Work, 15
   Natural and Unnatural, 9
Wants, Civilization multiplies, 13
   Development of Natural, 12
   Franklin on, 14
   of civilization, 14
   Power of false, 10
   Prime Natural, 12
Waste, annual average, 96
   Fixed Capital and, 90
   by burning, 95
   by drinking, 96
   Consumption, and, 62
   in care and support, 106
   in Production, 90
   in the Care and support of Productive, Life Wasted, 106
   momentum of, 86
   of human life, 78
   of Labor, 96
   of Labor and Product, 90
   of Production, 94
   of Products, 95
   of Time and Life, 98
   of Wages, 96
   Production's total, 97

Waste, wider field of, 98
Wasted Resources, 58
Water, 39
Waterford, England, 64
   Values in, 64
Wayland, Dr., 147
Wealth, consumers of, 108
   creation of national, 49
   Definitions of, 38
   How it comes, 47
   Immaterial, 44
   Individual, 46
   intelligence and, 44
   in the mine, 41
   Material, 38, 39
   National, 46
   Natural, 41
   Personal, 38, 39
   Reproductive Consumption and, 81
   requisites to production of, 33
   science of, 16
   the creation of, 38
   wage-earners and, 87
   wages will not equalize, 69
Webster's Dictionary, 1, 134
Wells, David A., 148
Wesley, John, 175
Wheeler, E. J., 101
Where the Line Breaks, 74
Whittier, John G., 40, 229
Whittier to the shoemakers, 40
   Revised, 234
Willard, Miss Frances E., 189
Witnesses, a cloud of, 173
Woolsey, President, 126
Work, the age of, 15
   Healthy, 14
   Want and, 15
   Waste of, 96
Worse than Wasted, 59
Woolen Goods, 60
Wright, Alfred, 21

Xenophon, 71

www.ingramcontent.com/pod-product-compliance
Lightning Source LLC
Chambersburg PA
CBHW032106220426
43664CB00008B/1148